S0-BAG-526

964.8   146851
W19 WITHDRAWN
L. R. COLLEGE LIBRARY

DATE DUE			

War and Refugees

War and Refugees
The Western Sahara Conflict

Edited by
Richard Lawless and Laila Monahan

CARL A. RUDISILL LIBRARY
LENOIR RHYNE COLLEGE

 Pinter Publishers, London and New York

© Refugee Studies Programme, 1987
except © E. G. H. Joffé, 1986 'The International Court of Justice and the Western Sahara
    Dispute'
    © A. Hodges, 1987 'The Origins of Saharawi Nationalism'
    © T. K. Smith, 1987 *Al-Mukhtufin* 'A Report on Disappearances in Western Sahara'
    © A. Lippert, 1985 'The Saharawi Refugees'
    © J. Firebrace, 1987 'The Sahara Refugees: Lessons and Prospects'

All rights reserved. No part of this publication may be reproduced,
stored in a retrieval system, or transmitted by any means,
without prior written permission of the copyright holder. Please direct all enquiries to the
publisher.

British Library Cataloguing in Publication Data
War and refugees: the Western Sahara
    conflict.
    1. Western Sahara—Politics and
    government—1975–
    I. Lawless, Richard I.   II. Monahan, Laila
    964'.805   DT548
    ISBN 0-86187-900-7

Library of Congress Cataloging in Publication Data
War and refugees.
    Includes index.
    1. Western Sahara—Politics and government—1975–
2. Refugees—Western Sahara.   I. Lawless, Richard I.
II. Monahan, Laila, 1944–
DT346.S7W35   1987   964'.8   87-15302
ISBN 0-86187-900-7

964. 8
W19
146851
June, 1989

Typeset by Joshua Associates Limited, Oxford
Printed in Great Britain by Biddles of Guildford Limited

Contents

List of contributors

James Firebrace

War on Want Programme Officer for North Africa and the Middle East. He previously worked as coordinator for the Catholic Institute of International Relations programme in the Yemen Arab Republic and Somalia. He is the author of 'Infant Feeding in the Yemen Arab Republic' (1981), a study of the problems caused by bottle feeding; co-author of 'The Hidden Revolution' (1982) which examines the social changes occurring in Tigray province of Ethiopia in the context of war and drought; and co-author (with Stuart Holland) of 'Never Kneel Down' (1984) which examines the situation of Eritrea and the gains of the EPLF revolution.

Dr Thomas Franck

Director of the Center of International Studies, New York University Law School, and Director of Research at the UN Institute for Training and Research. Author of 'The Stealing of the Sahara', *American Journal of International Law*, (1976).

Tony Hodges

Currently Africa Editor at Economist Publications, Ltd., London, he was formerly an analyst of African affairs at International Reporting Information Systems, Washington, D.C. He is the author of *Western Sahara: The Roots of a Desert War* (1983), *Historical Dictionary of the Western Sahara* (1982) and, with Colin Legum, *After Angola: The War over Southern Africa* (1976).

George Joffé

Consultant Editor for the Middle East and North Africa at Economist Publications Ltd., he writes and broadcasts on North African and Middle Eastern affairs, has been involved in several issues before the International Court of Justice at The Hague relating to maritime and border disputes and has written widely on issues of colonial border delimitation in North Africa and on the growth of nationalism and the nation state in the Arab speaking world. He is co-author (with K. S. McLachlan) of *The Gulf War: A Survey of Political Issues and Economic Consequences*, and is currently drafting studies of Libya and the modern political history of North Africa.

Dr Richard Lawless

Senior Lecturer and Assistant Director of the Centre for Middle Eastern & Islamic Studies at the University of Durham, England. He is joint editor of *Changing Middle Eastern City* (1980) and *North Africa: Contemporary Politics and Economic Development* (1984). The emphasis of his research is on economic and social change in the Maghreb.

Dr Anne Lippert

Professor, Ohio Northern University and Chair, The Saharawi Peoples Support Committee, Ohio. She has been researching the conflict in Western Sahara since 1976 and has stayed in the refugee camps frequently.

Laila Monahan

Publications Officer, Refugee Studies Programme, Queen Elizabeth House, Oxford.

Dr Werner Ruf

Professor of Political Science at the University of Kassel, West Germany. He has written numerous works in French, German and English. He is the editor and a contributor to *Transnational Mobility of Labour and Regional Developments in The Mediterranean* (1984); is currently preparing a report on a personal visit to the Western Sahara in which he had extensive contact with the Polisario.

Biancamaria Scarcia Amoretti

Lelio Basso Foundation for the Rights and Liberation of Peoples, Rome, Italy.

Dr David Seddon

Reader in Development Studies at the University of East Anglia, he teaches, among other things, courses on 'contemporary world development' and 'North African and Middle Eastern Development' in the School of Development Studies. He has done research in Morocco, Tunisia, Turkey and Nepal. He is the author of, among other things, *Moroccan Peasants* (1981); 'Winter of Discontent: Economic Crisis in Tunisia and Morocco', *MERIP Report no. 127* (1984) and 'Riot and Rebellion: Political Responses to Economic Crisis in North Africa' in B. Berberoglu, ed., *Class Struggle and Change in the Middle East*, forthcoming.

Teresa Smith

Director of the Western Sahara Campaign for Human Rights and Humanitarian Relief, USA; a member of the Executive Board, the Association of Concerned Africa Scholars: Institute for African Studies, Columbia University; she has participated widely in conferences relevant to the Western Sahara and refugees.

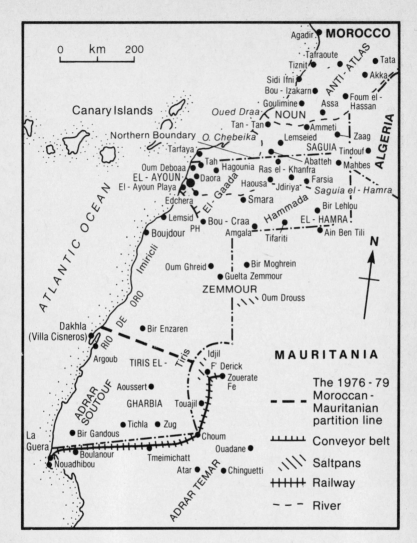

Map 1 The Western Sahara

Map 2 Greater Morocco

Plate 1 Saharawi women in Polisario camp, 1979 (*by courtesy of Christine Spengler, Sygma*)

Plate 2 Saharawi women at school (*by courtesy of James Firebrace, War on Want*)

Plate 3 Polisario fighters (*by courtesy of Christine Spengler*)

Plate 4 Koranic school in Saharawi Camp (*by courtesy of Christine Spengler*)

Plate 5 Saharawi troops on parade before refugees at Tindouf

Plate 6 A Saharawi camp (*by courtesy of James Firebrace, War on Want*)

Plate 7 Saharawi women demonstrate support for Polisario at the refugee camp near Tindouf in Algeria

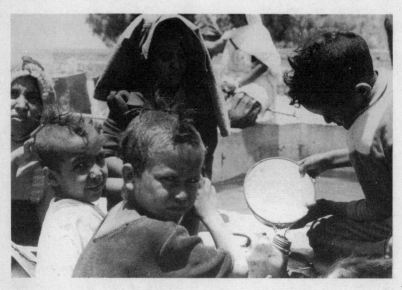

Plate 8 Most of the Saharawi refugees in Algeria are women and children (*by courtesy of Fredrick Schjander, United Nations*)

Introduction

TONY HODGES

There is a tradition among the Arosien, one of the Western Saharan tribes, that their founder was a marabout by the name of Sidi Ahmed el-Arosi who lived in the first half of the sixteenth century. He is said to have travelled from Tunis to Marrakesh, where he begged for alms and drew water from wells to perform his ablutions. One day, however, he was accused of sorcery and flung into a dungeon upon the orders of the sultan. He placed his hopes in God and was rewarded with a visitation from a long deceased saint who burst through the prison roof and spirited him away, carrying him off by the belt of his trousers. Together they flew through the skies towards the Sahara. They continued on into the desert until they reached a place called Tbeila, twenty-five miles west of Smara (now Western Sahara's second largest city). Thereupon Sidi Ahmed's belt snapped and the fugitive marabout fell to earth to dedicate himself to a saintly life in the desert and marry three local women from whose sons sprang the main branches of the Arosien.[1]

This myth, typical of its kind, is revealing in its symbolism: it depicts the Sahara as a sanctuary, a place of refuge from the oppression of unjust rulers. In pre-colonial times the writ of the Moroccan sultanate, the most powerful state in western Islam, did not extend to the nomadic tribes of the region now known as Western Sahara. No supra-tribal authority could have subjugated the Saharawis, who wandered in very small groups over huge tracts of wilderness in search of water and pastures for their camels.

This is not to say that there were no links between Morocco and the Sahara. There were important trade routes across the desert, between the Maghreb and the African societies south of the Sahara. At times the strongest Moroccan sultans, men like Ahmed al-Mansour (1578–1603) and Moulay Ismail (1672–1727), tried to control this trade by sending armies into the desert and administering strategic oases, but they never subjugated the Saharawi tribes. They did not tax them and they could not halt their incessant inter-tribal raiding. To have attempted to do so would have been fruitless given the mobility, dispersal and military prowess of these nomads and the sheer size, remoteness and inhospitality of their desert homeland.

Even in the modern colonial period it was difficult to bring these tough desert people to heel. Indeed, it took Spain fifty years to 'pacify' Western

Sahara—from 1884, when the initial settlement at Dakhla (baptized Villa Cisneros by the Spanish) was founded by the Sociedad de Africanistas y Colonistas—to 1934, when Spanish troops finally succeeded in occupying Smara and other points in the interior. Only then did Spain effectively secure control of its colony of 102,703 square miles (an area slightly larger than Great Britain) whose borders with Mauritania, Algeria and Morocco had been arbitrarily defined by a series of Franco–Spanish agreements between 1886 and 1912.

Since 1973 the Saharawis have been fighting to regain their lost freedom. In a chapter in this volume I argue that rapid changes in economic, social and political conditions in Western Sahara from the late-1950s to the early-1970s gave birth to a modern nationalist movement, differing in character and objectives from the anti-colonial resistance that ended in 1934. In May 1973 the Frente Popular para la Liberación de Saguia el-Hamra y Río de Oro, the liberation movement better known by its acronym Polisario, was founded as the 'unique expression of the masses, opting for revolutionary violence and the armed struggle as the means by which the Saharawi Arab African people can recover their total liberty and foil the manœuvres of Spanish colonialism'.[2] Polisario immediately began a guerrilla war against Spain, at that time still ruled by the Franco dictatorship.

Within two years the Spanish government was resigned to abandoning Western Sahara despite its value as one of the world's largest sources of phosphate, a raw material used in the production of fertilizer. However, instead of achieving independence, like other former European colonies in Africa, Western Sahara was handed over by Spain to neighbouring Morocco and Mauritania. This transfer of powers, which began after the signing of a secret tripartite agreement in Madrid on 14 November 1975, had been completed by the end of February 1976. On 14 April 1976 the country was partitioned, Morocco receiving 65,637 square miles in the north and Mauritania 37,066 square miles in the south.

All this happened without the indigenous inhabitants being consulted, even though the United Nations General Assembly had voted in successive resolutions since 1966 that the territory's future should be decided by a referendum. Moreover, there is little doubt that, if this referendum had been held, it would have produced a landslide vote for independence. In May 1975, just six months before the Madrid accord, a United Nations' mission of inquiry had found 'an overwhelming consensus among Saharans within the territory in favour of independence and opposing integration with any neighbouring country'.[3] In the first chapter in this book, Professor Thomas Franck notes that in the process of the dismantling of the European powers' colonial empires one rule emerged as the *sine qua non* of decolonization and self-determination: that the established boundaries of a territory could be altered only by the consent of its inhabitants. Western Sahara is a rare, though not unique, example of the violation of this principle.

King Hassan II's motive for annexing Western Sahara at this time was essentially political: by playing on the patriotic sentiments of his subjects he succeeded in emerging as the leader of a national crusade, thereby restabilizing a monarchy which had been gravely weakened by two coup attempts (in 1971 and 1972) and extensive social and political unrest. The territorial claim to Western Sahara was justified, like earlier forgotten claims to Mauritania and parts of Algeria (elaborated in the 1950s by the ideologue of Moroccan nationalism, Allal el-Fassi), on the grounds that it had historically formed part of the Moroccan empire before being 'amputated' by Spain. The evidence for this view was slim and, in an advisory opinion issued in October 1975, the International Court of Justice (ICJ) at The Hague dismissed Morocco's claim to pre-colonial territorial sovereignty. George Joffé argues below that the Moroccan claim, based on concepts of Islamic state practice in pre-protectorate Morocco, could not be properly assessed in terms of contemporary international law. However, in reaffirming the primacy of the principle of self-determination over the claim to historic title, the ICJ could be said to have rendered irrelevant the entire body of evidence presented to the court about the pre-colonial legal status of Western Sahara. It was of purely historical interest.

What happened to Western Sahara in 1975–6 could justly be described as a 'decolonization disaster'. The territory's arbitary cession to Morocco and Mauritania spawned a large refugee exodus, described by Anne Lippert in her contribution to this book, and a war that has continued for more than a decade. Tens of thousands of Saharawis fled to Algeria, fearing repression at the hands of the Moroccan authorities whose human rights violation in Western Sahara are recorded in a chapter below by Teresa Smith.

Algeria, for a mixture of ideological and strategic motives (a traditional commitment to national liberation movements and concern about the regional implications of Moroccan 'expansionism'), gave Polisario the bases, arms, vehicles, fuel, food, training and money needed to wage an effective war of resistance against the new colonizers. Meanwhile, in February 1976, Polisario unilaterally proclaimed the founding of its own state, the Saharawi Arab Democratic Republic (SADR).

By August 1979, the weaker of its enemies, Mauritania, had given up. In a peace treaty with Polisario, Mauritania renounced its territorial claims and withdrew its troops from Western Sahara, whereupon Morocco immediately laid claim to the erstwhile Mauritanian sector too. Since then Morocco has poured resources into what has become a seemingly interminable struggle to consolidate its hold over the territory. By 1987, King Hassan II had about 120,000 troops there, most of them strung out along a continuous defence line, a kind of Saharan equivalent of the Great Wall of China. These fortifications, 650–700 miles long, enclose about two-thirds of the territory's land area but are permanently harassed by the Polisario guerrillas. Polisario has also been pursuing an intense and extremely successful diplomatic struggle abroad: in 1984 the SADR was able to take its seat in the Organization of African Unity, prompting Morocco to renounce its membership, and by the beginning of 1987 the Saharawi republic had gained diplomatic recognition from sixty-seven states.

In his contribution to this book, David Seddon assesses the Moroccan government's ability to sustain its Western Saharan policy on three levels: military, diplomatic and socio-economic. He argues that Morocco faces a war of attrition and is incurring serious diplomatic losses, while the financial costs of the war effort are exacerbating Morocco's domestic economic and social strains. Morocco's greatest strength, however, is its ability to'draw on substantial Arab and Western aid, both military and financial. The role of the world powers, in particular the United States and France, is the focus of the chapter by Werner Ruf, who examines these countries' strategic interests in the region and how their aid has enabled Morocco to sustain its war in the desert.

While the military and diplomatic struggle grinds remorselessly on, more than 165,000 refugees remain in camps in the Tindouf region of western Algeria, awaiting the day when they will be able to return home. But with the Western Saharan drama already in its second decade and neither side showing any disposition to capitulate to or compromise with the other, these refugees may remain in exile for many years more. The hardship they have faced in Tindouf has been daunting for this part of the Algerian Sahara is particularly inhospitable—a windswept, gravel plain known as the *hammada*, where both livestock raising and animal husbandry are exceedingly difficult. The refugees can never achieve self-sufficiency. Yet, as the chapters by Lippert and Firebrace of War on Want so graphically show, the refugees have not lost hope and have made remarkable achievements in the spheres of education, health, vegetable cultivation, crafts and social organization. This progress can be attributed partly to favourable external factors such as the support of the host government, but it is also due to the quality of leadership within the refugee community notably its stress on self-reliance, popular participation, equity, social cohesion and the development of skills. As such, the Saharawi refugee experience is rich in lessons for refugee situations in other parts of the world.

The interplay between tradition and change in this refugee society is a theme to which both James Firebrace and Biancamaria Scarcia Amoretti turn, especially with respect to the position of women. Since most of the able-bodied men are enrolled in Polisario's guerrilla army, the adult population in the refugee camps is almost entirely female. Great strides have been made to raise the women's level of education and enhance their social and political responsibilities in the camps. Yet change need not imply a total rejection of the past. Oppressive features of the past are being broken down, in Firebrace's view, while the best features of the old society are being developed. For Scarcia Amoretti, Saharawi women are applying traditional behaviour in a new context—extending, for example, their traditional responsibilities for the nomad camps (*friq*) to the new setting of a large refugee settlement. Likewise, old concepts of blood solidarity (*assabiya*) have been widened from their traditional tribal framework to a modern, national dimension.

This book aims to cast a fresh light on the multiple facets of the Western Saharan conflict and the lessons of its associated refugee problem. Most of the chapters that follow were first presented as papers to a conference held under the auspices of the Refugee Studies Programme at Queen Elizabeth House, Oxford University, in March 1986. This brought together academics, aid workers, politicians and diplomats, among others, for a frank exchange of views on a regional conflict that, in the organizers' view, had received far less attention than it warranted. Three other contributions to this collection have been selected from other sources: the chapters by Teresa Smith and Anne Lippert were presented as papers to a panel at the November 1985 annual meeting of the African Studies Association of the United States, held in New Orleans, Louisiana, and my own contribution was first published in *Third World Quarterly* in January 1983.

Notes

1. Julio Caro Baroja, *Estudios Saharianos*, Instituto de Estudios Africanos, Madrid, 1955, pp. 401–2.
2. Political Manifesto of 10 May 1973 in *Sahara Libre*, Polisario Front, Algiers, no. 13, 20 May 1976.
3. Report of the United Nations Visiting Mission to Spanish Sahara, 1975 in *General Assembly Official Records*, 30th Session, Supplement 23, UN Document A/10023/Rev. 1, p. 59.

Part I: Nationalism, frontiers and decolonization

1 The theory and practice of decolonization: the Western Sahara case

THOMAS M. FRANCK

In the evolution of the organizing principle of mankind from empire to nation-state during the four decades following World War II, more than a billion persons navigated the transition from subjects of foreign rulers to citizens of independent political entities. This transition may not have benefited all of those billion persons in absolute economic or even socio-political terms, as we once hoped. The average Ghanaian may today feel poorer and less in control of his or her destiny than did the subjects of the Gold Coast in 1955. Nevertheless in many instances—from India to Singapore to the Ivory Coast to Kenya—the transition has been accomplished in the context of rising standards of gross national production, personal income, literacy, health care and, that most unmeasurable but crucial of commodities, human dignity. Moreover, the transition has not impoverished the former metropolitan imperial powers. Belgium, France, The Netherlands, the United States and, to a lesser extent, Britain, Spain and Portugal have decolonized amid continued overall growth in their national standards of living.

More important: the transition—perhaps the most revolutionary social transformation in human history—has been achieved, by and large, peacefully. There are notable and painful exceptions. France, Spain, Belgium and Portugal, too sentimentally attached to what they regarded as 'overseas provinces' and to a messianism which sought to make Africans and Asians into évolués, consumers of the culture of Cervantes and de la Rochefoucauld, had to be fought for control of the destinies of Algeria, Angola and that Congolese territory which is now Zaïre. Britain, not necessarily to its credit, never regarded Asians or Africans as suitable mass consumers of Shakespeare or Lord Byron. In East Africa, it was the British who learned Swahili and, in Nigeria and elsewhere, it was the traditional rulers whose powers were shored up by Lord Lugard's belief in indirect rule through chiefs and tribal councils. What the British instilled in Africa and Asia was not a sense of socio-cultural integration with the metropolitan culture, except at the very top of the colonials' cultural pyramid, but a respect for law, lawyers, courts and judges. British imperialism, essentially mercantilist rather than socio-culturally messianic, was dismantled with good grace as local demands became more clamorous, making continued British rule expensive and altering the mercantilist equation. Moreover, the

British colonial leaders, having been trained for the most part at the British bar, were pragmatic negotiators who knew how to make deals which, together with such legal fictions as the Commonwealth, eased the transition for the mother country by protecting the links and commercial interests that were allowed to remain, or appear to remain, untouched by the transition.

Belgium, by contrast, when it pulled out of the Congo, left that nation a shambles. The French, when Guinea dared to vote itself out of the French Overseas Community, took everything: telephones, administrators, lapdogs—vanished all, to paraphrase Alexander Pope. The Portuguese communists, after the revolution at home, sought to hand over Angola to their indigenous ideological disciples. In Timor, the Portuguese rulers, after four hundred years, surrendered ignominiously to the Indonesian invaders.

But even in the few disorderly transitions and in all of the orderly ones, one rule emerged as the *sine qua non* of decolonization: whether or not the boundaries of empire—decreed by cultural messianism, mercantilist greed, the Congress of Berlin or all three—made sense in ecological, geographic or demographic terms, those boundaries could only be altered with the consent of the governed.

Thus it was that the United Nations General Assembly, in its landmark resolution 1514, in 1960, decreed self-determination for all nonselfgoverning territories but linked that mandate to respect for the territorial integrity of each territory as it proceeded towards independence. The resolution stated that 'immediate steps shall be taken . . . to transfer all powers to the peoples of those territories, without any conditions or reservations, in accordance with their freely expressed will and desire, without any distinction as to race, creed or colour, in order to enable them to enjoy complete independence and freedom'.[1] To further these aims the Assembly established a Special Committee that to this day oversees and promotes the achievement of those objectives,[2] monitoring elections and plebescites preceding self-government, investigating progress towards self-rule and establishing the conditions and timetables for progress towards the mandated objective.

In the vast majority of cases of transition—both the normative, peaceful ones and the ones accompanied by violence—the objective of preserving the colony's territorial integrity was not seriously challenged. When elections in the Belgian trust territory of Ruanda-Urundi indicated clearly that the people wished to form two separate states upon achieving independence, the United Nations reluctantly agreed. There was greater approval when the British Togolese Trust Territory, voting under UN supervision, agreed to achieve independence in union with the Gold Coast (Ghana) with which it had long been administered by Britain. So, too, when the British Cameroons voted, under UN supervision, to become independent in reunion with the hitherto French Cameroon Trust Territory.

When on the eve of its independence, the Belgian Congo (Zaïre) began to disintegrate into warring tribal states, the UN raised a multinational force to hold it together. It next convened the interregional negotiations which allowed Zaïre to survive with its territorial boundary and national unity more-or-less intact.

All of these experiences underscore the respect for the principle of territorial integrity of the international community, as manifested by the UN and, overwhelmingly, as implemented by the colonial powers and colonial peoples on the verge of independence. To the very limited extent that a colony was permitted to become independent either by dividing into two states—as in the case of Rwanda and Burundi—or by joining another nation—as happened in British Togoland, British Somaliland, Sarawak and North Borneo, British Cameroons and the Arab Emirates—it was only after the indigenous population concerned had been consulted in a democratic electoral process under supervision or observation of the United Nations.

In the entire four-decade history of the decolonization of a billion people, there were only three exceptions to this rule of decency, reason and good order: Western New Guinea and Timor—colonies, respectively, of The Netherlands and Portugal, which were seized by Indonesia without the democratic consent of the inhabitants—and the Western Sahara—a Spanish colony which was occupied by Morocco against the clearly evident wishes of its inhabitants.

Most decolonization, at least in terms of numbers of new states involved, took place in Africa. It is important, therefore, that The Organization of African Unity (OAU), the regional organization of African governments, has heartily endorsed the UN rule of territorial integrity not merely because it is morally right but because the alternative would lead to endless bloodshed and chaos as expansionist states, directly or using disaffected groups, sought to dismember or absorb their more peaceful or weaker neighbours. In particular, the OAU has strongly opposed irredentism based on 'historic title'—claims to the territory of neighbours about to become independent on the theory that at some earlier time in history those territories had belonged to the claimant. 'Territorial integrity' means that good order demands that decolonization occur within the boundaries established by colonial usage. These boundaries are not immutable. It was the dream of the ruler of the first decolonized African nation, Kwame Nkrumah, that there would come to be a United States of Africa. But Nkrumah too, understood that if colonial boundaries were to give way to unification, that must come only with the consent of each new nation as part of its exercise of self-determination.

Exactly the same point was made by the International Court of Justice in its advisory opinion on the Western Sahara.[3] Asked by Spain and Morocco to determine whether, before its colonization by Spain, the Western Sahara had belonged to the Moroccan empire (or,' even, to the Mauritanian 'entity'[4]) the Court found those questions of historic title largely irrelevant. Instead, the judges asserted the supremacy of the norm developed by UN resolutions and by the practice of decolonization: the Saharawi population was entitled to self-determination within the perimeters of the existing colonial entity. During the past fifty years, the large majority of judges said, self-determination had become the rule, superseding such earlier concepts as 'historic title'.[5] In declaring self-determination the absolute right of colonial peoples as the *sine qua non* of decolonization the Court reaffirmed the same principle enunciated three years earlier in its advisory opinion on Namibia.[6] In the Western Sahara case the ICJ cited with approval UN General Assembly resolution 1514 of 1960 which decreed that a colony could become independent as a part of a neighbouring state only as a 'result of the freely expressed wishes of the territory's peoples acting with full knowledge of the change in their status, their wishes having been expressed through informed and democratic processes, impartially conducted and based on universal adult suffrage.'[7] The Court explicitly rejected the notion that there were between the Western Sahara and Mauritania or Morocco such ties of historic title 'as might affect the application of Resolution 1514 in the decolonization of Western Sahara and, in particular, of the principle of self-determination through the free and genuine expression of the will of the peoples of the Territory'.[8] In other words, it is the will of the people of the colony at the moment of its liberation from colonialism which must determine their future status.

The events which followed the rendering of the ICJ's opinion were flagrant violations of international law, globally accepted practice, moral imperatives and the requirements of peace and good order. The day after the opinion was handed down, Rabat proclaimed a massive 'green' march of civilians into the Sahara. When the UN Security Council failed to act decisively against this obvious violation of the self-determination rule,[9] Spain, weakened by the prolonged dying of the incapacitated Generalisimo Franco, decided to accede to the claims of Morocco and Mauritania. On 14 November 1975, a joint Moroccan, Mauritanian and Spanish communiqué was issued in Madrid which reported that secret negotiations, carried on in a 'spirit of the utmost friendship, understanding and respect for the principles of the Charter of the United Nations ... have led to satisfactory results in keeping with the firm desire for understanding among the parties and their aim of contributing to the maintenance of international peace and security'.[10]

The secret Madrid pact in effect stipulated Spain's agreement to Moroccan and Mauritanian partitioning of the colony. In return, Spain was permitted to keep a 35 per cent interest in Fosbucraa, the 700-million dollar Saharan phosphate company.[11] Spain agreed to establish an interim regime in which a Spanish governor, assisted by Moroccan and Mauritanian deputy governors, would function until 28 February 1976, at which time its responsibilities would terminate. Algeria, left out of the Madrid negotiations, declared that it would accord no validity to the agreement[12] and that it intended to arm Polisario, the pro-independence movement in the Sahara. By the end of February 1976, 60,000 Saharawis had become refugees, primarily in Algeria, as the Moroccans moved to crush resistance.[13]

At the United Nations, the General Assembly on 10 December 1975, passed Resolution 3458A(XXX) which reaffirmed 'the inalienable right of the people of the Spanish Sahara to self-determination . . .' and called on the Secretary-General 'to make the necessary arrangements for the supervision of the act of self-determination'. The president-elect of the Thirty-First General Assembly, Sri Lanka's Ambassador Shirley Amerasinghe, condemned Morocco's opportunism and the indifference with which it had been met, warning the Third World that its failure to unite in opposition to the Moroccan and Mauritanian usurpation of the Western Sahara would condone a trend 'to replace the old imperialism by another form of foreign control founded on territorial claims'.[14] Ambassador Salim of Tanzania, the chairman of the Special Committee, further pointed out that 'cardinal principles were involved' and that the United Nations must avoid condoning an evil precedent which 'would have consequences not only in the Territory itself but also beyond its borders and even beyond the African continent'.[15]

The Secretary-General of the United Nations, through his Special Representative, Olof Rydbeck, refused to put the UN imprimatur on the 'act of free choice' by a 'rump' Djemaa[16] which was hastily organized by the Moroccans at the end of February. Thus, the international requirement that the Saharawi people exercise their right to self-determination remains unfulfilled to this day.

The United Nations continues to adhere to these norms, demanding that they be fulfilled by Morocco, one of only two nations to have chosen to act in deliberate defiance of this clear and most basic of international laws.

What is then at stake is not only the patrimony of the Saharawi people but, much more broadly, the continued efficacy of a fundamental norm of law. International law is not an Austinian system, in the sense that there is no global sovereign served by a global police force capable of compelling offenders to act in accordance with the reciprocal normative expectations of the community. Instead, international law is still in that early stage of development characterized in common law as the phase of self-help. In other words, it is the global community itself together with the victimized party which must establish that the contingent benefits of the legal norms to all members of the system are far too great to permit any one member to deviate with impunity precisely because unhindered, successful violation of the law undermines the law itself and, in consequence, the regime of good order which it was intended to uphold. This is to say, merely, that if Morocco can get away with breaking the law of territorial integrity in the name of historic title in violation of the right of self-determination, then the next breach of the law becomes easier until respect for the law gives way to unfettered self-aggrandizement. The Argentine attempt to assert historic title in the Falkland Islands might not have been contemplated had

Morocco not been seen to get away so easily with its taking of the Western Sahara.

The United Nations and the OAU have been the main instruments for asserting the continued legitimacy of the right of self-determination as against claims of historic title.

In Africa, a significant majority of states have recognized the SADR, the Saharawi Arab Democratic Republic proclaimed by Polisario for the Western Sahara and have legitimized it by voting its accession to the OAU, even at considerable sacrifice to that organization's unity. On 27 February 1984, even Mauritania extended its recognition, having evacuated its part of the Western Sahara. The OAU's *Ad Hoc* Committee of Heads of State on Western Sahara at its sixth session also adopted recommendations calling for a democratic referendum under international supervision,[17] a recommendation accepted in principle by King Hassan of Morocco but not yet implemented. It has also asked the United Nations to provide a peacekeeping force to ensure tranquility during the referendum.[18]

The United Nations General Assembly for its part has continued to assert the right of self-determination for the Sahara, has welcomed the OAU initiative and has urged the parties to the conflict to negotiate directly the cease-fire and terms for implementing the required referendum.[19] A number of other UN members outside Africa have recognized SADR including Yugoslavia and Colombia.

A General Assembly resolution adopted in December 1985 once again 'reaffirms that the question of the Western Sahara is a question of decolonization which remains to be completed on the basis of the exercise by the people of Western Sahara of their inalienable right to self-determination and independence'.[20] That normative right is not necessarily convenient to the nations of the West. Polisario, realizing Morocco's close ties to NATO states, has turned, inevitably, to Warsaw Pact nations, as well as to the Third World, to support and supply its cause. Thus the conflict has become ensnared in the cold war trap. Nevertheless, it is difficult to understand Britain's failure to vote for straightforward General Assembly restatements of the law when the law in the Sahara has direct implication for the British case in the Falklands, Gibraltar, Belize and even Northern Ireland. In each instance, the British case turns precisely on the priority of the right of self-determination, as well as on the principle of territorial integrity and non-use of force to change boundaries in the name of historic title, the same case being asserted by the SADR.

Nations must realize that, whatever their short-term interest in the outcome of any particular dispute, all have a far greater interest in ensuring habitual deference to normative principles which have been legitimized by reason and practice. The successful, peaceful decolonization of a billion persons has been accomplished by habitual deference to self-determination within each of the existing colonial territories. What a tragedy it would be if, in these last few unfinished cases of decolonization, that benevolent, tried and sound norm were allowed to unravel, perhaps plunging who-knows-how-many areas of the world into chaos and bloodshed. That justice be done in accordance with the established fundamental norms evolved during four decades of decolonization is thus of direct, practical self-interest to all persons, everywhere.

Notes

1. General Assembly Resolution 1514, 15 UN GAOR Supp. 16, UN Document A/4684, 1960, paras. 66–7.
2. Established by General Assembly Resolution 1654, 16 UN GAOR Supp. 17, UN Document A/5100, 1961, para. 65.
3. *Advisory Opinion on Western Sahara*, ICJ, 1975, 12.
4. General Assembly Resolution 3292, 29 UN GAOR Supp. 31, UN Document A/9631 1974, paras. 103–4.
5. *Advisory Opinion on Western Sahara*, op. cit., p. 32.
6. ICJ, 1971, p. 31.
7. *Advisory Opinion on Western Sahara*, op. cit., pp. 32–3.
8. Ibid., p. 68.
9. The initial Security Council resolution, passed on 22 October, appealed to the parties 'to exercise restraint and moderation' so that the Secretary-General could arrange consultations'. Security Council Resolution 377, 1975. It was not until 6 November that the Council summoned the will to deplore the march and call for Morocco to withdraw. Security Council Resolution 380, 1975.
10. Third Report by the Secretary-General in pursuance of Security Council Resolution 379, 1975 relating to the situation concerning Western Sahara, UN Document S/11880, Annex 1, 1975, p. 1.
11. Morocco and Mauritania published an agreement under which two countries would divide the proceeds from the Bou Craa mines (*The Times*, 17 April 1976, p. 5, cols. 1–2). This, in fact, never happened.
12. Third Report by the Secretary-General, op. cit., Annex IV, pp. 2–3.
13. Interview with Spanish diplomats and UN Secretariat personnel.
14. UN Document A/C.4/SR.2175, Fourth Committee, 15 November, 27, 1975.
15. UN Document A/C.4/SR.2174, Fourth Committee, 22 November, 24, 1975.
16. The Djemaa was created by Spain in May 1967 as the highest representative body of local administration in the territory. For further information on the history and functions of the Djemaa, see 'Report of the United Nations Visiting Mission to Spanish Sahara', in the *Report of the Special Committee*, UN Document A/10023/Add.5, Annex, 1975, pp. 29–39.
17. Ad Hoc Committee of the OAU/Resolution 103(XVIII)B, Annex I, 1981.
18. Ad Hoc Committee of the OAU/Resolution 104(XVIII), 1981.
19. General Assembly Resolution 39/40, 5 December 1984.
20. General Assembly Resolution 40/50, 2 December 1985.

2 The International Court of Justice, and the Western Sahara Dispute

GEORGE JOFFÉ

The conclusions reached by the International Court of Justice at The Hague in its advisory opinion on the Western Sahara issue are by now well known to most observers and commentators.[1] However, the significance of the fact that the Court was asked to intervene in an issue which, originally at least, appeared to be simply one of decolonization has not been so widely considered. One observer, however, has implied that the Court's involvement in the issue arose in large measure because of the United Nations' unwillingness to apply—with its usual resolution—established principles regarding decolonization.[2] The Court itself was aware of this problem and some of the judges, in separate opinions, made their anxieties on this score abundantly clear.[3]

Indeed, the Court's opinion, in itself, became part of the technique by which the usual procedure for decolonization was circumnavigated since, although it denied that the legal ties of allegiance which it identified constituted ties of territorial sovereignty, it did, nevertheless, accept that such ties did exist.[4] It was this aspect of the judgment which, after all, was used by Morocco to justify its occupation of the Western Sahara in early November 1975, just a few days after the Court issued its opinion on 16 October 1975.

Nationalism and decolonization

However, both the contents of the Court's Opinion and the context in which it was requested do give rise to other anxieties over the question that it was requested to consider and, in this respect, the Western Sahara issue is of particular importance. For instance, the one group most directly affected by the Court's deliberations, the Saharan population itself, did not contribute to the debate, being excluded by the conventions of the Court and the formulation of the application to the Court according to the terms of UN General Assembly Resolution 3292 (XXIX) of 13 December 1974. Yet, between 12 and 19 May a UN mission visited the Western Sahara, Morocco, Algeria, Spain and Mauritania. Its report made it clear that support for the idea of independence and for the Polisario Front was widespread and profound amongst the population of the Western Sahara.[5] It even recommended that a self-determination referendum be held[6]—a recommendation that would seem to vitiate the reference to the International Court for an advisory opinion as to whether such a referendum would be appropriate.

In effect, the UN mission was implicitly enunciating the basic principles which have always underlain the decisions of the UN over decolonization— first, the concept of the intangibility of international frontiers and second, the priority of the right of colonial populations to self-determination over all other rights, particularly historic rights. It was also articulating the basic assumption behind the Cairo Declaration of the Organization of African Unity (OAU) in 1964[7] and Article 3 (3) of the Charter of the OAU drawn up in 1963. Ironically enough, it was also giving practical expression to the arguments put before the International Court by the Algerian representative in the case, Mohammed Bedjaoui.[8]

The Algerian arguments before the Court highlighted one of the major contradictions inherent in the approach taken by the UN General Assembly to the Western Sahara issue. At one level, the Algerian arguments were based on the principle of *uti possidetis*, a legal principle which provides that successor states accept international boundaries set by a predecessor regime.[9] The principle, which is derived originally from Roman law, was first applied in 1810 in Latin America to justify the territorial limits of the newly independent states created from the old Spanish colonial empire. In fact, the *uti possidetis* principle was abandoned in Latin America by the start of the twentieth century largely because it was found to be too restrictive in rectifying obvious errors and injustices. One major problem with the concept was that there was often confusion over the location of provinces and other subdivisions of colonial control and thus over which successor state had the right to the territories in question. In the end, legal rights were abandoned in favour of physical occupation to define the territorial extent of a state according to the principle of *uti possidetis*. In particular, one juridical interpretation considered that the principle could not be applied to adjacent territories which had been governed under different colonial regimes.[10] This has always been the attitude of the Moroccan government—amongst others— towards the principle, particularly when it is applied to the creation of states that, before their colonial experience, had no status in international law.

In the African context, the principle has not been used explicitly but is clearly inherent in the stand of the OAU over colonial frontiers. The one state that has been particularly anxious to make use of it has been Algeria, in large measure because it is extremely difficult to define a pre-colonial Algerian state with the same territorial extent as modern Algeria. Furthermore, as the issue of the Algerian–Moroccan border demonstrates, without the justification of *uti possidetis*, it would have been impossible for Algeria to settle to its advantage the conflicting claims that exist over contiguous regions in Algeria—Morocco having been willing to compromise its stand on the principle on this occasion. Although that particular border settlement has not been ratified, it has been delimited.[11]

In the case of the Western Sahara issue, it is clear that although Algeria was anxious to apply the principle in defining an entity different from Morocco—on precisely the same grounds as applied in Algeria itself[12]—Morocco had been most unwilling to do so again because the colonial regimes involved were very different and reflected different colonial approaches, and not owing to any inherent difference in the nature of the contiguous territories involved. Furthermore, the Western Sahara was not already integrated into Algeria, nor was this the declared purpose of decolonization. However, it is here that the second of the major legal principles enunciated by Algeria applies—the priority of self-determination. In short, the Algerian case argued before the Court assumed the existence of a separate Saharan people and thus its inherent right to self-determination, as laid down in the UN 1960 declaration.[13]

Implicit in this statement is the assumption that at the time of decolonization a nation exists—an entity that by identifying itself within an ethnic boundary sees itself as unique and separate.[14] Undoubtedly, such a nation existed in the 1970s in the Western Sahara. Not only had it been able to organize, quite independently from surrounding states, a resistance to Spanish colonial rule but it also demonstrated its awareness of its own uniqueness during the visit of the UN mission in 1975. Indeed, the Polisario Front leaders suggested to its members that the proposed referendum was unnecessary, given the evident nationalist sentiment that had been expressed.

As Tony Hodges describes, the growth of Saharawi nationalism arose in the late 1950s as a by-product of sedentarization and modernization as traditional tribal structures came under pressure and centralized administration broke down traditional differences.[15] It was, in short, a quite typical example of the growth of nationalist sentiment in a colonial situation: the same argument could be advanced for the development of almost any North African nationalist sentiment as a result of the colonial experience.[16] It was the interplay of colonial economic and political integration, together with the growth of indigenous resistance to a colonial presence within territorial limits set by the colonial administration that defined a popular consciousness which expressed itself through such a nationalist sentiment.

The crucial factor—and implicit in the attitude adopted by the UN, the OAU and Third World states towards decolonization—is that demands for self-determination in such circumstances are self-justifying. Their very expression inherently legitimates the existence of the nation that demands them and thus, under UN decolonization practice, the right of that nation to a state—territorially defined under the principle of *uti possidetis*. It is for this reason that issues of historic rights by other states have rarely been considered to be relevant to decolonization processes by the UN, or by international legal practice.[17] Such an approach, by definition, excludes any question of 'historic rights'—an approach which generally accords with reality, for the colonial experience creates such profound changes in economy, society and political attitudes, and even in the extent of geographical control or of the definition of territorial limits that, normally, it would be unreasonable to resolve the post-colonial situation in terms of the very different conditions of the pre-colonial era. It then, however, becomes difficult to understand why the UN General Assembly felt it necessary to refer the issue to the International Court of Justice for its advisory opinion. After all, the colonial experience had defined a set of boundaries which were internationally recognized and there existed a 'people' (to use the UN's own term) who had expressed their own sense of national identity and uniqueness, however recently that might have been acquired. The issue of a historic context to this newborn nationalism was quite irrelevant as far as the issue of decolonization was concerned. Equally, from this point of view, any claims over historic rights by neighbouring states would also have been irrelevant, however well founded they might have been.

Territorial integrity

Nevertheless, the UN General Assembly referred the issue of Saharan self-determination to the International Court for advice as to whether historical claims by Morocco and Mauritania were well founded. The reasons for this were three-fold and involved the attitude of Spain towards the issue of Saharan decolonization in 1974, the claims to historic rights in the region by Morocco and Mauritania and the objections to the principle of *uti possidetis* that originally led Morocco to express reservations over the famous OAU 1964 Cairo resolution on the intangibility of colonial frontiers and that is provided for in the 1960 UN General Assembly Resolution 1514 (XV), the Declaration on the Granting of Independence to Colonial Countries and Peoples.

Until mid 1973 Spain had been quite unwilling to accept the idea of abandoning its Saharan colony, apart from a mild aberration between 1958 and 1964 when it considered exchanging the Sahara for a Moroccan concession of sovereignty to Spain[18] over the *presidios* of Ceuta and Melilla. In the face of repeated calls from the UN, Spanish policy changed in 1973 largely because the Franco government had come to realize that Spanish economic interests in the Western Sahara could still be maintained by granting political independence to a state that would have to depend on Spanish economic aid. As a result, in September 1973, Spain offered the region autonomy and, in August 1974 it informed the UN Secretary-General that it was prepared to accede to demands for a referendum on self-determination.

The Spanish proposal met with fierce Moroccan opposition, not only because of Morocco's own claims to the region, but also because Spain made it clear that the referendum would only allow a choice between remaining attached to Spain or full independence. The legal grounds for this austere choice were simply that Spain considered that, before its occupation in 1884, the region had been *terra nullus*, i.e. there had been no political authority to claim sovereignty over it.[19] Thus, in accordance with UN resolutions, there would be no other choice offered to its inhabitants as part of the process of decolonization. Of course the real reasons for the choice were economic: Spain was determined that Morocco should not be able to squeeze it out from the Bou Craa phosphate industry, or prevent the Andalusian and Canary fishing fleets from exploiting the Sahara fishing grounds.[20] Such an approach automatically meant that Morocco's claims to the Western Sahara on historical grounds would fall. As a result, the Spanish referendum proposal was subject to considerable opposition and it was made quite clear that Rabat would oppose any referendum proposal which included independence as an option and did not include the possibility of integration with Morocco.[21] To resolve the issue, Morocco proposed a referral to the International Court of Justice over the issue of whether or not the Western Sahara had been *terra nullus* on 17 September 1974. Spain, predictably enough, refused, so on 13 December 1974, with Mauritanian support, the UN General Assembly was persuaded to support the Moroccan proposal, despite considerable misgivings. The Court was to be asked for an advisory opinion on whether or not the Sahara had been *terra nullus* at the time of Spanish occupation and, if not, what the legal ties between it and Morocco on the one hand and Mauritania on the other had been.[22]

The justification for this procedure—which, in terms of usual UN decolonization procedure, would otherwise appear to be quite inappropriate—lay in UN General Assembly Resolution 1514 (XV) of 1960. The original resolution allowed for one of three possibilities in the process of decolonization: sovereign independence, free association with an independent state or integration with an independent state. Resolution 2625 (XXV) 1970 confirmed this choice by stating that any political status could be chosen by a population seeking decolonization provided only that such a choice was 'freely determined by a people'.[23] Thus, it was clear that choices other than those offered by Spain—such as integration into Morocco—could be legitimately included in any referendum of self-determination in the Western Sahara.

This, however, does not reduce the primacy of self-determination as the means by which decolonization should be effected. If that were the case, then the question raised in the UN General Assembly Resolution 3292 (XXIX) 1974 would still be irrelevant, for the fact that there were pre-existing legal ties between Morocco or Mauritania and the Western Sahara could not influence the fact that the ultimate, indeed, the sole test was a referendum. However—and here the far earlier disputes over the universal validity of *uti possidetis* come into their own—the crucial UN General Assembly Resolution 1514 (XV) 1960 contains a further qualifying clause.

In Paragraph (6) of the resolution, it is stated that disruption of national unity or territorial integrity is incompatible with the UN Charter and that, in these circumstances, the territory should be reintegrated. It is for this reason that the quality of the pre-existing legal ties between the Western Sahara and Morocco have been so important. If, indeed, they amounted to full territorial sovereignty, as understood in international law, then Spanish colonial occupation could have been held to have disrupted territorial integrity or national unity and reintegration would have been the appropriate decolonization solution. If not, then the usual provisions of UN General Assembly Resolution 1514 (XV) 1960 would apply, and the referendum for self-determination amongst the 'people' of the Western Sahara would be the ultimate and sole test.[24]

Sovereignty

The key to this complex issue is the meaning of the word 'sovereignty' and the way in which it has been interpreted in international law. Typical dictionary definitions of the word suggest that it means 'pre-eminence'; 'supreme and independent power'; 'the territory of a sovereign or of a sovereign state'.[25] Most historians of international law would agree with the last of these definitions: 'sovereignty' means, for all intents and purposes, 'territorial sovereignty'. Although the concept of territorial sovereignty probably goes back to the end of the Middle Ages, it is generally considered that the modern international system dates from the Peace of Westphalia, which was signed on 24 October 1648, bringing the Thirty Years War to an end, and which allowed independent states to reject the concept of 'transcendent and superior authority'—in the form of the Holy Roman Empire.[26] States now had sovereign authority, as autonomous and independent bodies, and rulers had ultimate authority within their respective territories. Sovereignty was thus necessarily territorial. Between states there was sovereign equality—all would be equal in terms of international legal sanction, in so far as states allowed this to exist.

Over the subsequent centuries a corpus of practice and principle governing belligerent and non-belligerent relations between sovereign states grew up and, particularly during the nineteenth century, began to cover an elaborate set of activities governing inter-state activity. It was fundamentally concerned with European inter-state relations and has been the basis of international law ever since. Thus territorial sovereignty was a fundamentally European conception.[27]

During the nineteenth century a further addition was made to the concept of the sovereign state, although the germ of the idea may be perceived in the development of France and Britain far earlier. This was the idea that states also related to unique and specific communities, identified by a set of unique cultural values and perceiving themselves to be unique—nations, in short.[28] The apogee of this vision came at the start of the French Revolution. In the words of Article III of the Declaration of the Rights of Man, adopted by the National Assembly on 26 August 1789, 'The Nation is essentially the source of all sovereignty'.[29] The point was made even more forcibly by Sieyes in his famous pamphlet, *Qu'est-ce que le Tiers Etat?* 'The Nation exists before all things and is the origin of all. Its will is always legal, it is the law itself . . . In whatever manner a nation wills, it suffices that it does will; all forms are valid and its will is always the extreme law.'[30] Thus, the original vision of the sovereign state was amplified by the addition of the concept of nation, in which sovereignty was enshrined. The sovereign state, in short, became the sovereign nation–state. It has been this concept that has tended to be exemplified in the decolonization process—hence references to 'peoples' in UN resolutions on the subject and the close relationship between 'people' and 'territory'. Nation–states express their sovereignty through supreme control over national territory. The UN Charter, after all, owes much to the Declaration of the Rights of Man, its illustrious predecessor.

In discussions of decolonization it is perhaps often forgotten that the colonial experience, as well as being an experience of confrontation, was also one of dialogue. European colonial powers imposed territorial divisions that may, or may not, have coincided with indigenous patterns of political organization and, within these territorial limits, imposed radical social and political changes.[31] Indigenous populations, in struggling against such impositions, had to adapt to a set of inherently alien values as part of that struggle and this often meant accepting philosophical and legal constructs that were innately European. The reason was quite simple. No dialogue was ultimately possible unless a common vocabulary existed and that vocabulary, by virtue of the permanent changes wrought by colonialism and as a result of the colonialist assumption of cultural and ideological superiority, had to involve European political concepts and values. Yet, in making this adjustment, national liberation movements—whatever the level of struggle, whether open military confrontation or a propaganda struggle for popular support—inevitably absorbed some of that vocabulary and ideology into their own visions of the futures they wished to create. The process was inevitable, for they would have to manipulate a colonial inheritance in a post-colonial world and that inheritance itself was fashioned by the European political vision. It was additionally inevitable because many of the organizers of such movements were beneficiaries of colonial education who absorbed such ideological abstractions along with more indigenous values.

This became particularly crucial in the post-colonial era when independent successor states to former colonies had to cope with the problems of colonial organization and assumptions, particularly those relating to the nation–state. The result has been that virtually all such states have devoted considerable efforts to constructing nations—that homogeneous European ethnic vision[32]—within former colonial frontiers for territories in which political control was, in theory, geographically uniform and universal. This course was followed in order to justify their claim to sovereign statehood and sovereign territorial integrity and accounts for the obsession with territorial sovereignty and national integrity (see Paragraph 5 of UN General Assembly Resolution 1514 (XV) 1960).

In North Africa, this has meant that the ethnic diversity of Algeria or Morocco, with their different ethno-social or ethno-cultural groups of Berberophones and Arabophones (Berber, Tuareg or Arab; sedentary or transhumant nomad), has had to be crushed into a single homogeneous mould of Arabo–Islamic origins, as well as an artificially uniform historical experience being cited to ensure national cohesion within the post-colonial state. This has often been a difficult experience as the tensions of the Kabyle riots of April 1982 in Algeria, or the Rif Revolt in Morocco in 1958 have made clear. Yet the attempt cannot be avoided, if post-colonial states are to fulfil their own perception of their political identities. This is even true in the cases of such multi-ethnic or multi-national states as India or China, the United States or the Soviet Union. In all cases, either through conscious government policy or simply as a result of administrative and economic homogeneity, a single national consciousness is forged. The process occurs, furthermore, within the defined and unique territorial boundaries.

This process of nation-building is not synchronous. It is not confined to the present or the recent past. It extends back beyond the colonial experience, for the creation of a sense of national uniqueness involves the creation of a historical pedigree. National uniqueness also lies outside the confines of historical time yet, in so far as it has always existed, this uniqueness must be historically demonstrable. As a result, the process of nation-building requires the construction of a myth—a national history which, once defined, is jealously guarded against criticism or question as the nation attempts to set it within the indisputable and undisputed historical record. Such a historical record may, indeed, exist already, in that the nation concerned really did exist in the past. However, this is not the real point, for even if it did not, nationalist consciousness demands that it should. It is in this sense that national history is essentially a myth.

The Moroccan case

Set against this background, it is quite clear why Morocco and Mauritania were so anxious to demonstrate that in pre-colonial circumstances one or other or both had exercised territorial sovereignty over the Western Sahara and why the Court—although finding that legal ties had existed— considered that these did not correspond to ties of territorial sovereignty.[33] After all, under international law this was the only way in which the pre-colonial situation could be squeezed into the narrow confines set by the UN and international law to allow the application of paragraph 6 of UN General Assembly Resolution 1514 (XV) 1960. To justify the claim of disrupted territorial integrity and national unity, demonstrable territorial sovereignty was essential.

Apart from bringing various treaty relations between Morocco and European powers in as evidence, Morocco's case was substantially based on the internal nature of the Moroccan state in the pre-colonial era. Morocco argued that authority was demonstrated by the ability of the Sultan to appoint local officials in the region, collect taxes and obtain oaths of allegiance and fealty from local officials or representative leaders and from the communities they controlled or represented. This concept of authority, it argued, applied even when the Sultan's direct temporal authority was lacking for his spiritual status was still respected, providing the basis for an effective political authority. Apparently autonomous local potentates were, in reality, sultanic delegates because of the Sultan's overriding religious status and prestige. In some cases, such as those where local communities acted in the defence of the political collectivity (*thaghr*), the Sultan's political authority would be delegated to local authorities who thus acquired the appearance of political autonomy, although the underlying reality was political delegation. Thus, one of the crucial conditions of territorial sovereignty, that of exercising supreme and undisputed authority, was satisfied.[34] Furthermore, this pattern of political behaviour had a long precedent and was consequent on the unique nature of the Moroccan state.

The Court did not agree—although it did accept the uniqueness of the pre-colonial Morocco state—arguing that oaths of fealty were personal and not indicative of sovereign control since their validity was limited to the person of the Sultan. Furthermore, despite the accepted uniqueness of the Moroccan state at the moment of Spanish colonial occupation, religious ties did not constitute a basis for sovereignty.[35] This was particularly important in the context of the *bled as-siba*, where, it was agreed, sultanic control was not directly exercised, as opposed to the *bled al-makhzen*, where it was. The Moroccan argument that in such areas the reality of sultanic power was one of delegation was rejected by the Court.

Underlying the Court's objections was the fact that, in terms of European definitions, the arguments advanced by Morocco about the internal organization of the pre-colonial Moroccan state—all of which related to *communal* links—could not satisfy the stringent requirements of territorial sovereignty, even though they did contribute to the decision that the Western Sahara was not *terra nullus*, as Spain had claimed. The Court was careful to clarify that it accepted that such links existed with some, though not all tribes in the Western Sahara, for control of community does imply territorial control. However, even here, the Court was dubious of the Moroccan claim since the groups concerned were nomadic, scattered and not confined within strict territorial limits—circumstances which previous decisions of the Court had identified as inadequate for territorial sovereignty.[36] Yet it was precisely this that Morocco (and, under slightly different conditions, Mauritania) had to show if it were to benefit from the provisions of Paragraph 6 of Resolution 1514 (XV) 1960.

The problem of sovereignty

The usual response to the International Court's decision over Morocco's claim to the Western Sahara has been that it demonstrated the cynicism of the Moroccan case in flying in the face of accepted international law and the practice of the United Nations.[37] This may or may not be true, but it does not explain how the Moroccan government was able, during 1974 and 1975, to obtain support from not only the vast majority of the Moroccan population for its case, but also from every point of the political spectrum except the clandestine far-left group Ilal Amam. Nor does it explain how it has been possible for this national consensus to be sustained, despite evident war weariness, over the past decade. Nor, indeed, does it explain how it was possible, quite apart from the attitude of the Moroccan government, that there should have been a substantial strand of political thought since the nationalist movement of the 1940s and 1950s which argued for a long-standing claim, stretching back to pre-colonial times, to Moroccan *territorial* rights to an area comprising not only the Western Sahara, but also part of the western Algerian Sahara, Mauritania and parts of Mali as far south as the Senegal river. It was a claim that had originated with the veteran nationalist leader Allal al-Fassi, but which had been sustained and incorporated into official dogma as early as 1958 by King Mohammed V.[38]

An alternative explanation might conclude that in addition to practical considerations of Moroccan domestic policy and issues of hegemony in North Africa the problem resides, in part at least, in a lacuna in international law and in the consequences of the imposition of European political philosophy in regions where different and, on occasion, competing political philosophies applied. International law is conventionally considered to derive ultimately from Roman legal precepts and to have found its first codified expression in Grotius (*De Jure Belli ac Pacis*).[39] Such an approach, it has been argued, ignores the vast body of legal practice from different legal systems that also reflects on relations between states, particularly Islamic legal practice.[40]

The concept of sovereignty in Islam is derived from the organization of the early Muslim state as laid out in the 'Constitution of Medina' drawn up by the Prophet Muhammad in AD 632, after the hegira from Mecca to Medina. It finds its basic form in the system developed under the first four Islamic caliphs in which the Islamic world was organized under the precepts of the Quran (the revealed word of Allah), the *hadith* (the traditions of the sayings of the Prophet), which supplemented the inevitable lack of political and social detail in the Quran and the *sharia* (the code of law derived from the Quran and the *hadith*). The primary duty of the caliph was so to order polity and society that the *sharia* could be practised and daily life be ordered in accordance with the precepts of Islam. In fact, the primacy of that duty was such that should he fail to fulfil it the Islamic community had a right and duty to replace him with someone who could. This was formally embodied, certainly in later Islamic practice, by the *bayaa* and became incorporated into modern Islamic political theory.[41] The *bayaa* was, in short, a contractual agreement whereby the Muslim community offered a conditional loyalty to its caliph in response to his recognition of his obligations under the *sharia*. It was the popular legitimation of his religious status and, as such, a crucial element in Islamic concepts of political sovereignty.

Although the initial Islamic concept of the state envisaged its ideal as a single political unit, the *umma* (community) which formed the *dar al-Islam* Islamic world), the reality was that separate political units developed in which power (*sultah*) could be delegated. Those who acted politically autonomously from the caliph were restrained, in theory at least, by the same concept of communal contractuality as had existed for the first four caliphs. Once again this was expressed through the institution of the bayaa. Although there was a clear idea of territoriality, the primary legitimization of the system was the communal link between ruler and ruled and the conditionality of that link. Furthermore, even though the ideal prescribed a single political entity, legal prescript provided for a plurality of states within an encompassing legal framework, the sharia. Sovereignty was a communal concept, the link between community and a ruler legitimized by his practice of power in order to preserve conditions for the practice of Islam within the community.

The pre-colonial Moroccan state was, in theory, this ideal writ small— writ small because the Moroccan sultan claimed accession to the caliphate as the result of historical events connected with the collapse of the Ummayad caliphate and the growth of kharajite sentiment in North Africa during the early Islamic period in North Africa.[42] Its territorial extent was defined by the range of communities that had habitually accorded fealty through the bayaa to the sultan–caliph which stretched down from modern Morocco to the Niger bend as a result of the sixteenth-century Moroccan occupation of Timbuctoo, the justification of the claims put forward by Allal al-Fassi and Istiqlal in the 1950s. The bayaa was a crucial element in the legitimization of the sultan–caliph and, certainly up to the imposition of the Protectorate in 1912, a clearly conditional contract. It was for this reason that the Moroccan sultanate could be described as a religious institution in which fealty and allegiance were essential components of power and sovereignty.[43] It is also the reason why, in Morocco's submissions before the Court, such emphasis was laid on 'fealty' and 'allegiance'.[44] According to the precepts of Islamic law on the subject, such acts did provide a basis for political sovereignty—through control of community, rather than territory.

The potential within Islamic precepts for delegation also provided the justification for the Moroccan claim that, even in areas of the *bled as-siba* (those areas which were not directly controlled by sultanic authority) as opposed to the *bled al-makhzen* (those areas which were under direct administration by the sultan) Moroccan sovereignty still applied.[45] It has been argued by several historians of Morocco that the sultan's role inside the region of *siba* was essentially one of arbitration and legitimization of local authority.[46] This was particularly important in border regions, where *dal al-Islam* came into contact with the *dar al-harb* —that region outside Muslim control. Here authority could be delegated (*thaghr*) for the specific purpose of defending the limits of the Muslim world; hence the Moroccan claims over the relations of the Ma al-Ainin family with the sultans Abd al-Aziz and Abd al-Hafidh.[47] Furthermore, the Sultan had an obligation to aid in such resistance through his obligation to organize *jihad* to defend the *umma*.

The consequences

There was, therefore, a self-sustaining legal system that, in pre-colonial times at least, justified the theoretical constructs of Morocco's submissions to the International Court. The arguments were rejected, not least because the underlying principles of the Moroccan case could not and did not coincide with those of territorial sovereignty under the precepts of international law; hence the Court's decision that the ties were legal in nature but did not constitute sovereignty.[48] The problem was succinctly articulated by King Hassan himself, according to *Le Matin du Sahara* (9 March 1986) in a press conference, when he said:

Without doubt the law in Arab countries, particularly Islamic law, gives the *bayaa* an importance and a value which is not given by any other law. To us, the *bayaa* is not related in any way to territory or frontiers. The *bayaa* is bestowed upon those who accept its responsibilities. These provisions are legal but, although they have been obligatory since the advent of Islam, unfortunately they were not applied before Islam, especially once Roman law was re-introduced in the Mediterranean basin. Roman law is based on conquest by force unlike the *bayaa* with inherent spiritual and religious ties uniting its guardians and those who provide the basis of its action.

In any case, the Moroccan argument rested on a necessary contradiction in that the reality it attempted to describe was a historical situation defined originally and given legal force under Islamic law through constructs related to communal links, but the terms in which it did this were those of a legal justification relating to territorial control, as international legal practice demands. Indeed, Morocco as a successor state to the colonial Protectorate imposed by France and Spain was bound to adopt such an approach—just as Moroccan public and intellectual opinion after World War II translated the communal vision of the pre-Protectorate past into the territorial vision imposed by European political philosophy and the nationalist–colonialist dialogue.[49] It is small wonder then that Moroccan public opinion has clung so tenaciously to its Saharan claims over the past ten years and that the Moroccan government is not prepared to negotiate on the one essential for a settlement, a compromise over territorial sovereignty.

Given these inherent contradictions in philosophical and legal approaches, it seems almost inevitable that the International Court of Justice should have found the Moroccan and Mauritanian claims of territorial sovereignty over the Western Sahara wanting and that the requirements of Paragraph 6 of UN General Assembly Resolution 1514 (XV) 1960 had not been fulfilled. The basic assumptions of international law made no provision for the legal principles that had historically been involved. This would still have been the case even if the principle of intertemporal law had been applied, whereby the question of title or sovereignty is evaluated in terms of the law in force at the time. International law, quite simply, had no place for the principles involved in the sharia—at least as far as state practice was concerned.

It could even be argued that if the fact of the existence by the 1970s of a Western Saharan nation ready to exercise its right to self-determination was accepted—as the UN mission to the region in 1975 established—then any independent assessment of sovereignty by the Court, even if at the request of the UN General Assembly, only underlined the contradiction implicit in Resolution 1514, as the Court itself appeared to realize in paragraphs 71 and 72 of its opinion.[50] If nations have inalienable rights, as laid down in Paragraph 2 of UN General Assembly Resolution 1514 (XV) 1960, then it would seem impossible for these to be limited by Paragraph 6 of the same resolution. In short, sovereignty and self-determination form uncomfortable bedfellows in the process of decolonization and the Western Sahara issue provided the basis for an inevitable conflict which international law could not have resolved.

Notes

1. Hodges, T., *Western Sahara: The Roots of a Desert War*, London, Croom Helm, 1964, p. 368; Franck, T. M., 'The stealing of the Sahara', *American Journal of International Law*, 70, October 1976, p. 704.
2. Franck, op. cit., p. 694.
3. ICJ, *Western Sahara, Advisory Opinion*, 16 October 1975, paras. 70, 174, 131, 121, 111–15.
4. Ibid., paras. 62, 68.
5. Hodges, op. cit., p. 199.
6. Franck, op. cit., p. 709.
7. OAU Assembly AHG/Res 17(1), Cairo Ordinary Session, 17–21 July 1964. Interestingly enough, Morocco did not accept this resolution.
8. ICJ, *Western Sahara, Volume IV*, p. 497.
9. Bougaita, B., 'Les frontières, méridionales de l'Algérie', unpublished dissertation, University of Paris 1, 1979, pp. 233–74; Brownlie, I., *African Bound-*

aries: a Legal and Diplomatic Encyclopaedia, London, Hurst, 1979 p. 11; Murty, T. S., *Frontiers: A Changing Concept*, Delhi, Palit and Palit, 1978, p. 169.

10. Bougaita, op. cit., p. 246.
11. Prescott, J. R. V., *Boundaries and Frontiers*, London, Croom Helm, 1978, p. 68.
12. Trout has a long discussion of this issue. See Trout, F. E., *Morocco's Saharan Frontiers*, Geneva, Droz, 1969, pp. 216–81.
13. ICJ, *Western Sahara, Volume V*, pp. 320–2; Franck, op. cit., p. 698; see UN General Assembly Resolution 1514 (XV) 1960.
14. See Gellner, E., *Nations and Nationalism*, Oxford, Blackwell, 1983 and Smith, A., *Theories of Nationalism*, London, Duckworth, 1983.
15. Hodges, op. cit., p. 151; Assidon, E., *Sahara occidental: un enjeu pour le nord-ouest africain*, Paris, Maspero, 1978, pp. 38–9.
16. Joffé, E. G. H., 'Nacionalismo y el mito democrático', *Cuadernos de Alzate*, 1, 1984–5, pp. 35–51.
17. ICJ, *Western Sahara, Opinion*, paras. 31–4, 40.
18. Laroui, A., *L'Algérie et le Sahara Marocain*, Casablanca, Serar, 1976, pp. 35–6; Trout, op. cit., p. 441.
19. Hodges, op. cit., pp. 167–70; Laroui, op. cit., p. 49.
20. Assidon, op. cit., pp. 30–7, 47.
21. Hodges, op. cit., p. 182.
22. ICJ, *Western Sahara, Opinion*, para. 14.
23. ICJ, ibid., paras. 24–5.
24. ICJ, ibid., paras. 32, 80.
25. *Chambers' Dictionary*, p. 1056.
26. Thomas, C., *New States, Sovereignty and Intervention*, London, Gower, 1985, p. 3.
27. Thomas, ibid., pp. 4–5.
28. Smith, op. cit.
29. Paine, T., *Rights of Man*, Harmondsworth, Middx, Penguin, 1969, p. 132.
30. Cobban, A. *A History of Modern France*, Vol. I, Harmondsworth, Middx, Penguin, 1963, p. 165.
31. Muller, M., 'Frontiers, an imported concept: an historical review of the creation and consequences of Libya's frontiers' in Allan, J. A., *Libya since Independence*, London, Croom Helm, 1982, p. 165.
32. The term 'ethnic' is used in its anthropological sense in the context of the 'ethnic boundary'.
33. ICJ, *Western Sahara, Opinion*, para. 68.
34. ICJ, *Western Sahara, Opinion*, paras. 44–9. *Volume IV*, paras. 252–84. Volume III paras. 170–87.
35. ICJ, *Western Sahara, Opinion*, para. 44.
36. Ibid., para 45.
37. Cf. Hodges, op. cit.; Franck, op. cit. Interestingly enough Assidon, who is strongly opposed to the Moroccan case, on this point accepts that there was a reasonable basis: Assidon, op. cit., p. 61.
38. Knapp, W., *North West Africa—a Political and Economic Survey*, Oxford, Oxford University Press, p. 335; ICJ, *Western Sahara, Opinion*, para. 127.
39. Thomas, C., op. cit., p. 77.

40. Ibid; Murty, op. cit., pp. 88–106.
41. Joffé, E. G. H., 'Arab nationalism and Palestine', *Journal of Peace Research*, 20, 1983; see also Mardin, S., *The Genesis of Young Ottoman Thought: a Study in the Modernization of Turkish Political Ideas*, Princeton, N.J., Princeton University Press.
42. Lahbabi, M., *Le gouvernement marocain à l'aube du XXe siècle*, Casablanca, Atlantides, 1968, p. 23; see also Laroui, op. cit., p. 56.
43. ICJ, *Western Sahara, Volume IV*, paras. 259–62; *Volume III*, paras. 178–9.
44. ICJ, *Western Sahara, Opinion*, paras. 43, 48.
45. ICJ, *Western Sahara, Volume III*, para. 179.
46. Laroui, A., *Les origines sociales et culturelles du nationalisme marocain (1830–1912)*, Paris, Maspero, 1977, p. 163; Ayache, G., 'Les fonctions d'arbitrage du makhzen' in Pascon, P., *Les actes du colloque de Durham*, Rabat, Smer, 1978.
47. ICJ, *Western Sahara, Volume III*, para. 187.
48. ICJ, *Western Sahara, Opinion*; para. 68.
49. See Memmi, A., *The Coloniser and the Colonised*, London, Souvenir Press, 1965.
50. ICJ, *Western Sahara, Opinion*, para. 28.

3 The origins of Saharawi nationalism

TONY HODGES

Over the past eleven years Western Sahara has become the theatre of one of Africa's most determined guerrilla wars. Since the Madrid accords of 14 November 1975, by which Spain handed its phosphate-rich, desert colony to Morocco and Mauritania, the nationalist guerrillas of the Frente Popular para la Liberacion de Saguia el Hamra y Rio de Oro, or the Polisario Front for short, have fought doggedly and with considerable success against vastly superior military forces. By 1979 they had obliged the weaker of their adversaries, Mauritania, to sue for peace; and since then they have forced the 40,000 or so Moroccan troops in the territory to pull back into two small coastal enclaves, which together cover only about one-sixth of the territory's total land area of 103,000 square miles. Meanwhile, in the international arena, their state-in-exile, the Saharan Arab Republic (SADR), which was founded in February 1976, has won diplomatic recognition from sixty-seven countries and, with the backing of the majority of African states, gained admission as a full-member state to the Organization of African Unity (OAU) in February 1982, though not without provoking a paralysing boycott of subsequent OAU meetings by King Hassan's conservative African allies.

The Polisario Front is fighting for independence, or, as its leaders sometimes say, to liberate the remaining occupied zones of the SADR's national territory. Like many African nations, however, Western Sahara has no historical antecedent. The Western Saharans never constituted a nation in pre-colonial times, and their present-day nationalism is a very recent phenomenon, which took root only in the latter part of the Spanish colonial period.

The Saharawi

Before the arrival of the Spanish, who first set up a colony on the Rio de Oro bay in 1884 but proved unable to pacify the desert hinterland until as late as 1934, no supratribal authority had ever regulated Western Saharan society. The harsh world of the desert, in which small nomadic groups had to migrate over vast areas in search of pastures for their animals, was not conducive to the rise of large and complex state structures. Moreover, there was frequent inter-tribal conflict. The Saharans possessed ample means of war (camels, fire-arms) and an ingrained pride in the bearing of arms. In a society centred on the rearing of livestock, the *ghazzi*, or raid, was primarily staged to acquire animals, and it was organized on commercial principles, with customary rules governing the distribution of the booty; but, since agnates were customarily held responsible for murders, the spilling of blood could spark off endless rounds of mutual raiding, in which each attack by one side led remorselessly on to a reprisal raid by the other until eventually one side sued for peace, exhausted.[1]

Western Saharans' prime loyalties were to tribe (*gabila*, plural—*gabael*), tribal faction (*fakhd*) and family. These were the social groups within which political, military and judicial leaders were appointed, assemblies and councils would meet, collective defence or raids were organized, civil disputes were resolved and crimes punished. Likewise, it was by virtue of his place on the genealogical tree of his *fakhd* or *gabila* that the Western Saharan acquired an array of rights and obligations relating to such matters as the finding of marriage partners and responsibility for blood debts.[2]

Moreover, tribal identity was reinforced by the caste inequalities between tribes. At the top of the social scale were the free tribes, who were known either as *shorfa*, if they claimed (by virtue of their forebears' astute genealogical manipulation) to be descended from the Prophet Mohammed, or as *ahel mdafa* (people of the gun), though the *shorfa* usually depended as much on their military prowess as their claim to holy ancestry to assure their social position. Beneath these two castes were the *znaga*, tribes that had to pay tribute for protection to powerful free tribes. This tribute could take different forms, but its most exacting variant was the *horma*, tribute paid by each family head in a vassal tribe to a designated family in the protector tribe. The *znaga* were sometimes known as *lahma*, or 'flesh without bones', a designation that rather aptly summed up their unenviable social place, though their predicament was marginally preferable to that of the despised castes of bards (*iggawen*) and craftsmen (*maalemin*) and, in the social gutter, the slaves (*abid*) and ex-slaves (*haratin*), all of whom were attached to tribes of warrior, sherifian or tributary status, rather than forming tribes of their own.[3]

Not surprisingly, notions of blood loyalty (*asabiya*) and agnatic solidarity were particularly strong in such a society.[4] And, although the final establishment of a *pax gallica/hispanica* in the desert wastes between Adrar (Mauritania) and the Oued Draa (southern Morocco) in 1934 terminated inter-tribal raiding, eroded the protection system at the root of the caste inequalities between tribes and also diminished the day-to-day significance of the *fakhd* by allowing migration in much smaller groups to make better use of scarce pastoral resources, notions of tribal fraction identity and loyalty had changed little even by the late 1950s from what they had been centuries earlier. They remained much stronger than any incipient sense of supratribal national identity, whether Western Saharan, Moroccan or, for that matter, Mauritanian.

None the less, the territory which today goes under the name of Western Sahara corresponds rather roughly with the geographical region known traditionally to the *qabael* who roamed it as the Sahel, or the littoral, since it bordered the Atlantic coast. The nomads of this region saw themselves, broadly speaking, as the *ahel es-Sahel*, the people of the Sahel or of Atlantic Sahara.[5] In the nineteenth and twentieth centuries the main *gabael* to comprise the *ahel es-Sahel* have been the Reguibat, the Izarguien, the Oulad Delim, the Oulad Tidrarin, the Ait Lahsen and the Arosien.

These Saharawis did, in a broad cultural sense, have a common identity with the predominantly Berber sedentary or semi-nomadic populations to their immediate north, in southern Morocco, beyond the Ouarkziz and Bani mountains and the Oued Draa. Besides their distinctive way of life as great camel-herding nomads and their total political and military independence, their language—the Hassaniya dialect of Arabic—distinguished them from the Tashelhit-speaking Berbers to the north.[6]

But the Saharawis of Western Sahara are part of the same broad ethnic group as the *beidan*, or Moors, of Mauritania. They are all the descendants of Sanhaja Berbers, the Beni Hassan Arabs who began migrating into this region of the Sahara from the end of the thirteenth century, and black Africans. The long process of vassalization and fusion between Beni Hassan and Sanhaja brought the gradual decline of the Sanhaja language (still spoken widely at the time of the first Portuguese expeditions along the Western Saharan–Mauritanian coast in the fifteenth century) and the adoption of Hassaniya even by the tribes of purest Sanhaja ancestry. The *trab el-beidan* (the 'land of the Moors') came to be bordered, broadly speaking, by the Oued Draa and its flanking mountain ranges in the north, by the valley of the Senegal River and the bend of the Niger in the south, and by the barely inhabitable Erg Chech, Tanezrouff and Majabat al-Koubra to the east, which separated the Moors from the lands of the Tuareg, except in the south-east, in the region of Timbuctoo,[7] A number of common features characterized this swathe of desert: among them a common language (Hassaniya), an economy based on pastoral nomadism and commerce, the frequent practice of raiding and a host of distinguishing cultural features, ranging from poetry to diet and clothes.

However, there was a certain distinctiveness about the *ahel es-Sahel*. It was made up of a number of autonomous, often conflicting emirates, confederations and tribes. In the plains of the south and centre-west, which enjoy slightly better rainfall and whose oases and relatively better pastures can support a higher concentration of population, embryonic supratribal states had been imposed from the seventeenth century in Trarza, Brakna, Adrar and Tagant by certain powerful warrior tribes of Beni Hassan origin (that in Tagant coming under the domination of a tribe of Sanhaja origin, the Idou Aich, in the eighteenth century). But the exceptionally arid desert between Adrar and the Oued Draa was the domain of *gabael* who were effectively beyond the reach of and never subservient to either the sultans of Morocco or the emirs to the south.[8]

However, the specificity of the *ahel es-Sahel* might have had no political importance for the latter part of the twentieth century. On the face of it, the Saharawis of Western Sahara might appear to have far more in common with the Moors across the border in Mauritania than do the latter with their fellow-Mauritanians, of Pulaar, Soninke and Peul ancestry. Likewise, there is no intrinsic reason why the cultural differences between the Saharawis and their Moroccan neighbours to the immediate north should have been any more of a barrier to political integration today than those, say, between Arabophone and Berberophone Moroccans.

Indeed, thousands of Saharawis became part of a broad, trans-frontier anti-colonial struggle only as recently as 1957-8, when they responded to the insurrectionary appeals of the Moroccan Army of Liberation (Jaich at-Tahrir). In January 1956, the Army of Liberation appointed a Fifian, Benhamou Mesfioui, as commander of its southern zone; and, on the eve of Morocco's independence (March 1956), his men took control of huge areas of Morocco to the south of Agadir. Headquarters were set up in such towns as Tiznit, Bou-Izakarn and Goulimine. Since Goulimine was an important trading centre for the Saharawis, word of the arrival of these liberation fighters in the extreme south of Morocco soon reached the desert. Inspired by the success of the Moroccan independence struggle, Saharawis began to enrol in the Army of Liberation. In June 1956, its units began a series of attacks on French positions near Tindouf, in south-western Algeria.[9] In February 1957 guerrillas staged the first of several attacks against the French in the extreme north of Mauritania, near Bir-Moghrein.[10] In Western Sahara itself, the Spanish governor-general, General Mariano Gómez Zamalloa, ordered a strategic withdrawal of Spanish troops to a handful of enclaves on the coast (even Smara was abandoned) in the second half of 1957, while further north the guerrilla movement, supported by the local Ait Ba Amaran, began a full-scale invasion of Ifni in November, finally forcing the Spanish army to retreat to a small enclave around its capital, Sidi Ifni, the following December.[11]

However, though the Saharawis were inspired by Morocco's independence and though the top commanders of the Army of Liberation were Moroccan, the Saharawis may not have had, as it were, a Moroccan national consciousness. The units that actually fought in the Sahara were almost exclusively Saharawi in composition; and it was through their traditional assemblies, the *djemaas*, that Saharawi fractions gave their support to the movement. Perhaps some Saharawi participants in this struggle did embrace the ideal of becoming part of independent Morocco, but it is probable that most had a more traditional approach, viewing their struggle as a resumption of the anti-colonial *ghazzian* that had ended only twenty-three years earlier, in 1934, and intended to restore the total liberty to which they had been accustomed in pre-colonial days. Yet, had the Army of Liberation succeeded in driving the Spanish from Western Sahara, the territory would have been integrated into Morocco and Saharawi nationalism would probably never have emerged as a political force, just as Tuareg nationalism has not become a significant political phenomenon in southern Algeria.

In fact, the Saharawi wing of the Army of Liberation was crushed in February 1958 by a combined Franco-Spanish counter-insurgency operation, involving 14,000 troops and 130 aircraft, known as Operation Ouragan.[12] Its remnants sought refuge in southern Morocco, where they were disarmed, disbanded and partially integrated (1958–60) by the Forces Armées Royales (FAR), which had finally succeeded in establishing the royal government's authority in the extreme south of Morocco early in 1958. Spanish Sahara remained Spanish, with the exception of a small strip of territory between the Oued Draa and parallel 27°40′, known as the Tarfaya Zone or Spanish Southern Morocco. Its cession, or 'retrocession', to Morocco had been promised by Spain since, unlike the outright colonies of Saguia el-Hamra and Río de Oro, it had formed part of Spain's Moroccan protectorate zone under the 1912 Franco-Spanish convention on Morocco; but the hand-over had been delayed because of Madrid's insistence that the insurgents first be brought under control. The cession was finally made by the Agreement of Cintra, signed on 1 April 1958.

The ensuing decade saw no significant expression of Saharawi opposition to Spain in the territory that remained under Spanish rule. However, this was to be a period of profound economic, social and political change and, when a new anti-colonial movement did begin to take shape, at the end of the 1960s, it took a decidedly different form from the Saharawi units of the Army of Liberation.

The mineral bonanza and social change

Until the late 1950s, the colonial presence had not only been extremely recent; it had also left but a modest mark on traditional society. Western Sahara had had minimum economic interest to Madrid. Under a decree issued in 1934, after the final Franco-Spanish pacification of the region, it had been administered by a *delegado gubernativo* as a kind of minor appendage of the Spanish protectorate in Northern Morocco. And, from 1946, it was administered by a sub-governor as part of Africa Occidental Española (AOE), which had its capital in Sidi Ifni.[14] The pace of change had been exceedingly slow. Graphic indicators are that, by 1952, there were still only 216 civilian employees (155 of them Saharawis), twenty-four telephone subscribers and 354 school-children (189 Saharawis) in the whole territory (including the zone ceded to Morocco six years later).[15] None of the Spanish settlements was larger than a medium-sized Spanish village, and very few Saharawis had settled in them. Indeed, the Saharawis had continued since 1934 to engage in their own pastoral economy, albeit with increased trading ties to the Spanish settlements, to apply their own justice (the customary *orf* and koranic *sharia* law) and to regulate their affairs through the traditional *djemaas*, while coexisting pragmatically with the Spanish. The latter, enclaved in their little settlements, were perfectly happy with such a *modus vivendi*. They had neither the means nor the desire to bring the nomads under direct administrative control or even to tax them.

However, from the late 1950s, Western Sahara experienced belated but quite rapid changes. One of the principal causes was a sudden awakening of interest in the territory's mineral resources. At first the main focus was on oil exploration. Between 1960 and 1964 more than forty concessions, covering around 100,000 square kilometres (two-fifths of the territory's total land-area), were awarded to eleven consortia, involving nineteen oil companies, and by 1964 a total of twenty-seven discoveries had been made. The search then shifted off-shore. But, probably because of the country's inadequate infrastructure and the low world oil prices at the time, no oil was exploited.[16] None the less, the arrival of scores of oil exploration teams in the early 1960s awakened the Saharawis to their territory's possible interest as a source of natural resources.

Of much greater importance was the development of the territory's famous phosphate resources, which had first been discovered by the Spanish geologist, Manuel Alia Medina, in the 1940s. In July 1962, the Spanish state's Instituto Nacional de Industria (INI) set up the Empresa Nacional Minera del Sahara (ENMINSA) with a brief to examine the feasibility of exploiting Western Sahara's phosphates. ENMINSA soon claimed that Western Sahara had ten billion tons of phosphates and that there was a proven reserve of 1.7 billion tons of very high-grade ore at Bou-Craa, about 107 kilometres to the south-east of El-Ayoun. In August 1969, a new INI subsidiary, Fosfatos de Bu-Craa (Fosbucraa) was founded to exploit the deposits there. By 1974, pesetas (pta) 24.5 billion had been invested there and exports had reached 2.5 million tons, making Western Sahara the world's sixth-largest phosphate exporter. But, with plans to raise mining capacity to ten million tons by 1980, Western Sahara seemed destined to become the world's second major exporter, surpassed only by Morocco (which exported 16.4 million tons in 1984).[17] There was also considerable investigation of the territory's iron ore deposits during the 1960s.

One of the consequences of this new interest in Western Sahara's mineral resources was that the Spanish government began for the first time to make large-scale investments in the territory, to improve its basic administrative and economic infrastructure. The territory's budget was quadrupled from pta 53.5 million in 1960 to pta 207.3 million in 1961. In 1965 an extraordinary budget for public work projects, totalling pta 225.7 million, was adopted by the Madrid government, bringing the territory's total annual budget to pta 552 million; and, in November of the same year, a director of social and economic planning was appointed for the territory.[18] By 1972, the territorial budget had risen to pta 1,277 million; and, by 1974, it had doubled again to pta 2,460 million, with 69 per cent of expenditure financed by subsidies from Madrid.[19] New wells were sunk to increase the water supply, and new ports, roads and power stations built. A measure of the economic change was that annual imports rose tenfold in value between 1959 and 1971, from a mere pta 170 million to pta 1.6 billion.[20]

As the modern sector of the economy grew, Spanish workers began to arrive, mainly from the high-unemployment Canaries, to take up jobs. By 1967 there were 9,726 Spanish civilians in the territory; by 1974 there were 20,126.[21] Despite the influx of Spanish labour (and the fact that Spaniards held 60 per cent of the capital-intensive phosphate industry's 2,550 jobs in 1975), many Saharawis also entered waged employment in this period. By 1974 there were around 8,000 Saharawi wage-earners in all: 5,465 of them unskilled labourers, 345 industrial workers, 707 drivers, 190 office employees, 141 teachers and 1,341 soldiers, among others.[22] A Saharawi working class, albeit miniscule, was germinating. Meanwhile, other Saharawis put their age-old commercial skills to use by setting up shop in the growing small towns as traders, taking advantage of the expanding urban market and also the opportunities, resulting from Western Sahara's status as an extension of the Canaries' special customs zone, to engage in a flourishing smuggling trade into neighbouring African countries. By 1974, the census authorities could count 981 Saharawi traders.[23]

The growth of employment, trading and also educational opportunities in the towns encouraged a large part of the Saharawi population to abandon its precarious nomadic way of life. Droughts were another factor. A serious drought in 1959–63 is estimated to have killed off 46 per cent of the country's camels, reducing their numbers from 44,848 to 24,300.[24] There was a gradual recovery in the mid-1960s, but another great drought, in 1986–74, is thought to have wiped out 60 per cent of the livestock.[25] Sedentarization occurred on a mass scale in many parts of the Sahara; and in Mauritania, for example, the nomadic proportion of the population fell from 65 per cent in 1965 to only 36 per cent in 1977, while the population of the capital, Nouakchott, grew tenfold, from 12,300 to 134,986.[26]

Although the statistics are not totally reliable, it would appear that a majority of Western Saharans had abandoned nomadism by 1974. The number of Saharawis living in the three main towns—El-Ayoun, Smara and Villa Cisneros (now Dakhla)—tripled between 1967 and 1974, reaching 40,660, or 55 per cent of the total number of Saharawis recorded in the 1974 census, which put the total population at 95,019 of whom 73,497 were Saharawis, 20,126 Europeans and 1,396 from other countries, but which may have underestimated the nomadic element of the population

Table 3.1 The growth of the urban Saharawi
population

	1967	1974
El-Ayoun	9,701	28,010
Smara	1,916	7,280
Villa Cisneros (Dakhla)	2,364	5,370
Total: 3 main towns	13,981	40,660

Sources: Instituto des Estudios Africanos, *Resumen estadistico del Sahara español [Año 1969]*, Madrid, p. 10; *Censo-74*, Servicio de registro de población, censo y estadística, El-Ayoun, 1974, p. 44.

since the census authorities themselves noted the reluctance of some of the Saharawi population to cooperate with their efforts.[27]

Sedentarization brought the Saharawis into much more direct and permanent contact with the Spanish, notably in employment and schools. It was really during the 1960s that large numbers of Saharawis came within the effective purview of Spanish administrative structures and the Spanish judicial system for the first time. These Saharawis were thus no longer living in pragmatic coexistence with Spanish settlements that were essentially external to their own nomadic world, but were now part of a Spanish-dominated urban society, even though the towns remained very small by international standards. With its administrators and bureaucrats, soldiers and policemen, laws and regulations, schools and hospitals, Western Sahara started to look, to settled Saharawis, like a country. Here surely was one of the principal seeds of a sense of nationhood.

In this new urban world, Saharawis of different tribal origins lived and worked, or went to school, side by side. Moreover, they were all, in a sense, *znaga*, or tributaries, in relation to the Spanish, who were now the undisputed *ahel mdafa*, or people of the gun. In short, the Saharawis, whatever their tribal background, faced the common denominator of Spanish colonial rule.

A distinct colonial experience

Moreover, a series of political changes, introduced by the Spanish from 1958, tended to reinforce the impression that the territory was becoming a coherent political entity. Ironically, this began with its conversion, on 10 January 1958, a month before Ouragan, into a fully fledged province of Spain, upon the dissolution of AOE.[28] Western Sahara ceased to be an adjunct of Ifni and was henceforth ruled by its own governor-general, resident in El-Ayoun. A senior military officer, he took orders in military matters from the captain-general of the Canaries, but otherwise he was responsible to the presidency in Madrid through its colonial office, the Dirección General de Plazas y Provincias Africanas, or, after the Spanish withdrawal from Rio Muni, Fernando Po and Ifni in 1968–9, the Dirección General de Promoción del Sahara. Within the province, he was assisted by a secretary-general, who headed the civil administration.[29]

Additionally, provincial and municipal councils were established for the first time, albeit within the undemocratic, corporatist framework of the Francoist system, following the enactment of two laws on the province's political structure in 1961–2.[30] These established a fourteen-member Cabildo Provincial for the territory as a whole, while El-Ayoun and Villa Cisneros were designated municipalities (*terminos municipales*), with town councils (*ayuntamientos*) comprising elected *concejales* (twelve in El-Ayoun and eight in Villa Cisneros) and state-appointed mayors (*alcaldes*). The two smaller urban settlements of Smara and la Guera were designated *entidades locales menores*, with local *juntas*. The first elections to the Cabildo Provincial, the *ayuntamientos* and *juntas* were held in May 1963; and a Saharawi, Khatri Ould Said Ould el-Joumani, a *sheikh*,[31] or chief, of the Reguibat, was appointed by Madrid to become the Cabildo's first president. In view of the territory's new provincial status, it was also to be represented in the Cortes under the new legislation, and so, in true corporatist style, Khatri and the two *alcaldes* of El-Ayoun (a Spaniard) and Villa Cisneros (a *sheikh* of the Oulad Delim, Souilem Ould Abdellahi) took their seats in the Cortes the following July.[32] After the second elections, in 1965, Khatri was replaced as president of the Cabildo by another Reguibi, Saila Ould Abeida; and in 1967 the number of *procuradores* from the Sahara in the Cortes was raised to six.[33]

Finally, albeit as a Spanish province, Western Sahara was beginning to have a structured political system of its own. Still, in the early 1960s, most of the Saharawis, as nomads, remained only marginally affected by these changes, though the November 1962 decree on the territory's local administration did attempt to integrate the nomads' own traditional forms of political organization into the province's administrative system by requiring the *djemaas* to elect councils headed by *shioukh* whose election (by the respective fraction's heads of families) was subject to the governor-general's approval.

However, as the urban Saharawi population grew, the Spanish authorities feared that neither the Cabildo Provincial, which had only six Saharawi members (and eight Spaniards) in 1967, nor the *ayuntamientos* could provide adequate channels for communication between the colonial government and the Saharawi population or for the satisfaction or appeasement of Saharawi political aspirations. In 1967 the colonial authorities established an all-Saharawi consultative territorial assembly, known as the Asamblea General de Sahara or, more popularly, as the Djemaa. Saila Ould Abeida was elected its president and Baba Ould Hasseina, a *sheikh* of the Oulad

Delim, his deputy, at the Djemaa's inauguration on 1 December 1967. The assembly had no real legislative powers; and its members, initially numbering eighty-two, were not elected by universal adult suffrage in geographically defined constituencies but were either *ex officio* or chosen by the *djemaas* of tribal fractions.[34] Despite these limitations, the very creation of a territorial assembly and its subsequent debates on the territory's economic, social and other problems tended to encourage a sense of supratribal territorial identity.

The backdrop to these changes, moreover, was Western Sahara's status as the sole remaining European colony in the region—after the achievement of independence by Morocco in 1956, Mauritania in 1960 and finally Algeria in 1962. The Western Saharans, in other words, were now living a distinct and unique colonial experience. Despite the territorial claims of both Morocco and Mauritania, neither country played any significant role in assisting the birth of a new anti-colonial movement within the Spanish colony.

The Moroccan and Mauritanian claims

King Mohammed V had formally endorsed Allal el-Fassi's 'Greater Morocco' theses when, in a famous speech at M'hamid, an oasis town near the bend of the Draa, at 'the gate of the Moroccan Sahara' on 25 February 1958, he had pledged to 'continue to do everything in our power to recover our Sahara and all that which, by historical evidence and by the will of its inhabitants, belongs as of right to our kingdom'.[35] He had done so to prevent the Istiqlal party from outpacing the monarchy in nationalist fervour and because, by glorifying the conquests of the more powerful of Morocco's pre-colonial sultans, Allal el-Fassi's ideology could easily be turned to royal ends, to boost the prestige of the monarchy.

Yet Mohammed V's drive to reinforce monarchical power also meant that Operation Ouragan, which terminated on the eve of his M'hamid speech, was not unwelcome to the king. Along with the entry of his own troops into the extreme south of Morocco, including the Tarfaya Zone, in the early part of 1958, it spelt the end of the 'irregulars' whom he had so distrusted. Thereafter, the royal government had no intention of authorizing a new guerrilla struggle against Spain and, although the claim to Western Sahara remained official policy, nothing was done, until quite different circumstances in 1974, to give Madrid real cause for alarm.

Indeed, after his ascent to the throne in 1961, King Hassan II adopted a particularly pragmatic policy towards Spain, putting the accent on economic cooperation rather than the traditional territorial claims to Western Sahara, Ifni and the *presidios* of Ceuta and Melilla on Morocco's Mediterranean coast. The king's *entente* with Spain was highlighted by a summit meeting with General Franco at Madrid's Barajas airport on 6 July 1963, where they agreed to 'study all the problems of common interest with a view to reaching solutions which can serve as a basis for subsequent agreements'.[36] There was a close ideological affinity between Franco and Hassan.[37] And Spain held out an attractive economic carrot. 'I am sure that there are vast domains in which Morocco and Spain can work together', suggested the Spanish industry minister Gregoria López Bravo in Rabat on 2 March 1964.[38] The 'spirit of Barajas' governed Spanish–Moroccan relations for more than a decade, despite occasional friction over Spanish fishing rights off the Moroccan coast.

The Moroccan writer Rachid Lazrak has observed that Spanish–Moroccan negotiations on territorial issues during the decade after Barajas were conducted almost entirely in private, between Hassan and Franco.[39] The claim to Ceuta and Melilla was not brought before the United Nations, even though Spain continually raised the analogous issue of Gibraltar there from 1963.[40] Both cities continued to receive their water from Morocco.[41] The claims to Ifni and Spanish Sahara were promoted sporadically in diplomatic forums, but no attempt was made by the Moroccan government to organize an anti-Spanish struggle by their inhabitants. Having disbanded the remnants of the Army of Liberation at the end of the 1950s, when he was Crown Prince and chief-of-staff of the FAR, Hassan had no intention of re-creating a guerrilla movement. During the 1960s and early 1970s, Hassan was much criticized by Moroccan nationalists for playing down the struggle against Spain, although the King did succeed, by means of his private diplomacy, in persuading Spain to hand over Ifni in 1969, but, unlike Western Sahara, Ifni had no economic interest for Spain.

On a purely verbal plane, there was a short-lived revival of drum-beating by the Moroccan government about Western Sahara in 1965–8, occasioned by the adoption of the first resolution on Western Sahara (and Ifni) by the United Nations Committee of 24 in 1964. A Ministry of Mauritanian and Saharan affairs was established in 1965, under Moulay Hassan Ben Driss, a cousin of the king. He encouraged the formation of the Frente de Liberación del Sahara bajo Dominación Española (FLS), which sent a delegation led by Ma el-Ainin el-Abadila Ould Sheikh Mohammed Laghdaf, a grandson of Sheikh Ma el-Ainin, to New York to lobby the United Nations in November–December 1966, on the eve of the adoption of the first UN resolution advocating a referendum of self-determination. The FLS also began publishing a Spanish-language journal, *Neustro Sahara*, under the editorship of Brika Zaruali, an Istiqlalian, in March 1967. However, the FLS was barely active. It was never more than a circle of Saharawi exiles in Morocco who were dependent on the largesse of the Moroccan government for their limited literary and diplomatic ventures. The FLS never attempted political activity within Western Sahara. In mid-1968, *Neustro Sahara* ceased publication; the grouplet's final death followed a year later when King Hassan wound up the Ministry of Mauritanian and Saharan Affairs to permit the establishment of diplomatic relations with Mauritania.[42]

The Mouvement de Resistance 'les Hommes Bleus' (Morehob), which was set up in 1972 by a former Moroccan policeman Bachir Figuigui who took the bizarre Christian pseudonym of Edouard Moha, had even less political significance. Based first in Rabat, where it advocated Western Sahara's 'return to the mother country', it mysteriously shifted base to Algiers in March 1973, declaring that it refused to be used by the Moroccan authorities as a 'fifth column'.[43] However, Moha was expelled from Algeria within six months of his arrival, settled in Belgium and then in January 1975, re-emerged as a supporter of the Moroccan claim. A UN mission of inquiry, which toured Western Sahara in May 1975, reported that it did not meet a single supporter of Morehob there and that 'the Spanish authorities and the political movements encountered within the Territory consider that Morehob does not have many members and point to the fact that there is no evidence of it having engaged in armed activities within the Territory.'[44]

The playing down of the Western Sahara question by the Hassan regime meshed, from the late 1960s onwards, with a muting of its enthusiasm for the whole Greater Morocco cause. In January 1969, at a summit meeting in Ifrane, Hassan and President Houari Boumedienne signed a twenty-year treaty burying the differences of the past that had led to a border war in 1963.[45] At a second summit on 27 May 1970 at Tlemcen, Hassan and Boumedienne decided to set up a joint commission to 'proceed to the fixing of the border-line between the two countries.'[46] Finally, two years later on 15 June 1972 Morocco and Algeria signed a joint declaration affirming their intention to 'establish a permanent peace for centuries to come' and a border convention which gave *de jure* recognition to the *de facto* Algerian–Moroccan frontier which Morocco had previously contested. Morocco thus renounced its old claim to large tracts of the Algerian Sahara'.[47]

The *détente* with Algeria was accompanied by a belated recognition of Mauritania, which Morocco had refused to recognize since its independence in 1960. Hassan also broke the ice by inviting President Mokhtar Ould Daddah to an Islamic summit conference in Rabat in September 1969. Then on 8 June 1970 Morocco and Mauritania signed a treaty of friendship and cooperation.[48]

The Istiqlal party and the Moroccan communists vigorously expressed their displeasure in their press at the Hassan regime's abandonment of the claims to Mauritania and parts of Algeria and of its soft-pedalling of the claim to Western Sahara. The Union Nationale des Forces Populaires (UNFP), which had not shared the Istiqlal's enthusiasm for the claim to Mauritania and had opposed the 1963 war with Algeria, was also critical of the government's warm relations with Madrid and demand a 'clear position concerning the occupied territories'.[49] However, in practice, the Moroccan opposition parties limited their Western Saharan activity to the writing of editorials in party newspapers and the making of speeches. They made no attempt to begin political work underground within Western Sahara itself.

It is one of the great ironies of the Western Saharan affair, in fact, that it was partly as a result of the failure of the Moroccan government and the Moroccan opposition parties to pursue their claim to Western Sahara with real vigour after the demise of the Army of Liberation that the anti-colonial Saharawis began to organize on their own account and to turn further afield than Morocco, to such countries as Algeria and Libya, for external support. This self-reliance also helped to mould the distinctly Saharawi nationalist character of the anti-colonial movement when it resurfaced at the end of the 1960s.

Anti-colonial Saharawis also received only limited practical support from the Mauritanian government. Although President Mokhtar Ould Daddah had laid claim to Western Sahara consistently since an appeal at Atar on 1 July 1957 to 'our brothers of Spanish Sahara to dream of this great economic and spiritual Mauritania', he had had no wish to jeopardize relations with Spain, which provided valuable aid to his impoverished country (notably from 1964 for the Nouadhibou fishing industry), so long as Spain did not hand Western Sahara to Morocco. That, in view of Morocco's designs on Mauritania itself and Western Sahara's proximity to the Zouerate-Nouadhibou iron industry on which Mauritania was dependent for about 85 per cent of its export revenue by the mid-1960s, would have constituted a real strategic danger for Nouakchott. But Madrid, which was adept at playing on the rivalries of Rabat and Nouakchott, continually reassured Mokhtar Ould Daddah that it had no intention of bowing to Moroccan pressure. So, from a *realpolitik* standpoint, the Mauritanian government found the colonial status quo a rather satisfactory arrangement, though it naturally never said so publicly. As a Spanish buffer zone, Western Sahara kept the Moroccans at arm's length.[50]

The UN and self-determination

Meanwhile, better-educated Saharawis knew, from the mid-1960s onwards, that the United Nations was advocating self-determination for the Spanish Sahara. It was in December 1965 that the United Nations General Assembly adopted its first resolution on Western Sahara (and Ifni) by a majority of one-hundred to two (Spain and Portugal), requesting Spain to 'take all necessary measures for the liberation of the Territories of Ifni and Spanish Sahara from colonial domination and, to this end, to enter into negotiations on problems relating to sovereignty presented by these two territories.'[51] However, whereas there seemed to be no reason to doubt that the population of Ifni would wish to be integrated with Morocco, the problems relating to sovereignty appeared to be more complicated in the Western Saharan case, if only because Morocco and Mauritania had rival claims to the colony. It had become standard practice by the early 1960s for the United Nations to organize or monitor plebiscites or elections in colonies where, on the eve of the colonial power's departure, there seemed to be an open question as to which state(s) their inhabitants wished to join or form. In December 1966, the United Nations General Assembly adopted a second resolution, by 105 votes to 2 (Spain and Portugal) which, while requesting Spain to transfer its powers to Morocco in Ifni, proposed a UN-supervised referendum of self-determination in Western Sahara. Spain was asked to

determine at the earliest possible date, in conformity with the aspirations of the indigenous people of Spanish Sahara and in consultation with the Governments of Mauritania and Morocco and any other interested party, the procedures for the holding of a referendum under United Nations auspices with a view to enabling the indigenous population of the Territory to exercise freely its right to self-determination.[52]

Six similar resolutions, all reaffirming the Western Saharan's right to self-determination and urging a referendum under United Nations auspices, were adopted by overwhelming majorities in the United Nations General Assembly between 1967 and 1973. Furthermore in 1972 and 1973 the resolutions went further to affirm explicitly the Western Saharan people's rights to independence, rather than, as before, simply self-determination.[53]

Similarly, the OAU Council of Ministers, in its first resolution on Spain's African colonies, adopted in 1966, appealed to Spain to initiate resolutely a process giving freedom and independence to all those regions.[54] Several resolutions, endorsing the UN resolutions on Western Sahara, were adopted by the OAU Council of Ministers over the following years. Thus, a resolution adopted by the Council of Ministers in June 1972, at a session held in Rabat, called on Spain to 'create a free and democratic atmosphere in which the people of that territory can exercise their right to self-determination and independence without delay in accordance with the Charter of the United Nations'.[55]

By repeatedly asserting the Saharawis' right to determine their future, and at times also their specific right to independence, the United Nations and the OAU helped to legitimize the idea of Saharawi sovereignty, and perhaps also created the impression that a bid for Saharawi independence would receive international support.

Moreover, in response to the growing pressure for decolonization from the United Nations the Spanish government announced, in a letter to the president of the UN's Committee of 24, on 8 September 1966, that it would accept self-determination in Western Sahara.[56] In the Fourth Committee a few weeks later, on 17 November, the Spanish representative Jaime de Piniés reaffirmed that 'we are prepared to decolonize, in accordance with the will of the population of the Sahara', while warning that Spain would not tolerate interference from neighbours of the territory with 'imperialist appetites'.[57]

Indeed, by endorsing the UN doctrine of self-determination, albeit without the intention of putting it into practice in the foreseeable future, Spain could rebuff the Moroccan and Mauritanian territorial claims. The future of the country, the Spanish government now said, was a matter to be determined exclusively by the Saharawis and Spain, without external interference by third parties. In Spanish propaganda much was now made of Morocco's supposed desire to acquire Western Sahara's new-found mineral wealth. 'It is certain that, with the scent of these riches, the jackals are beginning to prowl around your *khaimas*', was, for example, the colourful warning given to the Saharawis by the Spanish army minister, Lieutenant-General Camillo Menéndez Tolosa in El-Ayoun on 16 May 1967. He promised:

But now more than ever you will have us by your side, to the end and the last sacrifice, to guarantee your will, without foreign pressure or interference, to protect you against the manœuvres and false fraternity in whose name it is intended to bring you into a household to which you have never belonged and in which, if they achieved their goal (something they will never do), you would be considered a poor relative to be exploited like a domestic.[58]

Hypocritical though they were (since the Spanish had been particularly attracted by the 'scent' of Western Sahara's phosphates and other minerals), the general's words struck a chord in the Saharawi soul. Why should the Moroccans, who had never had to cope with the rigours of the arid Sahara, now arrive from the north to reap the advantages of its newly discovered mineral wealth?[59] But why too should the Spanish? Moreover, the phosphate bonanza doubtless suggested to the Saharawis that an independent Western Sahara would be a viable state, indeed a relatively prosperous one.[60]

Until 1974, however, the Spanish government had no intention of implementing its commitment to self-determination. It was hoping to reap the benefits of the territory's mineral wealth itself. So, while paying lip-service to the principle of self-determination, in practice Spain dragged its feet. It was not until August 1974, almost eight years after its formal endorsement of self-determination, that the Spanish government finally announced that a referendum would be held—in the first six months of 1975. As an excuse for its tardiness, the government tried to convince the United Nations that self-determination could not be rushed because of the nomadic character of the population and the territory's low level of economic development.

For Madrid in the mid-1960s, a policy along these lines appeared to carry no serious political risks within the territory itself since there was no organized nationalist movement pressing for the implementation of self-determination. Indeed, the Spanish authorities succeeded in persuading 800 *shioukh* to address a petition to the United Nations in March 1966 supporting continued union with Spain; and the following November, 91 per cent of the Saharawi adult men who took part in a referendum organized by the colonial authorities endorsed a similar declaration, which was taken to the United Nations by a 'comisión elegida por el pueblo del

Sahara', including Saila Ould Abeida, Souilem Ould Abdellahi and Baba Ould Hasseina.[61] 'An improvised independence would lead us to chaos and disorder', the commission told the Fourth Committee in December. 'The consequences and damage of such haste would fall on us and we cannot accept that a small minority of adventurers, backed by any other nation, disturbs our peace and tranquility.'[62]

Ironically, the Spanish government's oft-repeated yet hypocritically empty commitments to self-determination and its paternalist defence of Saharawi rights against the 'predatory' designs of neighbouring governments played a significant part in engendering a nationalist consciousness which was later to rebound against the Spanish. Indeed, the November 1966 declaration ended on this note: 'The signing of this statement does not bar the possibility of the Saharan people reaching complete independence in the future, simply by requesting Spain for it when we have capable leaders and adequate economic means.'[63] Additionally, it was the discrepancy between the Spanish government's abstract 'democratic' declarations and its actual practice and the failure of the *shioukh* of the Djemaa to challenge Spain to act upon its declared intentions that prompted young urban Saharawis to begin engaging in their own autonomous nationalist activity.

Furthermore, it is another irony that, despite their territorial claims to Western Sahara, both the Moroccan and Mauritanian governments also gave their blessing to the notion of Saharawi self-determination from 1966. Both governments tailored their policies, after the UN General Assembly's first resolution on the territory in 1965, to accommodate the standard UN principles regarding decolonization. At a meeting of the Committee of 24 in Addis Ababa on 7 June 1966, the Moroccan representative Dey Ould Sidi Baba went so far as to propose that Western Sahara and other Spanish colonies 'should as soon as possible be granted their independence, thereby enabling the people of those Territories to exercise all the responsibilities of power themselves, without any colonial presence'.[64] Although Dey Ould Sidi Baba hastened to add that this did not mean a renunciation of the Moroccan claim, the nationalists of the Istiqlal were aghast. 'We are absolutely opposed to any attitude, even one explicable for tactical reasons, which could engender confusion and put in question the integrity of Moroccan territory to the slightest extent', the party protested.[65] But the ultras of the Istiqlal Party were quietly ignored. On 13 October the Moroccan foreign minister Mohammed Cherkaoui reaffirmed Morocco's support for Western Sahara's independence and said that this must be 'a true independence which would put the future of these territories in the hands of their own nationals who, with their discretion and in fully recovered freedom, would know how to decide their destiny'.[66] Cherkaoui accepted the principle of a referendum in Western Sahara but insisted that prior to its being held the Spanish administration and troops there were to be withdrawn and Saharawi refugees allowed to return home.[67] Morocco accordingly voted in favour of General Assembly Resolution 2229 on

20 December 1966; and it voted for every one of the six pro-referendum resolutions adopted by the UN General Assembly between 1967 and 1974 except, mysteriously, that adopted in 1972. Indeed, King Hassan himself explained at a press conference on 30 July 1970 that, in his negotiations with Spain,

instead of going purely and simply to claim the territory of the Sahara, I went to request specifically that a popular consultation take place there, assured as I was that the first result would be the departure of the non-Africans and that then one would leave it up to the people of the Sahara to choose whether to live under the Moroccan aegis or their own aegis or any other aegis.[68]

Hassan was almost certainly unaware of the germination of a Saharawi nationalist consciousness in this period. He probably believed, until as late as 1974, that Morocco would win a referendum. 'Although the Moroccan character of this part of the Sahara is historically and geographically obvious', the semi-official *Maroc-Soir* noted in an editorial on 23 July 1973, Morocco had accepted the idea of a referendum 'certain that the population will vote in favour of returning to the motherland'.[69]

Mauritania also endorsed the principle of self-determination from 1966, while continuing, like Morocco, to maintain its territorial claim. 'Although the Sahara is an integral part of Mauritania', the Mauritanian representative at the Committee of 24 argued on 18 November 1966, 'the right of its inhabitants to choose their future, without their being converted into tools of the internal problems of other countries, must be recognised.'[70] Mauritania therefore voted for all seven of the pro-referendum resolutions adopted by the UN General Assembly between 1967 and 1973. It would seem that Mokhtar Ould Daddah also banked on a favourable outcome from the poll, perhaps because of the cultural links between the Saharawis and the *beidan* of Mauritania, and calculated that the United Nation's endorsement of the principle of self-determination would at least hinder the possibility of outright Moroccan annexation.

Finally, the UN resolutions on Western Sahara were formally approved by King Hassan and Presidents Mokhtar Ould Daddah and Houari Boumedienne at two tripartite summit meetings at Nouadhibou on 14 September 1970, and Agadir on 24 July 1973. The three heads of state proclaimed at Agadir, for example, their 'unwavering attachment to the principle of self-determination and their concern to ensure that this principle was implemented in a framework which guaranteed that the will of the inhabitants of the Sahara was given free and genuine expression in conformity with the United Nations decisions on this question.'[71]

The Saharawis of course knew that neither Morocco nor Mauritania had abandoned their territorial claims; but these governments' repeated declarations on the Saharawis' right to self-determination helped to legitimate the claim to Mauritania and by recognizing Mauritania's independence in 1969–70 King Hassan established a precedent that was not lost on the Western Saharans. If Mauritania could finally secure Moroccan recognition of its right to nationhood, why could not Western Sahara as well?

Mohammed Bassiri and the Harakat Tahrir

It should be noted that, during this period, the Western Saharans were becoming a rather well-informed people. The role of Arabic as a common lingua franca and the spread of transistor radios enabled them to obtain access to a wide range of information and political ideas.[72] In fact, the flood of cheap radios from the Canary Islands into the 'free zone' of Western Sahara meant that virtually no Saharawi family was without one. UNESCO statistics show that, for every 1,000 inhabitants, 340 Western Saharans had radios in 1972, compared to only ninety-five in Morocco and forty-seven in Algeria.[73]

With access to the plethora of Arabic-language radio stations, it was not difficult for Western Saharans to hear of the UN resolutions, the declarations on Western Sahara made by neighbouring governments—or news of the struggles for independence being fought elsewhere in the Third World, from Vietnam to Palestine, and Guinea-Bissau to Eritrea.[74]

The leadership of the new anti-colonial movement of the late 1960s and early 1970s was markedly different in background and experience from the nomad commanders of the Saharawi guerrilla units of the Army of Liberation. Although they had usually spent much of their early childhood in a nomadic environment, most had later become sedentary and received a modern education. Western Sahara's growing labour requirements and the settlement of European families had prompted the Spanish authorities to begin providing modern educational facilities, for almost the first time, in the 1960s. As late as 1959, there had been only six primary schools in the entire country, with a combined teaching staff of seven and a total pupil enrolment of just 366.[75] There was no secondary education at all until October 1963 when the General Alonso secondary school opened in El-Ayoun, with a branch in Villa Cisneros.[76] But, by 1974, there were 9,252 children in school, 6,170 of them Saharawis, though still only 111 of the 653 secondary school pupils were Saharawi.[77] However, to meet the need for skilled labour, two training schools had been set up by the Spanish ministry of labour's Promoción Profesional Obfera (PPO) in 1967, and they had trained 1,500 Saharawis in various industrial and office skills by 1972.[78] By 1975, seventy-five Saharawis were studying in Spain, fifty-two of them at universities or other institutions of higher education.[79]

It was a young Saharawi who had studied abroad, in the Middle East, who organized the first clandestine anti-colonial movement in Western Sahara after the demise of the Army of Liberation. A Reguibi, Mohammed Sidi Ibrahim Bassiri had been born about 1943 near Tan-Tan, then part of Spanish Southern Morocco.[80] During the Army of Liberation's 1957

Saharan campaign he seems to have been living further south, in Saguia el-Hamra, for he was one of several hundred Saharawi children evacuated by the guerrillas in September 1957 from Lemsid, near El-Ayoun, to Morocco, where he entered a school in Casablanca with the help of a government scholarship.[81] After passing the baccalaureat exams he travelled to the Middle East to study at the universities of Cairo and Damascus. He graduated with a diploma in journalism and returned to Morocco in 1966 to found a radical Saharawi journal *Al-Chihab* (The Torch). However, towards the end of 1967, he left Morocco to return to Western Sahara where he persuaded the Spanish authorities to grant him a residence permit. He started to teach the Koran and Arabic in the mosque at Smara; and there he used his influence as a teacher to recruit the nucleus of an underground anti-colonial movement, which came to be known as the Harakat Tahrir Saguia el-Hamra wa Oued ed-Dahab (Organization for the Liberation of Saguia el-Hamra and Oued ed-Dahab) or more simply as al-Hizb al-Muslim, the Muslim party. In an interview with the Algerian daily newspaper *La République* published in January 1971, a few months after the movement had been severely repressed by the Spanish authorities, two of its exiled leaders said that it had three principal objectives: 'internal autonomy, an agreement between the organization and the Spanish government fixing a time limit for the proclamation of the independence of the Sahara and the evacuation of the Spanish troops' and 'no exploitation of mineral resources without the organization's consent'.[82] The Harakat Tahrir was the first urban-based Saharawi political movement. It advocated wide-ranging social reform as well as national liberation. According to a Spanish military intelligence report written in June 1970, it sought 'the abolition of the *shioukh*, not just the current ones, whose incapacity and incompetence are recognized, but the institution in and of itself'. The movement's members 'are seeking to destroy the tribal structure' and 'also want the reorganization of the present institutions, including the General Assembly', i.e. the Djemma.[83] By the spring of 1970, the colonial authorities had detected widespread support for the movement among urban Saharawis. Most alarming of all, its supporters included 'a considerable number of soldiers in the Tropas Nomadas, policemen, interpreters, drivers, administrative auxiliaries and teachers of the Koran, that is to say practically all the personnel in the confidence of the *jefes de puesto*'.[84] The Harakat Tahrir had also begun seeking aid from neighbouring Arab governments. Taking advantage of the Tindouf *mouggar*, an annual trade fair which attracts visitors from throughout the Western Sahara region, the organization was able to submit a memorandum setting out its goals to Algerian officials in Tindouf on 8 May 1970.[85] Similar appeals to the Moroccan and Mauritanian governments were also planned, but they had not been dispatched by the time the Spanish axe fell, in June 1970.

The movement's fate was sealed when it decided to emerge from hiding by holding a counter-demonstration to a government-sponsored rally addressed by the governor-general General José Maria Peréz de Lema y Tejero in El-Ayoun on 17 June 1970. The Foreign Legion opened fire on the counter-demonstrators, killing a number of them—two according to the Spanish government itself, or ten to twelve according to Arab sources at the time.[86] The ensuing repression shattered the Harakat Tahrir. Hundreds were arrested. Most were released after a few days, but the movement's main militants were detained for several months, some of them in the Canaries, and then deported to Morocco or Mauritania. As for Bassiri, he was arrested on the night of 17 June and has not reappeared since. The Spanish government later claimed to have deported him to Morocco, but the Moroccan authorities deny that he ever arrived and many Saharawis believe that he was murdered by his Spanish captors.[87]

The Saharawi diaspora

Bassiri was not the only Saharawi nationalist leader to have spent much of his childhood or youth outside Spanish Sahara in one of the neighbouring territories. When the Polisario Front was founded three years after the Harakat Tahrir's collapse, in May 1973, many of its founding members hailed from the Saharawi communities of southern Morocco and northern Mauritania. The birth of this second movement also illustrated the role of young university-educated Saharawis.

Sedentarization among the *ahel es-Sahel* had proceeded on as large a scale in southern Morocco, northern Mauritania and south-western Algeria as within the borders of Western Sahara. Political as well as economic factors had prompted many thousands of Saharawis to settle in southern Morocco in 1958 after the collapse of the Army of Liberation. They had lost much of their livestock during the war with the French and Spanish, and many of their remaining animals perished in the ensuing 1959–63 drought. Impoverished, they squatted in such southern Moroccan settlements as Tan-Tan, Tarfaya, Zaag and Goulimine, where they could have access to welfare, jobs and education. To avoid destitution, many joined the FAR after the disbanding of the Army of Liberation. By 1966, there were 27,976 members of Western Saharan tribes living in the province of Tarfaya according to census results published by the Moroccan Ministry of the Interior. There were certainly a few thousand more further north; and it seems unlikely that there could have been fewer than 40–50,000 Saharawis in Morocco by 1974. Similarly, several thousand Reguibat and other Saharawis settled in northern Mauritania in the 1960s and early 1970s, partly as a result of the growth of employment in Zouerate and Nouadhibou brought about by the opening of the iron-mining industry and the development of economic and administrative infrastructure there. Reguibat sedentarization also occurred in south-western Algeria, mainly around Tindouf with the assistance of the Algerian government, which launched a settlement programme for the Reguibat in 1966. In the early 1970s, drought-stricken Reguibat were helped to set up agricultural villages at Abadla, south-west of Bechar, and at Oum el-Assel, Ain Naga and Hassi Abdallah near Tindouf. By 1975 there were some 18,000 Reguibat in Algeria, of whom at least 10,000 were sedentary.[86]

Despite this dispersal of Saharawis across several countries, a marked sense of kinship remained among the members of tribes and fractions separated by political frontiers. Excepting those born into a sedentary environment, all had previously been nomadic; most had close relatives who had settled in one or more of the other countries with Saharawi communities. 'Because of the close affinity between the Saharans of the Territory and those, for example, in the Moroccan province of Tarfaya or the border regions of Mauritania', a UN mission which examined conditions in Western Sahara in May 1975 noted, 'it is extremely difficult to determine who among them is a Saharan indigenous to the Territory.'[90] This of course posed problems for the referendum anticipated by the United Nations.

Clearly any census of indigenous persons undertaken outside the Territory would be a formidable task which, in the opinion of the Spanish authorities and the representatives of Saharan political movements, encountered within the Territory, would have to be based on proven membership of social and family groups (fractions and sub-fractions of tribes) existing within the territory.[91]

Since the Saharawis in the neighbouring countries retained such close family ties with those living within the Spanish colony, it was not surprising perhaps that they too should have come to play a prominent part in the Saharawi nationalist movement. This was especially true of Saharawis who had received secondary and higher education in the neighbouring countries. Bassiri, who had travelled even further afield, was just one example.

El-Ouali and the origins of Polisario

About 1,000 Saharawi children were admitted to Moroccan schools during or immediately after the 1957–8 war; and by the early 1970s, some forty of these had succeeded in gaining entry to Moroccan universities. By 1975, sixteen Saharawis had graduated from Moroccan universities with a *licence* according to one source.[92] It was at Mohammed V University in Rabat that several of the students who were in 1973 to play a part in forming the Polisario front, first came together. The most influential among them, the man who was later to become the Polisario Front's first secretary-general, was a Reguibi by the name of El-Ouali Mustapha Sayed, or 'Lulei'. Born about 1948, he had spent a nomadic childhood and then settled with his parents and five brothers and sisters in Tan-Tan after the defeat of the Army of Liberation when he was about ten. Like many of the Saharawis who settled in southern Morocco at this time, his family was almost destitute. None the less, with the help of government scholarships, he was able to attend a series of primary and secondary schools, and after passing the baccalaureat, enter the law faculty of Mohammed V University in 1970. Most of his fellow Saharawi students there had similar backgrounds.[93]

A number of these students, including El-Ouali, were members of a loosely structured Saharawi student collective in Rabat in 1970–2. Significantly, they did not at first specifically advocate the establishment of an independent state in Western Sahara. Their prime focus was on opposing the Spanish, rather than proposing any particular post-colonial status for the territory. Indeed, it is ironic that these students in 1970–2 worked hard to lobby support for their cause from the Moroccan opposition parties that were the main standard-bearers of the Greater Morocco idea. And so, to the Saharawi students in Morocco, it was only natural to turn initially for support to the Moroccan opposition which had for so long railed against the Hassan regime for its collaborative relations with Spain and its playing down of the Saharan question. Accordingly, at this time El-Ouali and his comrades sought support from Allal el-Fassi, Ali Yata, Abderrahim Bouabid and other Moroccan opposition figures.[94]

Although they were not, strictly speaking, 'Saharan nationalists' in these early days, the students around El-Ouali underwent a rapid political evolution in 1971–4. First, they began to tire of the Moroccan opposition parties, who seemed unprepared to go beyond a verbal anti-Spanish militancy to provide practical support for their plans to launch a new guerrilla struggle against Spain, the resort to arms being proven necessary in their opinion by the fate of the Harakat Tahrir. Second, as they made preparations for their new movement, they began (in 1971) sending emissaries to Western Sahara to investigate political conditions and make political contacts there; and, as they did so, they came across anti-colonial Saharawis, in many cases former members or supporters of the Harakat Tahrir, who did want to create an independent Saharawi state. At the same time, they began to make contact with Saharawis living further afield, in such centres of the Saharawi diaspora as Zouerate and Tindouf. A particular effort was made to recruit support from the Saharawis of southern Morocco. The self-reliant and exclusively Saharawi participation in this organizing work tended also to encourage ideas of Saharawi distinctiveness and autonomy. Fourth, by March 1972 this student group was beginning to appeal for support to a range of foreign Arab governments, notably those of Algeria, Libya, Iraq and Mauritania, as well as Morocco. And, finally, despite a formal request to the Moroccan government for aid, the El-Ouali group began to experience harassment from the Moroccan authorities in the spring of 1972. For this was a period of heightened political tension in Morocco, illustrated by two coup attempts in 1971 and 1972, political skirmishing between the Palace and the Kutlah al-Wataniya (a 'national front' uniting the UNFP and the Istiqlal party), a rash of labour disputes and student radicalization which culminated in the banning of the Union Nationale des Etudiants Marocains (UNEM) in January 1973. In March and May 1972, anti-Spanish demonstrations by Saharawi students and youth in Tan-Tan were broken up by the police and a number of the demonstrators, including El-Ouali, were briefly detained.[95]

The Tan-Tan incidents confirmed the group's fears that the constitution of a Saharawi liberation movement on Moroccan territory would carry serious political risks. Meanwhile, as a result of his incessant travelling, El-Ouali had established links with another nucleus of Saharawi militants, including two veterans of the Army of Liberation M'Hamed Ould Ziou and Ahmed Ould Qaid (who had also been active in the Harakat Tahrir), in Zouerate. At the same time, Libya provided some small-scale aid, from afar, while Algeria, apparently disillusioned by its experience with Morehob, refused to help (and did not aid Polisario significantly until the spring of 1975). But the Zouerate group was able to secure residence permits for El-Ouali and some of his comrades from Morocco, and so it was in Mauritania that the final preparations for Polisario's founding were made at the beginning of 1973. The founding congress was finally held somewhere near the Mauritanian–Western Saharan frontier, on 10 May 1973. 'The Polisario Front', it proclaimed, 'is born as a unique expression of the masses, opting for revolutionary violence and the armed struggle as the means by which the Saharawi people can recover its total liberty and foil the manœuvres of Spanish colonialism.'[96]

However, the front's founding manifesto did not explicitly mention independence as a goal. The formula of 'total liberty' was perhaps deliberately ambiguous. As late as January 1973 El-Ouali had written a memorandum, for the attention of UNFP exiles in Algiers, which seemed to approve the idea of Western Sahara's integration with Morocco.[97] Polisario itself admitted two years later, in a balance-sheet of its progress in July 1975 that 'in effect the Revolution was not clear in its first year about certain of its goals'.[98] The ambiguity reflected the different, contrasting backgrounds of, and influences on, the movement's earliest militants. It was seemingly the group of ex-students from Morocco that initially 'lagged' in their Saharawi nationalism, but they had now cut loose from their Moroccan links, been disillusioned by both the Moroccan government and opposition, forged the nucleus of a liberation movement with Saharawis of a quite different background and outlook from within the Spanish colony, as well as Mauritania, and were now fighting a difficult guerrilla war (the first attack came ten days after the front's founding) against the Spanish, with no appreciable material aid from any foreign government. They could really count only on their own commitment and whatever support they could muster from their fellow Saharawis, plus the convenience of being able, when necessary, to evade the Spanish army by slipping across the border into the vast desert zones of northern Mauritania. Their enforced self-reliance carried with it a sense of bitterness towards all the neighbouring governments. Thus a Polisario tract, distributed in March 1974, condemned 'the silence of Arab countries and notably those of the Maghreb, and

Morocco especially, with regard to the acts of colonialist Spain and its savage repression of the people'.[99] As for Mauritania, it is the view of Ahmed Babe Miské, a veteran Mauritanian politician who was to join the Polisario Front in 1975 and become a member of its political bureau (until 1978), that 'it would have sufficed for the Mauritanian government to have supplied aid to this movement in order, on the one hand, to have multiplied its chances of success and, on the other, to have reinforced and concretized the multiple ties linking the two peoples and to have promoted a process of unification between them'.[100] The Mauritanian government was prepared, in 1973–4, to harbour Polisario militants and to turn a blind eye to some of their activities on Mauritanian territory, but it never gave the movement military aid and it took care not to jeopardize its relations with Spain. On at least two occasions, in July and October 1973, Polisario guerrillas were arrested in Mauritania: on the latter occasion, so that the captured members of a Spanish patrol could be rescued and handed back to the Spanish authorities.[101]

It was thus at its second congress, held on 25–31 August 1974 that the front unambiguously came out in favour of full independence. This congress, Polisario later observed, marked a 'turning point' defining 'clearly and scientifically the objectives of the Revolution in the short and the long term'.[102] A manifesto issued by the congress declared that 'the Saharawi people have no alternative but to struggle until wresting independence, their wealth and full sovereignty over their land.'[103]

It is probably that the overwhelming majority of Saharawis within Western Sahara were nationalist in outlook by this date, but Polisario itself was still a very small guerrilla group. It was as a result of the dramatic political changes of 1974–5 that the Western Saharans rallied *en masse* to the movement. On account of the Lisbon coup in April 1974, and the approaching collapse of Portugal's African empire, Spain finally announced plans to implement its long-stalled commitment to Saharawi self-determination. In July 1974, plans were unveiled for an *estatuto político*, introducing internal self-government through the conversion of the Djemaa into a real legislature and the appointment of a partially Saharawi 'Governing Council'.[104] A month later, Spain announced that it would finally hold the long-delayed referendum, in the first half of 1975.[105] And, in the hope of conserving its substantial economic interests in the territory, the Francoist regime even set up its own 'moderate' Saharawi nationalist party, the Partido de la Unión Nacional Saharaui (PUNS), under the leadership of a young Reguibi, Kahlihenna Ould Rachid, who had trained as an engineer in Las Palmas and Madrid, to counteract the influence of the Polisario Front and lead the country to independence in close association with Spain.[106] Parallels with France's grooming of Mokhtar Ould Daddah, in the late 1950s, for the leadership of independent Mauritania are not far-fetched.

However, the sudden turn in Spanish policy brought a furious response from King Hassan. After years of virtual apathy about the Spanish presence in Western Sahara, the king pulled out all the stops to prevent the territory moving towards independence, permanently beyond Morocco's grasp, like Mauritania a decade and a half earlier. By generating an atmosphere of *jihad* to recover Morocco's Saharan provinces, he rallied unprecedented political support at home, outflanked the opposition parties and so engineered a spectacular domestic political recovery from the crisis-torn years of the early 1970s. The king harboured no doubts that if Spain's referendum went ahead it would result in a vote for independence; and so, on 20 August 1974, he announced that Morocco would oppose the inclusion of the option of independence in the referendum.[107] Spain, shaken by the vehemence of Moroccan objections to its plans, stalled. The referendum was postponed and the *estatuto político* shelved. The PUNS, whose *raison d'être* to its Saharawi supporters had been Spain's promise of constitutional progress towards independence, was discredited. Colonel Luis Rodríguez de Viguri y Gil, who was then secretary-general of the colonial administration in El-Ayoun, later recalled that the postponement of the internal autonomy plan under the Moroccan pressure dismayed the Saharawi population. 'Above all, the youth, who were very disillusioned, began to rally massively around the Polsario Front', he said, 'and the desertions to its Algerian camps, especially by the soldiers of the Tropas Nómadas and the Policía Territorial, became widespread.'[108]

It was the arrival of the UN mission of inquiry on 12 May 1975 that acted as the catalyst to bring the Saharawi population of the towns into the streets to demonstrate their support for Polisario publicly and on a mass scale for the first time—rather as the arrival of the Pearce Commission in Zimbabwe inspired African nationlists there to pour into the streets to show their opposition to Sir Alec Douglas-Home's 1971 Rhodesian settlement proposals.[109] Large pro-Polisario demonstrations, sometimes involving almost the entire Saharawi population of the towns in which they were held, greeted the UN visitors wherever they went. The PUNS was swamped by the outpouring of support for Polisario and gradually disintegrated over the following six months. Almost no Saharawis at all voiced support for integration with Morocco or Mauritania; and the United Nations' findings were unambiguous. At every place visited the mission was met by mass political demonstrations and had numerous private meetings with representatives of every section of the Saharan community, the mission members reported. 'From all these it became evident to the mission that there was an overwhelming consensus among Saharans within the territory in favour of independence and opposing integration with any neighbouring country.'[110] The mission believed

in the light of what it witnessed in the Territory, especially the mass demonstrations, of a support for one movement, the Frente Polisario, . . . that its visit served as a catalyst to bring into the open political forces and pressure which had previously been largely submerged. It was all the more significant to the Mission that this came as a surprise to the Spanish authorities who, until then had only been partly aware of the profound political awakening of the population.[111]

Six months before the Madrid accords of 14 November 1975, by which the Spanish government (in a radical reversal of previous policy) allowed Moroccan and Mauritanian troops to march into its colony, there could be no doubt that not only were the great majority of Saharawis within the territory in favour of independence, but they had now also demonstrated their allegiance to Polisario. None the less, as the threat from Morocco mounted during the summer of 1975, even Polisario indicated that it might be willing to sacrifice the prize of full independence by federating with Mauritania to keep out the Moroccans. The Saharawis' cultural ties with the *beidan* of Mauritania doubtless helped to make this a palatable second-best option, but perhaps the relative weakness of the Nouakchott regime compared to that of Rabat also made integration with Mauritania seem acceptable. Politically, Polisario's intention was to undermine the pact, hinged on the promise of future partition, which Hassan had reached with Mokhtar Ould Daddah at an Arab League summit in Rabat on 26–9 October 1974, to remove the embarrassment of Mauritania's counter-claim.[112] Sometime in May–June 1975, El-Ouali Mustapha Sayed visited the Mauritanian president in his Palace in Nouakchott and, during a two-hour conversation, proposed a Saharawi–Mauritanian federation, under Mokhtar Ould Daddah's federal presidency.[113] But it was to no avail. Misjudging the determination of both Polisario and its new powerful ally Algeria, Mokhtar Ould Daddah remained loyal to his allegiance with King Hassan. His government's subsequent signing of the Madrid accords, its military alliance with Morocco in the ensuing war and the April 1976 partition treaty finally put paid to any residual interest, on the Polisario side, in the idea of federation with Mauritania.

The bitterness of the war with Morocco and Mauritania, and the accompanying movement of refugees to Algeria, crowned the process of formation of a Saharawi national consciousness. It brought Saharawis of different tribal origins together in refugee camps and guerrilla units for an especially gruelling and difficult struggle. It deepened their sense of national pride and unity. Moreover, the strong sense of kinship between those from within and those from beyond the Western Sahara's old borders roused many thousands of Saharawis from southern Morocco, northern Mauritania and south-western Algeria to join the exodus to Polisario's Tindouf camps.[114] Thus it was that the number of Saharawis there came to exceed the total number counted within Western Sahara by the Spanish census authorities in 1974. In new supratribal dimensions, the old imperative of *asabiya* had brought together Saharawi from all corners of the Saharawi diaspora, as well as from within the old Spanish colony, to fight for the birth of a nation.

Notes

1. On raiding in Saharan society, see Pierre Bonte, 'La guerre dans les sociétés d'éléveurs nomades', *Cahiers du Centre d'Etudes et de Recherches Marxistes*, no. 133, Paris, 1977, pp. 42–67; Julio Caro Baroja, *Estudios Saharianos*, Instituto de Estudios Africanos, Madrid, 1955, pp. 92–3 and 341–7; and David M. Hart, 'The Social Structure of the Rgībāt Bedouins of the Western Sahara', *Middle East Journal*, 16, 4, Autumn 1962, pp. 525–6.
2. On the segmentary lineage system of Saharawi tribes, see Caro Baroja, op. cit., pp. 3–17; on the *diya*, or blood debt, ibid., pp. 17–18.
3. On the caste system of traditional Western Sahara society, see ibid., pp. 25–53; and Juan Bautista Vilar Ramirez, *El Sahara y el hamitismo norteafricano: estudios antropo-históricos sahárico-magrebíes*, Instituto de Estudios Africanos, Madrid, 1969, pp. 106–43. The singular of *shorfa* is *sherif*.
4. See Caro Baroja, op. cit., pp. 18–22; and Hart, op. cit., pp. 518–19.
5. Caro Baroja, op. cit., pp. 65–6. The term 'Sahel' is, of course, relative. It could refer strictly to the coast, in which case the *ahel es-Sahel* were the small fishing tribes which lived along it.
6. Frank E. Trout, *Morocco's Saharan Frontiers*, Geneva, Droz, 1969, pp. 144–5.
7. Francis de Chassey, *La Mauritanie, 1900–1975, de l'ordre colonial à l'ordre néo-colonial entre Maghreb et Afrique noire*, Paris, Editions Anthropos, 1978, p. 25.
8. Francis de Chassey, 'Des ethnies et de l'imperialisme dans la genèse des nations, des classes et des Etats en Afrique: le cas du Sahara occidental', *L'Homme et la société*, nos. 45–6, July–September and October–December 1977, pp. 115–16.
9. Trout, op. cit., pp. 420–3.
10. *Chroniques Etrangères: Espagne*, La Documentation Française, Paris, no. 181, 31 March 1957.
11. *Chroniques Etrangères*, no. 190, 31 December 1957.
12. For a detailed account of Operation Ouragan and its background, see George Chaffard, *Les carnets secrets de la décolonisation*, Paris, Calmann-Lévy, 1965, pp. 251–93.
13. Tomás Garcia Figueras, *Santa Cruz de mar Pequeña, Ifni, Sahara Law acción de Espâna en la costa occidental de Africa*, Madrid, Ediciones Fe, 1941, p. 310.
14. Francisco Hernandez-Pacheco and Jose Maria Cordero Torres, *El Sahara Español*, Madrid, Instituto de Estudios Politicos, 1962, p. 127.
15. *Resumen estadístico del Africa Española (1953–54)*, Madrid, Dirección General de Marruecos y Colonias e Instituto de Estudios Africanos, 1954, pp. 345–6, 381.
16. For a full account of the history of oil exploration in Western Sahara, see Tony Hodges and James Ball, 'Oil and the Western Saharan Conflict', *Quarterly Energy Review: Africa*, 2nd Quarter, 1982, pp. 1–4.
17. On the Bou-Craa phosphate industry, see *Fosfatos de Bu-Craa, SA*, Instituto Nacional de Industria, Madrid, 1972.
18. Manuel Melis Claveria, 'La Provincia de Sahara ante el plan de desarollo económica y social', *Africa*, no. 295, July 1966, p. 4.
19. Report of the United Nations Visiting Mission to Spanish Sahara, 1975, in

General Assembly Official Records: 30th Session, Supplement no. 23, UN Document A/10023/Rev. 1, p. 52.

20. Virginia Thompson and Richard Adloff, *The Western Saharans*, London, Croom Helm, 1980, p. 123.
21. *Resumen estadístico del Sahara Español (Año 1969)*, Madrid, Instituto de Estudios Africanos, p. 10; Report of the United Nations Visiting Mission to Spanish Sahara, op. cit., p. 38.
22. *Censo-74*, Servicio de registro de poblacion, cenos y estadistica, El-Ayoun, 1974, p. 74.
23. Ibid., p. 74.
24. J. Meastre, *El Sahara en la crisis de Marruecos y Espāna*, Madrid, Akal, 1975, p. 190.
25. UN Document A/9623/Add. 4, part 2, 13 November 1974, pp. 24–5.
26. *Seconds résultats provisoires du recensement général de la population (population au 1èr janvier 1977)*, Bureau central de la population, Ministère du plan et des mines, Nouakchott, pp. 13, 17.
27. *Censo-74*, pp. 5, 44; Report of the United Nations Visiting Mission to Spanish Sahara, 1975, op. cit., p. 38.
28. Decreto por el que se reorganiza el Gobierno General de Africa Occidental Española, 10 de Enero de 1958, *Boletín Oficial del Estado*, 14 January 1958.
29. Ibid.
30. Ley 8/61 de 19 Abril, sobre organización y régimen jurídico de la Provincia de Sahara, *Boletín Oficial de Estado*, 21 April 1961, p. 6062; Decreto de la Presidencia del Gobierno de 29 de noviembre por el que se aprueba el Ordenamiento de la Administracion local para la Provincia de Sahara, *Boletín Oficial del Estado*, 12 December 1962.
31. Plural *shioukh*.
32. *Chronique Etrangères: Espagne*, nos. 63–9, September 1963.
33. John Mercer, *Spanish Sahara*, London, George Allen & Unwin, 1976, p. 200.
34. Decreto 1024/67, 11 May 1967; see also 'La Yemaa o Asamblea General del Sahara', *Africa*, no. 309, September 1967, p. 18, and Mauel Castilla Ortega, 'Se constituye la Asamblea General de Sahara', *Africa*, no. 310, October 1967, p. 8.
35. Quoted in *Le Sahara occidental devant la Cour International de Justice: Mémoire présenté par le Royaume du Maroc*, Rabat, 1975, p. 36. Allal el-Fassi was the leader of Morocco's principal nationalist party, the Istiqlal (Independence) party.
36. 'Les relations hispano-marocaines', *Maghreb*, La Documentation Française, Paris, no. 3, May–June 1964, p. 11.
37. 'Spain and Morocco are the two pillars of Hercules which guard the entrance to the Mediterranean', stated Hassan on the day of the Barajas summit. 'It is upon our two countries that depends, in large part, the destiny of the free world.'
38. 'Les relations hispano–marocaines', p. 11.
39. Rachid Lazrak, *Le contentieux territorial entre la Maroc et l'Espagne*, Casablanca, Dar el Kitab, 1974, p. 285.
40. Ibid., p. 310.
41. Ibid., p. 352.

42. Interview with Mohammed Ma el-Ainin, Rabat, 16 October 1978, Reuters, Rabat, 13 January 1967.
43. Letters of Edouard Moha to ambassadors accredited to Morocco, July 1982, Reuters, Rabat, 5 March 1973.
44. Report of the United Nations Visiting Mission to Spanish Sahara, 1975, op. cit., p. 65.
45. Traité de fraternité, de bon voisinage et de coopération entre la République algérienne démocratique et populaire et le Royaume du Maroc, in *Journal Officiel de la République Algérienne Démocratique et Populaire,* 8th Year, no. 11, 5 February 1969, pp. 82–4.
46. *Communiqué commun algéro-marocain*, Royaume du Maroc, Ministère des Affaires Etrangères, Division Presse et Information, DAP/5, 1 June 1970.
47. Convention relative au tracé de la frontière d'Etat établie entre le Royaume du Maroc et la République algérienne démocratique et populaire, *Journal Officiel de la République Algérienne Démocratique et Populaire*, 12th Year, no. 48, 15 June 1973, pp. 546–8.
48. Traité de fraternité, de bon voisinage et de coopération entre la République islamique de Mauritanie et le Royaume du Maroc, *Journal Officiel de la République Islamique de Mauritanie*, 1970, pp. 233–4.
49. UNFP Central Committee resolution, 8 October 1972.
50. See Bertrand Fessard de Foucault, 'La question du Sahara espagnol (II)', *Revue Française d'Etudes Politiques Africaines*, no. 120, December 1975, pp. 75–6.
51. United Nations General Assembly Resolution 2072, 16 December 1975, in *General Assembly Official Records: 20th Session*, Supplement 14, UN Document A/6014, pp. 59–60.
52. United Nations General Assembly Resolution 2229, 20 December 1966, *General Assembly Official Records: 21st Session*, Supplement 16, UN Document A/6316, pp. 72–3.
53. For a detailed history of the evolution of UN policy on Western Sahara, see 'The Question of Western Sahara at the United Nations', *Decolonization*, United Nations, New York, no. 17, October 1980.
54. *Resolution on the Territories under Spanish Domination*, OAU Council of Ministers, Addis Ababa, 1966, OAU Document CM/Res. 82(VII).
55. OAU Document CM/Res. 272(XIX), Rabat, June 1972.
56. Lazrak, op. cit., p. 301.
57. *ABC*, Madrid, 18 November 1966.
58. *Maghreb Arabe Presse*, Rabat, 17 May 1967. The *khaima* is the Saharawi tent.
59. Zygmunt Komorowski has argued that this attitude is shared by Saharans who constitute minorities in states dominated by 'outsiders', whether from the black south or the Maghreb to the north. 'The road transport and mining business situated in the desert sign on representatives of all the tribes and natives of various regions. But, given the harsh climate, they are almost uniquely Saharans. This state of affairs creates an opposition between "us", who have lived here for generations, and "them", who have come from the fertile and rich lands of the north or the south, where drought is not a threat, and only come here, temporarily, to administer and exploit ...' Zygmunt Komorowski, 'Formation de la conscience sociale supratribale en partant des

conditions ethniques du Sahara occidental', *Africana Bulletin*, University of Warsaw Centre of African Studies, no. 23, 1975, p. 116.

60. Later, in May 1975, the Spanish government suggested to the United Nations that 'on the basis of present population statistics, the phosphates when fully developed would furnish a per capita revenue equal to that of some developed countries in Europe'. Report of the United Nations Visiting Mission to Spanish Sahara, 1975, op. cit., p. 52.

61. *ABC* (Madrid), 18 November 1966 and 19 November 1966.

62. *ABC*, 8 December 1966.

63. *ABC*, 19 November 1966.

64. Quoted in Thomas M. Franck, 'The Stealing of the Sahara', *American Journal of International Law*, 70, 4, October 1976, p. 702.

65. Editorial in *L'Opinion*, Rabat, 22 July 1966.

66. *Discours prononcé par SE Monsieur Mohammed Cherkaoui, ministre des affairs etrangères du Maroc, à la XXIème session de l'Assemblée Générale, 13 octobre 1966*, Moroccan government.

67. Ibid.

68. Conference de presse due Roi Hassan II, le 30 juillet 1970, in *Annuaire de l'Afrique du Nord, 1970*, CNRS, Paris, 1971, p. 807.

69. Reuters, Rabat, 23 July 1973.

70. *ABC*, 19 November 1966.

71. Joint Communiqué Issued by the governments of Algeria, Mauritania and Morocco, 24 July 1973, at Agadir, in UN Document A/10023/Rev. 1, pp. 126–7.

72. C. C. Stewart, *Human and Societal Factors*, paper presented to US State Department conference on 'The Sahara and US Policy', Washington, DC, 7–8 February 1979.

73. *Statistical Yearbook*, UNESCO, 1973, pp. 732–3, cited in Zygmunt Komorowski, op. cit., p. 115.

74. The influence of these nationalist struggles is particularly evident in the earliest issues of *20 de Mayo*, the bulletin published by the Polisario Front from 1973.

75. John Mercer, op. cit., p. 202.

76. 'El enseñanza media en el Sahara', *Africa*, no. 310, October 1967, p. 11.

77. Report of the United Nations Visiting Mission to Spanish Sahara, 1975, op. cit., p. 57.

78. Ramiro Santamaria, 'La cultura, arma de paz en el Sahara español', *Africa*, no,. 363, March 1972, p. 8.

79. Report of the United Nations Visiting Mission to Spanish Sahara, 1975, op. cit., p. 58.

80. Frederico Abascal, Sol Gallego and Enrique Bustamante, 'Sahara: documentos secretos', *Cuadernos para el Diálogo*, Madrid, 21 January 1978, p. 17; *El Pueblo Saharaui en Lucha: documentos del Frente Popular para la Liberacion de Saguia el Hamra y Río de Oro*, Polisario Front, 1975, p. 2.

81. Interview with Mohammed Ma el-Ainin, Rabat, 16 October, 1978.

82. Reuters, Algiers, 21 January 1971.

83. Informe del Estado Mayor del Sector del Sahara sobre 'el movimiento nacionalista denominado Organización del Pueblo Saharaui', 13 de Junio de 1970, in Frederico Abascal, Sol Gallego and Enrique Bustamante, op. cit., p. 16.

84. Informe del delegado gubernativo de la Región Norte, Señor López Huertas, sobre la 'Organización Avanzada para la Liberación del Sahara y los preparativos del dia 17 de Junio de 1970', in Frederico Abascal, Sol Gallego and Enrique Bustamante, op. cit., p. 15.

85. *El Pueblo Saharaui en Lucha: documentos del Frente Populat para la Liberación de Saguia el Hamra y Rio de Oro*, pp. 16–17, 1974.

86. Reuters, Madrid, 20 June 1970; Reuters, Nouakchott,, 20 June 1970; Reuters, Algiers, 21 January 1970; Maghreb Arabe Presse, 18 June 1970.

87. Report of the United Nations Visiting Mission to Spanish Sahara, 1975, op. cit., p. 39.

88. Attilio Gaudio, *Le dossier du Sahara occidental*, Paris, Nouvelles Editions Latines, 1978, p. 45.

89. Eugénie Muret, *Le procesus de sédentarisation des nomades reguiebat de la région de Tindouf*, Algérie, unpublished dissertation,' pp. 21, 74–9.

90. Report of the United Nations Visiting Mission to Spanish Sahara, 1975, op. cit., p. 39.

91. Ibid., p. 39.

92. Leila Badia Itani, *Al-Polisario: qaid wa thawra*, Beirut, Dar al-Masirah, 1978, p. 128; interview with Mohammed Ma el-Ainin, Rabat, 16 October 1978.

93. Among them, for example, was Mohammed Lamine Ould Ahmed, a member of the small sharifian tribe, the Taoubalt, who had been evacuated to Morocco by the Army of Liberation in September 1957, at the same time as Mohammed Sidi Ibrahim Bassiri. He was later, in February 1976, to become the first prime minister of the Saharan Arab Democratic Republic (SADR), but in the early 1970s he was, like El-Ouali, a law student at Mohammed V University. Studying political sciences there at the same time was the SADR's future information minister, Mohammed Salem Ould Salek, a Tidrarini who had attended secondary schools in both El-Ayoun and Marrakesh. In the faculty of letters was Omar Hadrani, a Reguibi born near Goulimine in about 1947 who was later to become one of the nine members of the SADR's Supreme Council for the Command of the Revolution. There were several other future leaders of the Polisario Front among these students in Morocco. Interview with Mohammed Ma el-Ainin, Rabat, 16 October 1978; Leila Badia Itani, op. cit., pp. 130–4.

94. At this time, El-Ouali contributed to a study of the Western Saharan problem, 'The Reality of Our Usurped Saharan Province', which was published by the pro-Moscow Parti de Libération et du Socialisme (PLS) in its journal *Al-Mabadi* in May 1972.

95. *El Pueblo Saharaui in Lucha: documentos del Frente Popular para la Liberación de Saguia el Hamra y Rio de Oro*, 1974, pp. 21–7; Interview with Mohammed Ma el-Ainin, Rabat, 16 October 1978; Reuters, Rabat, 5 March 1972, and 24 May 1972.

96. Manifesto of 10 May 1973, in *Sahara Libre*, Polisario Front, Algiers, no. 13, 20 May 1976.

97. 'Muthakkarat Mustapha el-Quali haoul al-Sahra', *Alikhtiar Athaouri*, Paris, nos. 19–22, 23 and 25, October, November and December 1977, and January, February and April 1978.

98. 'Bilan de deux années de lutte de notre peuple', *20 Mai*, Polisario Front, no. 21, July 1975, p. 15.

99. Reuters, Rabat, 20 March 1974.

100. Ahmed Baba Miské, *Front Polisario, l'âme d'un peuple*, Paris, Editions Rupture, 1978, p. 38.

101. *20 de Mayo*, Polisario Front, no. 1, 1 November 1973; *20 Mai*, no. 21, 1975, p. 14. On Polisario's early relations with the Mauritanian government in 1973–5, see also 'Omar Hadrami, Interviewed by Tony Hodges', *Africa Report*, March–April 1978, p. 42.

102. 'Bilan de deux années de lutte de notre peuple', op. cit., p. 15.

103. 'Manifeste politique', in *Le peuple saharaoui en lutte: document du Front Populaire pour la Libération de Saguiat El-Hamra et Río de Oro*, Polisario Front, 1975, p. 50.

104. On the *estatuto politíco*, see Report of the United Nations Visiting Mission to Spanish Sahara, 1975, op. cit., pp. 44–6.

105. Letter of the Permanent Representative of Spain to the United Nations Secretary-General, 20 August 1974, in United Nations Document A/9714.

106. On the PUNS, see Emilio Menendez del Valle, *Sahara español: una descolonización tardía*, Madrid, Editorial Cuadernos para el Diálogo, 1975, pp. 17–19.

107. *Discours de SM Hassan II, 3 mars 1974–3 mars 1975*, Ministère d'Etat chargé de l'information, Rabat, 1975, p. 67.

108. *Sahara 14-Nov-1975, La Traición*, Associación de Amigos del Sahara and IEPALA, Madrid, 1980, pp. 62–3. Polisario had been authorized by the Algerian government to establish camps in the Tindouf region early in 1975.

109. Martin Loney, *Rhodesia: White Racism and Imperial Response*, London, Penguin, 1975, pp. 178–80.

110. Report of the United Nations Visiting Mission to Spanish Sahara, 1975, op. cit., p. 59.

111. Ibid., p. 59.

112. Conférence de presse de SM Majesté le Roi sur les résultats de la 7ème conférence arabe au 'sommet', 30 octobre, in *Discours de SM Majesté Hassan II*, 3 mars 1974–3 mars 1975, Ministère d'Etat chargé de l'information, Rabat, 1975, p. 114.

113. *Remarques Africaines* (Brussels), 15 August 1976, *Jeune Afrique*, Paris, 1 April 1977.

114. Interviews with Polisario prisoners in Moroccan custody, El-Ayoun, October 1978.

Part II: The War, the Maghreb and the world powers

4 The role of world powers: colonialist transformations and King Hassan's rule

Like every problem in international relations the Western Sahara conflict has its history, and in this case it is, once more, a problem of colonialism and imperialism. Spain's claim over the territory of the Western Sahara was notified on 19 January 1885 to the so-called Congo conference which was held in Berlin in 1884–5. At this time France laid claim to the whole mass of land which later formed French West Africa and which included the present states of Senegal, Mali, Niger, Chad, and Mauritania. This land was linked with France's Algerian and Tunisian colonies. The small Spanish territory on the Atlantic looked almost like an island in the ocean of French possessions. In fact, the borders with the French-occupied parts of the region were delimited only much later in various agreements between the years 1900 and 1912.[1] In any case the colonial powers did not pay too much attention to this extremely dry and apparently poor region which was only inhabited by a few nomadic tribes. Those tribes, however, fought the colonial and military penetration of their territory fiercely until 1934. For the most part, they were struggling against the French who often did not respect Spanish sovereignty over the territory, whereas the Spanish merely deployed their Foreign Legion at a few points on the coast.

The question of the delimitation of the territory became important again in 1912 when France and Spain colonized Morocco, with Spain finally gaining recognition of its occupation of the Tarfaya zone and Ifni enclave, both north of the present territory of Western Sahara.[2] In fact, the Sultan's authority had never reached further than the Oued Noun, well to the north of the subsequent border between 'Spanish Southern Morocco' and Spanish Sahara.[3] In northern Morocco, Spain obtained a small strip of Tetouan-Nador, while all the rest of Morocco came under French rule.[4]

When Morocco became independent in 1956, the Spanish withdrew from the northern province of Tetouan and Nador without, however, leaving the so-called *presidios* of Ceuta and Melilla. In the south they continued to occupy the territory of Tarfaya and the enclave of Ifni. The struggle for the political independence of Morocco had united almost all political forces in Morocco, and it has to be remembered that in the same year, 1956, Tunisia

* Research for this study was largely made possible by a travelling grant of the Volkswagen Foundation, Hanover.

also won its independence. In Algeria the anti-colonial war had started in November 1954. In southern Morocco and in the territories occupied by Spain the so-called Moroccan Liberation Army had grouped together almost all of the tribes living in that area, as far as northern Mauritania and south-west Algeria. This movement intensified its struggle after the formal agreement to Morocco's independence was signed. Its leadership thought the agreement omitted the essential political, military and economic conditions of real independence.[5] Therefore, the Liberation Army guerrillas[6] continued their struggle, and even intensified it by attacking the Spanish troops in Tarfaya, Ifni and the Western Sahara. They started cooperating with the Algerian Front de Libération Nationale, thus also threatening French interests in the area. Not only did they escape King Muhammed's control, but they also refused his offer to integrate with the newly built up Royal Armed Forces. While the king could not crack down on these forces struggling for liberation from colonialism, he could not easily allow the French army, which was still in Morocco, to clear that area of 'irregulars' whom it feared to be a potential revolutionary danger to the monarchy.[7]

Under the threat of the growing strength of the Liberation Army which started to attack almost everywhere (in southern Morocco, in the Western Sahara and in Mauritania), France and Spain agreed to a joint military action, Operation Ouragan, also codenamed 'Tiede' by the Spanish and 'Ecouvillon' by the French. In heavy ground attacks supported by air cover the two armies smashed the guerrillas in February 1958. A few days later, regular Moroccan troops entered Southern Morocco. For many Saharawis, this is regarded as proof that the palace knew about the operation and had let the colonial powers do its dirty work in order to take military control over the region north of the border of Western Sahara.[8] After Operation Ouragan, Spain returned the Tarfaya zone to Morocco (10 April 1958); the enclave of Ifni was handed over to Morocco only in 1969.

The take-over of these two small territories was acclaimed in Morocco as a step towards the 'Greater Morocco' as it had been first defined by the Istiqlal party[9] just after Morocco's independence. This idea of a Greater Morocco was shared by all political parties and nationalist forces, including, though more half-heartedly, the UNFP, after it had broken away from the conservative branch of the Istiqlal in 1958, and the successor of UNFP, the USFP.[10] (In fact, the UNFP and the USFP did not support the claims to Mauritania and parts of Algeria, although they did support the claim to Western Sahara.) The idea was that the Moroccan border, which in the east had been defined in precolonial treaties from the Mediterranean southwards as far as the oasis of Figuig, should continue more or less straight towards the south until the Senegal river, thus including large parts of south-west Algeria, especially the important oasis of Tindouf, the whole of Mauritania and parts of Mali. Consequently, Morocco strongly protested against the independence of Mauritania in 1960 and broke off diplomatic relations with almost all states which recognized it.[11] Shortly after Algeria's independence in 1962, Morocco attacked the border between Bechar and Tindouf in 1963, in order to bring that part of south-west Algeria under Moroccan rule. The very heavy conflict was finally settled in 1964 by the Organization of African Unity (OAU). The actual border is still as it was left by the French colonials. However, the underlying issue of contention has not been definitively settled.[12]

A true understanding of the Western Sahara conflict, therefore, cannot be dissociated from the development of domestic Moroccan politics. Despite not being able to go into all the details in this chapter, a few determining elements have to be mentioned. The basis of the Moroccan regime, i.e. of the Moroccan monarchy, is still the feudal landed bourgeoisie[13] as it arose from the French colonial policy developed by its first administrator Lyautey.[14] At the head of this system, defined by strong personal relationships, stands the king who is both the civilian as well as the religious ruler, the commander of the faithful.[15] On the other hand, however, the colonialist and imperialist penetration of Morocco has resulted in huge transformations such as the setting up of industries, infrastructure (railroads, ports, roads etc.), and a steady modernization, i.e. the transformation of its agriculture into large-scale farming based on an increase in wage labour. This has led to the decline of the old politically as well as culturally dominant merchant bourgeoisie (which up to today is mostly represented in the Istiqlal party) and to the rise of a socialist party dominated by intellectuals (the UNFP and later USFP,[16]) the existence of a very small communist party (Parti du Progrès et du Socialisme, PPS) and to organized labour movements, among them especially the Union Marocaine du Travail (UMT) and the more recent Confédération Démocratique du Travail (CDT) which has close ties with the USFP.

This very complex social structure has brought about what has rightly been called Morocco's blocked process of transformation.[17] On the one hand, the king is the supreme representative of the old social order who draws his legitimacy from his religious authority stemming from his alleged descent from the prophet and, on the other hand, the transformation of that society through capitalist penetration has led to the rise of new groups and classes such as intellectuals, workers, and above all, a steadily growing lumpenproletariat. Their aspirations are increasingly blocked by the traditional order which is forced to ally itself more and more with foreign capitalist interests at the same time eroding its own social and political base.

In line with the interests of the dominant economic and political forces, Morocco has always followed an essentially liberal economic policy. French interests were not noticeably damaged as a consequence of political independence, and the Moroccan bourgeoisie has prospered since. However, in order to get around the restrictions on economic and financial transactions, favouritism and corruption became almost basic to the functioning of the social and political system. The resulting social unrest brought about repeated urban riots like those in Casablanca in 1965 and

1981,[18] the peasant revolts in the 1970s[19] or the hunger revolts of January 1984.[20] Not only did the population revolt periodically against the consequences of the economic and social policies of the regime, but unrest was also growing in the army as the two abortive military coups of 1971 and 1972[21] have made clear. The liquidation of the leading figure of the army and the commander-in-chief of the Royal Armed Forces in the Sahara, General Dlimi, in January 1983 may well have been related to more widespread discontent in the army.[22] In particular the two attempted military coups of 1971 and 1972[23] headed by the army's leading officers and its elite units,[24] which until then were believed to be particularly loyal to the king, had seriously brought into question not only the stability of the political system but also the legitimacy of the representatives of the *'alaoui* dynasty.

After the second coup the relationship between Morocco and the United States suffered some noticeable disturbances and the king seemed to become more and more isolated at the international level. In addition to this, domestic stability came under threat as peasant unrest increased,[25] and his main asset, the army, became more and more unreliable. After heavy purges, carefully selected units were sent to the Golan Heights front[26] where certain officers who were believed to be dangerous to the king's regime were killed in battle and glorified as martyrs.

At this same time tension mounted again in the Western Sahara. As early as 1969, Morocco had definitely given up its claim over Mauritania and signed treaties declaring fraternity and cooperation with its neighbours Algeria and Mauritania.[27] At a summit meeting in Nouadhibou on 14 September 1970, the three states declared in a joint communiqué that they intended to intensify their close cooperation in order to accelerate the decolonization of Western Sahara in conformity with the resolutions of the United Nations.[28] A coordinating committee was set up in order to follow closely the decolonization process in the territory, though in fact it turned out to be ineffective.

Saharawi nationalism and the coveted territory

Only ten years after Operation Ouragan, the Saharawi anti-colonial struggle started again, this time however on a different social basis.[29] The nucleus of truly nationalistic—no longer merely tribal—resistance comprised essentially young people whose parents had settled down and who had gone to school, sometimes to universities in Rabat, Spain or the Middle East. Their common social status and political experience were for them a closer link than the attachment to kinship groups. Very soon women started to play an important role in the movement as well. The Polisario Front (Frente Popular par la Liberación de Saguia el Hamra y Río de Oro) was created on 10 May 1973. It initiated armed resistance against the colonizer as early as 20 May 1973, by attacking Spanish military posts with considerable success. From the very beginning the Polisario Front, as the leading and truly representative movement among the different Saharawi nationalist organizations,[30] was suspicious about the expansionist tendencies of Moroccan politics.[31] In late 1974 the Polisario Front sabotaged, for the first time, the conveyor belt transporting the phosphates from Bou Craa to El-Ayoun.[32] OAU and the United Nations were exerting growing pressure upon Spain to hasten the decolonization of the territory.[33] In May 1975 a commission from the United Nations visited Spain, the Western Sahara, Morocco, Algeria and Mauritania, and, in its subsequent report to the General Assembly, clearly recommended a referendum to enable the self-determination of the Saharawi people.[34] During this visit, the UN mission had been especially impressed by the strength and representative nature of the Polisario Front.

Long before the situation in the Western Sahara had become as critical as it was in 1975, Morocco had begun its preparations on the political,[35] diplomatic[36] and military[37] levels. Nationalist propaganda, which had always been the main theme of the Istiqlal press, was mounted by the palace as well, and the leftist parties, the USFP and the PPS, joined in. Nationalist and expansionist policies towards the Western Sahara seemed, as far as the palace was concerned, to be the way to avoid isolation and the loss of legitimacy. By defending what was called territorial integrity, the palace managed to unify all national forces and give the distrusted army a new mission.

The international dimension to the Western Saharan conflict on the eve of the outbreak of the war should be seen on two levels. The first is the regional level, i.e. the relationships and interests of the neighbouring states like Spain, Morocco, Algeria and Mauritania, and to some extent Libya, Tunisia and Senegal. The second is the global level, in particular the interests of the United States and France. The Soviet Union and Great Britain (except for Gibraltar), having no stronghold in the region, may be ignored, at least during the period in 1975–6 when Spain was preparing to withdraw from its colony.

On the regional level there was the clear and well-formulated interest on the part of Morocco, which had always considered the territory as a component of Greater Morocco. Even though this was veiled by diverse tripartite negotiations with Algeria and Mauritania, it became quite clear that the support for Moroccan-steered nationalist organizations like MOREHOB and FLUE was aimed at turning the growing Saharawi nationalism into a pro-Moroccan movement, which would then have legitimized the annexation of the territory immediately upon Spain's withdrawal. Similarly, Morocco's irredentist attacks on Spanish colonialism, sometimes linked with the question of the *presidios* of Melilla and Ceuta, were intended to hasten Spain's withdrawal and incidentally to strengthen both the Moroccan territorial ambitions and the king's position at home.

The Mauritanian position in the emerging conflict was more complicated. As a very poor state depending completely on the export of its iron ore from Zouerate and on French aid, it is still unclear why Mauritania joined Morocco. From the very beginnning, President Mokhtar Ould Daddah knew that he could not deal with Morocco on an equal basis. Also, he must have realized that supporting the Moroccan position would disturb Mauritania's friendly relationship with Algeria, which for years had supported Mauritania against Moroccan irredentism. Of course, by moving closer to the Moroccan position, Mauritania improved bilateral relations even though, ten years after independence, Mauritania's sovereignty was no longer in danger. This had always been strongly supported by France and Algeria and, since independence, Mauritania had been a full member of both the OAU and the United Nations. One possible explanation seems to be that through Mokhtar Ould Daddah's alliance with Rabat, France could enlarge its influence in this area. Or perhaps, faced with a Moroccan juggernaut, Mokhtar Ould Daddah thought it better to get some benefit rather than none at all, to be on good, rather than bad, terms with Morocco in view of past historic claims. Perhaps one day French archives will clarify this none-too-clear matter.

Algeria's position was clear from the beginning and remained unchanged. It stressed the principle of decolonization and self-determination as laid down in the Charters of the United Nations and OAU. This is very much in line with Algerian foreign policy which has always supported anti-colonial liberation movements, not least out of the experience of its own extremely bloody struggle for liberation. However, besides these principles Algeria has, of course, no desire to have Morocco occupy a territory as rich in resources as Western Sahara, or have its border lengthened with a state which does not recognize that section of the common border from the oasis of Figuig southwest to the Oued Draa north of Tindouf, and which one day may claim sovereignty over the rich iron ore of Gara Djebilet in the Tindouf area.

In his very thorough examination of the political and diplomatic process which finally led to the Madrid Agreement[38] Barbier[39] comes to the conclusion that Spain originally intended to apply the recommendations of the UN mission[40] and to conform with the advisory opinion of the International Court of Justice,[41] both calling for self-determination of the Saharawi people. However, the Saharan crisis reached its peak as the Spanish dictator Franco was dying, a time when rivalries in the government and fear about the (possibly democratic) future complicated decision-making processes in Madrid.[42] It seems, however, that American and French pressure was also brought to bear to bring the Spanish government to agree to Morocco's demands.[43]

The rather conservative states of Tunisia and Léopold Sédar Senghor's Senegal[44] backed the Moroccan–Mauritanian position, and presumably their position was not arrived at without the influence of France and possibly the United States. Both invoked the danger of balkanization of Africa, and at least Tunisia found itself in contradiction with principles it had upheld in 1960, when it strongly backed Mauritania's independence against Morocco irredentism.[45] This position, of course, would give the Moroccan–Mauritanian annexation support in the OAU and the Arab League, the latter being dominated anyway by the wealthy and conservative Arab states. Very early, Libya gave some support to Polisario for its anti-colonial struggle against Spain. As soon as the war with Morocco intensified after the military occupation, following the withdrawal of the Spanish at the end of February 1976, Libya strengthened military support for Polisario without initially recognizing the 'Saharan Arab Democratic Republic' (SADR), proclaimed on 27 February 1976 in the liberated territories.[46]

Without question, further research is necessary to establish more detail about the French[47] as well the American intervention on the eve of the Madrid Agreement. What is certain is that both have a vested interest in the area, and this aspect is very important in so far as it is linked with the economic resources of the Western Sahara as well as with geostrategic interests, especially those of the United States. Here these interests can only be touched upon, but they will be discussed in greater detail later.

The Spanish Sahara, which during nearly one hundred years of colonization was believed to be one of the poorest and most hostile regions of Africa, turned out in the 1960s to be one of the most important areas with regard to its economic resources. Not only does it contain one of the largest reserves of phosphates (estimated at some ten billion tons,[48] but these phosphates can also be exploited by surface mining and are of the highest quality. For their extraction, the world's largest conveyor belt has been constructed between Bou Craa and El-Ayoun. The second resource is fish. The Western Saharan coasts are reputed to be one of the richest fishing areas in the world, and all international fishing fleets are quite active in the area.[49] In addition to these, it is maintained that in this territory there are other resources such as copper, nickel, chromium, platinum, manganese, gold, vanadium and uranium,[50] the two latter being of tremendous strategic importance. There have also been discoveries of oil and gas in the offshore areas of the Western Sahara;[51] it is highly probable that there is top quality iron ore as well.[52]

Besides these economic resources, there is the geostrategic location of the Western Sahara, close to Morocco and Algeria and opposite the Canary Islands. As in Morocco and Spain, the United States has an important military base in the Canary Islands which is reported to be of great importance to American spy satellites. It was argued too that the possibility of an independent Saharan state might have given additional strength to the Canary Island liberation movement, the MPAIAC,[53] which was also supported by Algeria. Additionally, at the time when Franco's death was imminent, the United States feared a development in Spain (such as that which occurred in revolutionary Portugal in 1974) which could have consequences for the American presence in that country. From the point of view of hawkish American foreign policy makers, the security of the western Mediterranean could have been seen to have been challenged.[54] Constantly reiterating this argument since the outset of his rule in 1962, King Hassan has always demonstrated his reliability as a partner for the West, further exemplified by his different direct military interventions in Africa on behalf of French and American interests:[55] 'Spain and Morocco are the two pillars of Hercules which guard the entrance to the Mediterranean. It is upon our two countries that, in large part, the destiny of the free world depends.'[56]

Therefore Spain as a regional power was at the same time the link to the international dimension of the conflict. She controlled the northern shore of the Straits of Gibraltar and her undisturbed presence in the Canaries seemed of supreme importance as well. It should be added that there are several important American bases on Spanish soil, among which is Rota, west of Gibraltar where American atomic submarines are located. With the imminent death of the Caudillo, Spain's membership of NATO finally became possible. In any event, the political and strategic importance of Spain had increased because of the politically unstable situation in Portugal after the Portugese revolution. Support for Morocco's position seemed to be even more important if the left came to power in Spain after Franco's death.

The evolution of the conflict

In 1975, while tension was mounting in the Western Sahara, especially because of the military actions undertaken by the Polisario Front against the Spanish occupation forces,[57] and because the visit of a UN mission in May signalled the hastening of the decolonization process, Morocco prepared a gigantic stunt, the so-called Green March.[58] On 16 October 1975, the king called for the reintegration of the 'despoiled' Saharan territory by means of a peaceful march of 350,000 civilians. The march was announced the very day that the International Court of Justice[59] published its advisory opinion. At the same time that the court's statement rejecting the Moroccan and Mauritanian claims to territorial sovereignty was published, the Moroccan media praised it as a victory for the Moroccan position[60] and mixed the already existing mood of *jihad* with (distorted) references to international law. Without any doubt there was a wave of nationalist enthusiasm in Morocco, and very soon the volunteers for the Green March surpassed by far the planned number of 350,000.[61]

The symbolic pressure which the Green March exerted on the Spanish government, as well as the diplomatic pressure, led to the Madrid Agreement which was signed on 14 November 1975.[62] This agreement enabled Morocco and Mauritania to secure control over the administration of the Western Sahara, even if from the point of view of international law Spain would still be held responsible for the decolonization of the territory.[63] Morocco and Mauritania took over administrative and military control as the Spanish evacuated the territory between November 1975 and February

1976. The struggle the Polisario Front had directed against Spain was now turned with renewed strength toward the new occupation. Resistance was strengthened because of the atrocities committed by the Moroccan army against the civilian population, including the bombing of women, children, men and herds as the Saharawi population fled to seek refuge in Algeria.[64]

Subsequently, Morocco and Mauritania divided the territory, the larger part being taken over by Morocco, the smaller and reputedly poorer part, with Dakhla as the main town, being occupied by Mauritania. The Polisario Front, which was at the same time making enormous efforts to protect its refugees who fled to the area of Tindouf in south-western Algeria, continued to fight the occupation forces with growing strength,[65] concentrating its forces mostly against Mauritania, which was the weakest link in the chain. At the very beginning of the war there were desertions from the Mauritanian army since many Mauritanians identified with the Saharawis. The Mauritanian army was small, poorly equipped and badly trained. The SPLA (Saharawi Popular Liberation Army) struck deep into Mauritanian territory, attacking the capital of Nouakchott twice and sabotaging the railway which transports Mauritania's major resources, the iron ore from Zouerate, to the port of Nouadhibou. During one of these attacks in May 1977, two French technicians were killed and several taken prisoner. The pressure exerted by the Polisario Front against Mauritania led to direct French intervention against the Saharawis.[66]

The direct intervention of the French air force from bases in Senegal in December 1977 not only constituted a dangerous escalation of the conflict but also the first step towards its possible internationalization. Yet many observers both within and outside Africa accept France's continued presence and influence in its former African colonies and consequently its repeated direct military interventions in African conflicts never attract much publicity.[67] In spite of French support in the form of large supplies of arms and military personnel as 'aid' to the Mauritanian army, Mokhtar Ould Daddah's government collapsed under the blows of the Polisario Front and was removed by a military coup in July 1978. The government of the SADR immediately called a cease-fire on the Mauritanian front (19 July 1978). Finally after protracted negotiations and in spite of heavy pressure exerted by France, Morocco and conservative Arab states upon the Mauritanian government,[68] a peace agreement between the Polisario Front and Mauritania was signed on 5 August 1979. Thereupon, Morocco immediately took over the southern part of the Western Sahara which had hitherto been under Mauritanian administration.[69]

The agreement with Mauritania was of central importance to the Polisario Front. From now on, instead of fighting on two fronts, it could concentrate its forces against the main enemy, Morocco. The years between 1978–80 saw the SPLA gain one victory after another, and by 1980 the Polisario Front controlled about nine-tenths of the Western Saharan territory. By 1981 Moroccan troops had been driven from almost all their posts and the Polisario Front was waging war even in the south and southeast of Morocco. Consequently, Morocco changed its strategy and started to build its famous Saharan 'walls'. These were constructed of sand which were protected by minefields, heavy armaments, radar installations and electronic sensors in order to detect enemy attacks as early as possible. The first wall was built around the so-called 'useful triangle' sealing off Smara, Bou-Craa and El-Ayoun. In 1982 Morocco was able to resume phosphate transportation on the conveyor belt between Bou-Craa and El-Ayoun. Since then Morocco has continued to construct walls and by 1986 it had finished its fifth wall.

Without question these walls pose a major problem for the Polisario fighters as they serve to cut them off from an important source of armaments, namely the Moroccan army's stocks. None the less, the units of the SPLA attack where and when they want, and the war of attrition simply continues on another level. The more walls Morocco constructs the more troops it is forced to deploy. Thus the war is expensive in terms of manpower and financial costs (particularly the sophisticated electronic equipment). A third problem is the morale of the Moroccan army. Attacks on the wall damage the electronic equipment and make it possible for the SPLA to break through and inflict casualties on the Moroccan army.[70] That this war of attrition is effective is evident from the increasing number of Moroccan deserters,[71] clear proof that the morale of the Moroccan troops is very low,[72] despite a relatively stable military situation. This may be the reason why General Dlimi, former chief of Morocco's espionage service and commander of the Moroccan troops in the Western Sahara, possibly undertook secret negotiations with the Polisario Front before he was killed in what was said to have been a car accident in late January 1983.[73]

Technically speaking the Moroccan army has greatly improved its position since 1980. However this does not mean that, as a consequence, the situation as a whole has improved for Morocco because there are additional levels to be considered, namely the diplomatic and the economic.

While its military success has decreased, the SADR has significantly improved its position on the diplomatic front. During the first two years of the Polisario's struggle against Moroccan occupation only fifteen states recognized the SADR. The *putsch* in Nouakchott and later the peace treaty with Mauritania opened the door to a series of recognitions from African, Latin American and Asian states. This was an indispensable precondition for the policy then pursued by the SADR in the OAU. By the end of 1981[74] some twenty-six African states had recognized the SADR. Slowly, but surely[75] the majority of states backing the SADR's position in the OAU was growing, partly reinforced by Morocco's rigid position on the issue.[76] Its constant rejection of the two main essentials put forward by the OAU (in its resolution AHG 104 of July 1983) a free referendum under international (United Nations and OAU) control and direct negotiations between Morocco and the Polisario Front caused a deadlock. The OAU finally admitted the SADR as a full member of the organization, whereupon Morocco withdrew from the OAU on 13 November 1984. This withdrawal became definitive a year later.[77]

In its plenary session on 2 December 1985, the 40th General Assembly of the United Nations, on the recommendation of the Fourth Committee, endorsed the OAU resolution AHG 104,[78] and subsequently Morocco declared its withdrawal from the Fourth Committee's deliberations on Western Sahara. Only seven states supported Morocco in the United Nations by voting against the resolution.[79] None voted against a similar resolution adopted by the General Assembly in October 1986, when Morocco refused to participate in the proceedings. Morocco's isolation on the international level and the implicit condemnation of its annexation of the Western Sahara seem complete. Moreover, Morocco has tried to apply the policy of breaking off diplomatic relations with every state which recognizes the SADR. Many important states in the Third World recognize the SADR including Mexico, Cuba and India together with Yugoslavia, a leading member of the non-aligned movement. All in all, a total of sixty-seven states have recognized the SADR. Therefore, this policy of punishment has turned into self-isolation, and Morocco is unable to pursue it rigorously anymore. In fact it has just resumed diplomatic relations with Mauritania.[80]

Unfortunately, UN resolutions do not change world politics. However, Morocco has isolated itself to such an extent that international support for its colonial war in the Western Sahara is now limited to a few Western and conservative Arab states. Governments around the world will be examining more and more carefully possible agreements with Morocco inasmuch as they could include precedents concerning the recognition of Morocco's claim to sovereignty over Western Sahara. Parallel to this, the diplomatic position of the SADR has been growing steadily, and sooner or later recognition either from a Western country or a socialist state may be expected.[81] This would give a new dynamic to the conflict.

The war economy: from underdevelopment to sell-out

Without any doubt Morocco is potentially one of the richest countries in the Third World. Not only does it have remarkable agricultural potential, fish resources and mineral resources such as phosphate, coal, gas, lead, iron ore and barytin, but it has a well developed infrastructure. However, its economy has never overcome the structural imbalance which resulted from colonialism and the country's integration into the world-wide capitalist division of labour.[82] This disequilibrium is bound to a social structure which is also the consequence of colonial penetration. The dominant groups in Morocco, even if the basis of some of them is feudalistic, truly constitute a comprador bourgeoisie[83] whose interests are closely linked with those of foreign capital. The latter never had great difficulty in operating in postcolonial Morocco—thanks to the political influence of these very groups, the most prominent being the palace itself.

Therefore, the liberal economic policies which have determined Morocco's development since its political independence in 1956 have always been closely linked with foreign interests. For those interests, however, a liberal economic policy was a precondition for their presence in Morocco as well as for the backing of the political regime. So, if we speak about the role of foreign powers in the region, and of their relationship to Morocco or to the Western Saharan conflict, we must always bear in mind that as well as the diplomatic and military levels there are also economic interests which indirectly, but forcefully, influence the behaviour of governments. That the application of the principles of a liberal capitalist economy, particularly in a Third World country, contribute to the sharpening of social antagonisms is a commonplace.

As early as the 1960s, when enthusiasm for the recovery of political independence was over and the economic consequences of the unbroken presence of foreign capital and its collaboration with the politically dominant groups became apparent, Morocco became the theatre of public rioting and violent protest.[84] It was the generally worsening economic and social situation and the growing corruption which motivated the two publicly known attempts at military coups in 1971 and 1972. The so-called Moroccanization of the economy was not proclaimed accidentally in 1972–3, though it did not introduce any noticeable change.[85] Foreign owners and companies just took on Moroccan associates. So, underdevelopment and social antagonisms were still growing while the regime seemed to become more and more unstable. The Western Saharan crisis came just at the right time to try to solve this problem of internal instability through an ideological effort, that is by building up national unity around the theme of territorial integrity and decolonization of allegedly 'stolen' Moroccan territory. By projecting this theme the king could mobilize and unify all the political parties behind him and give the army a useful, and as far as he was concerned, a safe occupation.

Furthermore the king could expect that the resources of the Western Sahara would contribute in the medium term to an improvement of the general economic situation, as well as the stabilization of his throne. It should be added that the sharp rise in the phosphate price on the world market in 1974 may have produced in Morocco the hope that by controlling the Western Sahara it could build up something similar to OPEC as far as phosphate exports were concerned. This dream however began to vanish by the end of 1975.

While it is impossible here to establish the dynamics of underdevelopment in the Moroccan case, it seems important to draw a brief picture of the Moroccan economy around the year 1985 in order to understand the situation, as well as the peculiar involvement of foreign powers with the Moroccan regime, and the contradictions resulting from both. In looking at data concerning the Moroccan economy or the country's budget one has to be extremely careful. Not only are the data often quite unreliable, referring mostly to planned projects rather than to real achievements, but there is an additional and crucial problem. Since the military budget is secret it is difficult to evaluate its role in the Moroccan economy. And even if its volume is evaluated at what seems to be a realistic 40 per cent of the state's total budget,[86] this would just be the part spent for unequivocal military expenditure. Considerable amounts may still be integrated into budgets such as infrastructure, housing and construction, telecommunications and administration. Finally, there is the priority given to the so-called southern provinces for 'development', resulting in many development projects being shelved in Morocco itself.[87]

As already stated, there was a sharp increase in the phosphate price in 1974, and Morocco, the world's largest exporter of phosphate accounting for a third of the world's trade, had hoped to be able to set up a controlling body for phosphates. However, phosphate prices dropped drastically in 1975–6 and again in 1981–2.[88] Morocco had started to set up its own fertilizer industries in order not to export only raw phosphate. By the time that the corresponding industries were complete, however, prices had dropped again[89] while prices for sulphur, which Morocco had to import for the processing, had gone up, together with the dollar. Furthermore, Morocco has heavily invested in the production of phosphoric acid, which can also be used for the downstream production of uranium. Since phosphoric acid became one of the most prominent export goods of other phosphate-producing countries as well, such as Tunisia and Jordan, there is strong competition among the producers to the detriment of the price of the product, while amortization of the investments is still going on. While the production of phosphates went up by 5 per cent from 1983 to 1984, exports went up by only 2 per cent.[90]

Another central problem faced by the Moroccan economy was its growing foreign debt, which at the end of 1984 was estimated at about $13 billion.[91] This means that in the absence of debt rescheduling, the debt service ratio would be up to 50 per cent, an absolutely unbearable situation. As early as 1983, Morocco faced a debt crisis because the country could no longer meet its commitments to foreign creditors. Negotiations on the rescheduling of the debt lasted two years, by which time further debts totalling $2.1 billion required rescheduling.[92] As a condition for according Morocco another stand-by credit, the International Monetary Fund imposed its classical conditions: cuts in state subsidies for basic foods, cuts in welfare and social infrastructure as well as in the state budget, reductions in public investment, devaluation of the Moroccan dirham and further liberalization of the economy.[93] These cuts happened at a moment when, according to official Moroccan figures, the inflation rate had gone up in 1984 to 12.5 per cent and the cost of living by more than 14 per cent.[94] Price increases for basic food which had been imposed under pressure from the

IMF had provoked widespread public riots in which several hundred people were killed in June 1981 and January 1984. During the January 1984 riots, which were particularly serious in northern Morocco, there were, for the first time, slogans against the war. In connection with these riots 1,600 people were sentenced. Although the price increases may have immediately provoked the riots, the reasons for the social unrest lie in the political and social system of Morocco itself.

The government responded to the pressure of the IMF—and probably to that of private capital inside and outside the country—by further liberalizing the economy and introducing a value-added tax (VAT) to hit the poor consumer again.[95] State enterprise may possibly be privatized. All this and the growing liberalization of foreign exchange for goods and capital will further ease the transfer of capital from Morocco to safer places and consequently damage the national economy. It seems unlikely that the government's plan to issue state bonds carrying 14 per cent interest in order to finance projects in the Western Sahara will raise much money;[96] those who have it will not commit their capital in Morocco for a period of at least three years. Moreover how would the government pay back the debt plus the interest when it is no longer able to service its foreign debt? Furthermore, this interest rate is identical to the actual inflation rate.

One of the crucial aspects of Morocco's economy is energy. In spite of an intensive search no significant oil reserves have been found in Morocco. Therefore heavy investments have been put into the Jerrada coal mine[97] and the search for oil.[98] For the first time exploration is in progress off the Western Saharan shore between Dakhla and Boujdor.[99] Until now Morocco has been able to overcome its tremendous deficits in energy thanks to gifts and continuously renewed, very advantageous, credits from Arab states, mostly from Saudi Arabia and partly from Libya.[100] It seems however that this aid is slowly drying up[101] and with the drastic drop in the crude oil price, together with the depreciation of the US dollar, this aid may almost disappear. Thus the prospects for the financing of Morocco's growing debt are decidedly gloomy. Another negative element affecting Morocco's extroverted economy has been the entry to full membership of the EEC by Portugal and Spain from the beginning of 1986. The agrarian exports of these countries are very similar to those of Morocco. A sharp drop in its exports into the Common Market is foreseen, implying that the foreign currency earnings of Morocco will further decrease.

In spite of all this the king seems to be optimistic as far as the purchase of new armaments is concerned. In July 1985, Prime Minister Lamrani made a three-day visit to Washington where he conferred with Vice-President George Bush and Defense Secretary Caspar Weinberger. He also attended a fourth annual general meeting of the United States–Moroccan joint military commission.[102] In fact, the Reagan administration budgeted $74 million in military aid for Morocco in fiscal year 1986. Consequently American military aid remains at its average level.

During his first visit to the capital of the Western Sahara after nearly ten years of occupation, the king had declared in El-Ayoun on 17 March 1985 that the government would spend $1 billion during the next five years to equip the Royal Armed Forces for their struggle in the Western Sahara.[103] If the United States continues its current level of support, this alone would already cover nearly half of this planned military investment, which of course excludes the operating costs of salaries and ammunition, fuel and repairs and maintenance. The real costs of the war are estimated to total nearly $4 million a day.[104]

For further modernization of his army the king also turned to his other important supplier, France. During a visit to Paris late in November 1985, he declared that Morocco intended to buy twenty-four Mirage 2000 aeroplanes—the most sophisticated system France has to offer,[105] indicating that Morocco plans to continue this war for at least another few years.

Though practically bankrupt, Morocco has continued to obtain credits for the purchase of new weapons, suggesting that France and the United States, by far Morocco's biggest suppliers,[106] must have a vested interest in seeing the Moroccan monarchy continue its war against the Saharawi people. Commercial consideration may also play a part in encouraging governments to sell arms, but there is a political consideration as well. Imports of arms create dependency with respect to spare parts and technology. They need highly qualified personnel for training, repair work and counselling. In other words, the supplier gets part control over the purchases, and he can test and eventually improve technology on the basis of practical experience.

Morocco's already shaky economy has been ruined by the war. The regime which started the war in order to stabilize itself and to broaden its popular base has become even more threatened by the social consequences of the war. Presenting itself as the reliable ally of the West it gets almost all the *matériel* it desires regardless of the possibilities of payment. Consequently, the direction of the national economy has been abandoned to the dictates of international banks and the IMF. In order to understand the involvement of the two most important arms suppliers, the few accessible and reasonably reliable pieces of data should be compared.

Relying on official American documents, Tony Hodges supplies certain information (see Table 4.1). Even if during the presidency of Jimmy Carter (1977–81), there was a noticeable slackening in military sales agreements, this did not affect the deliveries which were particularly high. Comparing the figures over the years there seems to be a relatively constant volume on average since deliveries are spread over several years. Besides this relative continuity, the figures also show that only a part of these deliveries is financed by loans or grants, although the provision of grants has grown since 1983 in recognition of Morocco's financial difficulties. Much of the other weaponry has been financed by Saudi Arabia.[107]

As far as France, Morocco's other most important supplier, is concerned,

Table 4.1 US arms sales and military aid to Morocco (in million dollars, for fiscal years)

	1974	1975	1976	1977	1978	1979	1980	1981	1982	1983	1984	1985	Estimated 1986	Proposed 1987
Foreign Military Sales Agreements (FMS)	8.2	219.8	95.6	27.5	6.9	2.8	266.0	28.7	12.8	68.3	33.9	69.1	80.0	80.0
FMS deliveries	4.0	2.4	15.8	33.7	86.2	133.5	50.9	124.7	56.0	54.4	68.6	53.5	n.d.	n.d.
FMS financing (credits and credit guarantees)	3.0	14.0	30.0	30.0	43.0	45.0	25.0	33.4	30.0	75.0	38.8	8.0	1.0	10.0
Military Assistance Programme (MAP) grants	–	–	–	–	–	–	–	–	–	25.0	30.0	40.0	33.5	60.0
International Military Education Programme (IMET) grants	0.5	0.8	0.9	0.8	1.1	0.9	0.9	1.0	1.1	1.3	1.6	1.5	1.4	1.9
Licensed commercial arms exports	0.04	1.0	4.1	21.6	12.0	8.9	17.4	3.1	5.0	14.0	10.3	1.9	5.0	10.0

Source: Hodges, Tony, Sahara Occidental: Origines et enjeux d'une guerre du désert, Paris, L'Harmattan, 1987, compiled from Foreign Military Sales, Foreign Military Construction Sales and Military Assistance Facts as of September 1985, Data Management Division, Comptroller, Defense Security Assistance Agency, Department of Defense, Washington, DC.; Congressional Presentation, Security Assistance Programme, FY 1987, Department of Defense Document, Washington, DC.

there are hardly any official figures obtainable. However the compilations made by Clément[108] seem to be highly reliable (see Table 4.2). Additionally France provides military personnel, which amounted in 1984 to a total of 265 persons, most of whom act as instructors for the Moroccan army. All personnel serve in the uniforms of the Royal Armed Forces.[109] These figures show not only the heavy involvement of France in the conflict, but also demonstrate clearly that since the socialist government came to power in France, arms supplies to Morocco have not been curbed, in spite of the friendly declarations of the French socialist party towards the Polisario Front when it was in opposition. In addition, the figures clearly contradict the argument often used by French officials that they had to observe agreements which were concluded before the socialists came to power in May 1982.

Table 4.2 French military supplies to Morocco (in million francs)

Year	Orders	Deliveries
1974–5	250	. . .
1979	over 350	. . .
1980	373	234
1981	338	285
1982	416	289
1983	291	331
1984 (estimate)	450 to 500	300

Arms are, or have also been, provided in considerable numbers by Egypt, Iran at the time of the Shah, Saudi Arabia, Jordan, Israel and South Africa. However, it is difficult to know the exact amount. Sometimes these supplies have been delivered through third countries or some of the above-mentioned countries have served as third country suppliers.

The international dimension: destabilizing the western Mediterranean

The war in the Western Sahara has been going on for more than a decade yet it still seems to be ignored in world opinion. Therefore, its crisis potential tends also to be unknown, or at least underestimated. The first question to ask is why it is so poorly known. The second concerns its potential for crisis on an international level, a question which is very much linked to the role of the world powers in the region.

The military involvement of the United States and France in Morocco as well as the interests of international financial capital in Morocco have already been discussed. On the other hand, it is well known that the Soviet Union is Algeria's main supplier of weapons, even if Algeria tends more and more towards diversification in this matter.[110] It must be stated too that Morocco's military equipment is somewhat superior to that of Algeria.[111] While on the military side the 'client–state' structure seems to be very simple and clear, it is very different on the commercial side.

The Soviet Union has substantial commercial interests in Morocco which is by far its most important trading partner in Africa. On 14 March 1978 an agreement was signed between Morocco and the Soviet Union which was called the 'contract of the century'.[112] The agreement foresees the growing supply of phosphates and phosphoric acid going progressively up to ten million tonnes a year over a period of thirty years. In exchange, during this period, the Soviet Union will supply Morocco with oil, chemicals, timber and ore-carrier ships. In addition, the Soviet Union gave Morocco a credit of over 20 million[113] at an interest rate of 3.5 per cent over a period of seventeen years for the development of a new phosphate mine at Meskala near Marrakesh. Furthermore, the Soviet Union is a large importer of Moroccan oranges and has concluded another agreement concerning cooperation in the fishing industry. However, the Soviet Union has made it clear that it interprets these agreements as covering Moroccan territory only, thus excluding the Western Sahara.

On the other hand, the United States is Algeria's most important commercial partner, importing over half of Algerian crude oil production and, until recently, much of its liquefied gas.[114] Cooperation on almost all levels of technological equipment is very intense too. For Europe both states are important commercial partners as well, even if there are qualitative and quantitative differences. The Federal German Republic has become the most important supplier to Algeria while France has fallen back, reflecting Algeria's policy of finding the best sources of high-technology products. France remains Morocco's most important trade partner for both imports and exports and still has some 55,000 nationals living in Morocco.

This short look at the commercial relations of the two countries gives the impression that commercial relations are completely opposite to the relations which result from the arms trade. However, it is too facile to reduce Soviet reluctance for direct support to the Polisario Front only to its commercial interests in Morocco. The Soviet Union has no stronghold at all in the western Mediterranean, and may well be aware of the fact that, even if it could and did interfere more directly in the conflict, this would constitute a dangerous escalation and increase the likelihood of its internationalization, a development which would be in the interests neither of the Polisario Front nor Algeria, the states of the western Mediterranean or the Soviet Union itself.

The United States and France, for their part, do not have this kind of reservation. They consider Morocco and the western Mediterranean as well as West Africa as a part of their traditional spheres of influence: 'Europe's southern flank is a critical part of NATO, vital to hopes for peace and security in neighbouring regions'.[115] Indeed, for the whole continent of Africa, the Pentagon's congressional presentation on security assistance for the fiscal year 1986 reads: 'This region is important for its vital mineral resources, US investment and command of the . . . sea routes.'[116] In spite of the often expressed doubts of the African Sub-committee of the House of Representatives Committee of Foreign Affairs,[119] successive American administrations have unconditionally supported King Hassan's position because of the simplistic and one-dimensional reasoning that he is a reliable partner of the United States and that, therefore, his regime must be 'stabilized'.

In fact, the United States has had some reasons to be grateful to Hassan. His military interventions in sub-Saharan Africa could give an African image to neo-colonial intervention. He was the only Arab head of state who supported the late President Sadat's Camp David policy, even if he had to break off diplomatic relations with Egypt later on because he badly needed Saudi Arabian support. He received the Shah after he was overthrown by the Iranian revolution and has remained a good client of the armaments business, having his own lobby in Washington.[118] There are good reasons to believe that in this simplistic and one-dimensional logic, it seemed useful and possible to upgrade Hassan to the status of a kind of 'regional gendarme' in the area.[119] Besides the interventions in Zaïre (in 1977 and 1978), Moroccan troops had participated in an attempt to overthrow the progressive regime in Benin in 1977, and for several years have been backing the reactionary regime in Equatorial Guinea.[120]

The Iranian trauma seems to have taught the American administration a strange lesson. Instead of analysing the reasons which led to the overthrow of the Shah, American policy seems to have turned into a strategy of 'stabilization at any price'. And this is being justified by apologists from the field of political science:

It is, however, in the US interest to continue supporting King Hassan of Morocco. The United States requires a friendly ruler in control of the Strait of Gibraltar with a foothold both in the North Atlantic and in the western Mediterranean. The United States has used Moroccan territory for air bases and communications and will need to do so again if the Rapid Deployment Force is to become a reality. If Hassan were to lose the Western Sahara, his regime would probably be toppled. An unstable or unfriendly Morocco will hurt the interests of Israel, Egypt and Zaïre. Morocco has been a moderate voice in Middle Eastern politics, and Hassan's support is still necessary in efforts to make the Egyptian–Israeli peace treaty work. The United States will have to provide money, arms, and food to help Morocco in the struggle against the Polisario. It is worth the price to keep Morocco friendly and stable.[121]

Consequently, the Reagan administration strengthened its military help to Morocco. Starting in 1981 diplomatic contacts and visits by American officials to Morocco became yet more frequent.[122] Regardless of the implications from the point of view of international law, high-ranking

American officials were touring the Western Saharan territories held by Morocco and inspecting troops there,[123] and in February 1982 the then secretary of state General Haig visited King Hassan in Marrakesh. As a result Morocco put two air bases at the disposal of the United States, to provide transit facilities for the planned Rapid Deployment Force.[124] The two bases are located at Morocco's biggest airport, Mohamed V airport near Casablanca, and at Sidi Slimane in the Gharb, where the United States maintained a base up to 1978. The unconditional support of the American administration for the regime in Rabat has continued.

American facilities in Morocco, however, are anything but popular. Their presence was already a big issue in the 1970s. American policy towards Morocco, with its continuously repeated intentions of stabilizing a more and more shaky regime, may turn out to provoke exactly the opposite result. This well-founded fear was articulated by an American congressional study mission which visited the region in August 1983:

Continuation of the conflict, along with the perceived US tilt towards Morocco, contains some serious risks for a number of important US interests. US traditional support for the principle of self-determination appears to be weakened by recent shifts in US policy. It is possible that the Saharan quagmire could eventually contribute to an anti-Western successor regime in strategically located, historically friendly Morocco. There is the potential for damaging US economic and political interests in oil-rich, non-aligned, and strategically located Algeria. . . .[125]

Or to put it in Tony Hodges' words:

US military aid therefore served to prolong the war without much chance of altering its final outcome. Ironically, it seemed likely to worsen, rather than relieve, Hassan's predicament in the long run. It risked promoting the process of destabilization in Morocco that it was designed to halt.[126]

However, the story does not just stop there. As has become clear from the above, for American, and most probably French, policies, the Western Sahara war is not just a question on its own or even of the survival of Hassan's regime. The southern flank of NATO is obviously of highest concern to NATO and the United States, and is sometimes described as a 'platform of attack' against the Soviet Union[127] and requires, in such scenarios, a deep and safe hinterland. Only from this point of view does it make sense that units of the American Navy are calling at Moroccan ports in growing numbers and that there are now joint American–Moroccan naval manœuvres.[128] American military aircraft fly over the Western Sahara,[129] violating principles of international law, as do the American and French military advisers who visit the Moroccan-held parts of the Western Sahara.

The American sixth fleet in the Mediterranean, however, is not under NATO command; it can thus act without consulting neighbouring member states of NATO. Additionally, the Moroccan navy and air force stage common naval and air manœuvres with the navy and air force of Spain, recently integrated into NATO.[130]

I am not about to make ironical speculations about whether Morocco is on its way to becoming a member of NATO, merely to show how far this military cooperation goes—and also to show what risks may be implied in a policy which draws Morocco, its shaky regime and the conflict in the Western Sahara closer and closer into European, American and NATO politics, i.e. into a higher and higher potential degree of internationalization.

As far as the famous stability of the Moroccan regime is concerned, different hypotheses or scenarios are possible:

1. The monarchy may feel so threatened either by the army, or parts of it, and/or by probable popular unrest resulting from the inevitable future rises in basic food prices that it may attempt to rebuild national unity on the old model but on a much higher qualitative level by using 'hot pursuit'[131] against either Mauritania, where the Polisario forces may be hiding at some time, or against Algeria, its main supporter. At least King Hassan has announced such a possibility on many occasions. Certainly, the United States would not favour such a decision by the king, but considering the degree of American military involvement in the conflict, it may be difficult for the United States to stay out should King Hassan make such a move. As a variation of this scenario, how would the United States react were some of the American experts present on the battlefields to be killed or taken prisoner?
2. If the regime were to collapse as a consequence of further rioting and rural disturbances with perhaps part of the army joining in or refusing obedience, and/or a major upheaval of the Islamic Fundamentalists, would the American bases (possibly even attacked by rioters) then be used to bring the RDF into Morocco in order to preserve 'American interests' or to prevent another 'Iranian case'?

However such questions—which are not at all unrealistic—are answered, they show one simple thing: the degree of American political involvement in the 'Western Sahara quagmire' throws into relief the dangers of the conflict spiralling out of control. Until the Israeli bombing raid against Tunis in 1985 and the American bombing raid against Libya in April 1986, the western Mediterranean had been calm. The destabilization of the Moroccan regime through the Western Saharan war and the large unconditional support of the Hassan regime by the United States could set this region on fire, as is already the case in the Middle East.

The war in the Western Sahara has shown that there cannot be a military solution on either side. Generally one has to recognize that military solutions can no longer be political solutions. That this obtains is graphically clear in this conflict with its direct American presence and the close proximity of a member of NATO (Spain), which still has some involvement.

There are, however, alternatives. On 10–12 December 1982 the International Association of Democratic Lawyers, held a conference on 'The Mediterranean: zone of peace' in Algiers.[132] This conference expressed its concern about the dimensions of the conflicts which have been and are taking place in the region, threatening the security of the people of the region itself as well as world peace in general. The participants in that conference urgently called for measures of disarmament for the banning of nuclear arms and arms of massive destruction. They called as well for the simultaneous withdrawal of the fleets of the big powers and for the elimination of foreign military bases. The conference also stressed that security in the Mediterranean can only exist if the territorial integrity of the states of the region is respected as well as the right of the peoples in the region to self-determination.

The conference ended with a proposal for a declaration of the United Nations, 'The Mediterranean, a zone of peace'. Besides the principles of the right of self-determination and of the right of every state to have internationally recognized and respected borders, the conference included the following specific points in its proposal:

— the right of the Palestinian people to self-determination;
— the right of Lebanon to sovereignty and respect of its territorial borders;
— the right of Cyprus to territorial integrity and respect of its sovereignty;
— the right of the Saharawi people to self-determination and the full sovereignty of the Saharawi Democratic Republic.

This study of the conflict in the Western Sahara has analysed the involvement of the United States and France and highlighted the danger of direct involvement by the United States, either through the internationalization of the conflict as a consequence of Moroccan aggression against Mauritania or Algeria or through the possible intervention of the United States in domestic Moroccan affairs in case of unforeseen events there. By contrast, retreat by the United States and France from the unwinnable war would be the only solution to prevent another possible crisis in which not only the United States but NATO could become involved.

To avoid such an eventuality, Morocco would have to recognize the Polisario Front as the only legitimate movement representing the Saharawi people and make peace with it, following the resolutions of the OAU and the United Nations. At the same time, Morocco could regain a large part of its sovereignty now compromised by the intervention of the IMF into its economic, social and political affairs and from the impact of the presence of American military forces in the country. Such a reassertion of national sovereignty could well be made understandable to the Moroccan people who, at the beginning of the war, were very enthusiastic about the question of national sovereignty but over the years have come to realize that Western

Sahara will never be Moroccan and that the country is losing more and more of its own sovereignty through this war. Finally, such a change in Moroccan policy would de-activate a conflict which is potentially dangerous to peace in the Mediterranean and the world and, finally, it would bring Morocco back into its natural setting as an African, Arab and non-aligned state.

Notes

1. An account of these agreements is given in Tony Hodges, *Western Sahara: The Roots of a Desert War*, Westport, Conn., Laurence Hill, 1983, pp. 45–8.
2. For Tarfaya and Ifni see also Hodges, op. cit., pp. 33–6, and 45–8.
3. Maurice Barbier, *Le Conflict du Sahara Occidental*, Paris, L'Harmattan, 1982. pp. 4–51; see also Maurice Barbier, *Voyages et explorations au Sahara Occidental au XIXe siècle*, Paris, Editions L'Harmattan, 1985.
4. The question as to how far the Sultan of Morocco extended his rule is very complicated and was later of interest to the International Court of Justice when it was asked to give an advisory opinion of the status of the Spanish colony from the point of view of international law. Morocco itself, at the time of colonization fell into two parts: the *bled el makhzen* (under control of the Sultan) and the *bled es-siba* (tribes which continuously revolted against the attempts of the Sultan to bring them under control and to collect taxes). The submission of these tribes was only achieved by French colonial troops who through so-called 'pacification' integrated them into what is now the territory of Morocco.
5. This was reported by formerly active Saharawi members of the Liberation Army in interviews in September 1985. Some of them had participated in the armed struggle against the French as early as 1904.
6. An excellent and comprehensive account of the role of the Liberation Army is given in Hodges, op. cit., pp. 73–84. It has to be said that the Liberation Army first started in the Rif and in the Atlas Mountains, then spread further south. For the French as well as for the sultan, who was brought back from his exile in Madagascar in order to calm down the rebellion, this must have been a true reminder of the best times of *siba*.
7. See Hodges, op. cit., p. 75.
8. Interviews with old Saharawis who participated in the battles, September 1985.
9. Union Nationale des Forces Populaires, a party of social-democratic tendency.
10. Union Socialiste des Forces Populaires which broke away from the UNFP in the early 1970s and had a stronger socialist orientation. Soon after, the UNFP almost disappeared.
11. Werner Ruf, *Der Burgibismus und die Aussenpolitik des unabhängigen Tunesien*, Bielefeld, Guetersloh, 1969, pp. 132–5.
12. An agreement on this border problem was reached between King Hassan II and the Algerian President Houari Boumedienne at the meeting at Ifrane on 15 January 1969. The border line essentially fixed the status quo as left by the French. This agreement, however, has never been ratified by Morocco and, thus, has no validity from the point of view of international law.
13. For what is meant by this unusual definition invoking two rather opposite

concepts like 'feudal' and 'bourgeoisie' see Baber Johansen, 'Die feindlichen Staedte—Marokkos blockierter Transformationprozess', *Das Argument*, Nr. 65/1971, pp. 394–432, and Abdelhaq Esch-sch'abi, 'Marokko—eine imperialistische Basis', *Dritte Welt Magazin*, Bonn, no. 4, 1977, pp. I–XXX.

14. In the case of Morocco, France broke with its old tradition of highly centralized direct administration by using local notables, the so-called *grands caids* which later on were also called 'local elites' (see Remy Leveau, *Le Fellah marocain—défenseur du trône*, Paris, Presses de la Fondation Nationale des Sciences Politiques, 1976). This process led to the transformation of many tribal chiefs into big private landowners who still rely for their legitimacy on the old tribal structures.

15. See John Waterbury, *The Commander of the Faithful: The Moroccan Political Elite*, London, Weidenfeld-Nicolson, 1970. The very problem of this thorough study of Morocco's political system is whether it is (or even ever was) possible to explain Moroccan domestic politics in terms of segmentarity as Waterbury does. The segmentary model as developed by anthropologists may to some extent be helpful for the description of patterns of loyalty and conflict in traditional tribal societies. However, it hardly grasps the newly emerging social forces and classes as well as the economic interests which also determine the behaviour of that part of Moroccan society which is formally still feudal. A much better analysis of Morocco's social structure is, in my opinion, that of the former leader of the UNFP assassinated in 1965, Mehdi Ben Barka, *Option Révolutionnaire au Maroc*, François Maspero, Paris, (Cahiers Libres no. 84–5) 1966.

16. See notes 9 and 10.

17. Johansen, op. cit.; and Esch-sch'abi, op. cit.

18. See among many others *Annuaire de l'Afrique du Nord, 1965*, pp. 412–14 and *Annuaire de l'Afrique du Nord, 1981*.

19. Esch-sch'abi, op. cit.

20. David Seddon, *Bread and Riots*, International Labour Reports, May–June 1985, pp. 10–11.

21. Esch-sch'abi, op. cit.; *Annuaire de l'Afrique du Nord, 1970*, pp. 249–50; *Annuaire de l'Afrique du Nord, 1971*, pp. 414–15.

22. In fact, Ahmed Dlimi was *chef des aides de camp* of King Hassan. He was widely suspected of playing a key role in the assassination of the opposition leader Mehdi Ben Barka in Paris in 1965, and for many years he was a close collaborator of General Oufkir, minister of the interior and chief of the Moroccan secret service, the DGDE. When Oufkir died after the unsuccessful 1972 coup plot, Dlimi became head of the DGDE. See *Le Monde*, 27 January 1983; *Maghreb-Machrek*, no. 100 (April–June 1983), p. 70; *Le Monde*, 2, 4, 5, 8, 24 February 1983; *El País*, 7 February 1983.

23. On 10 July 1971, the cadets of the military school at Ahermoumou, led by their officers, attacked the King's birthday party near Rabat. They killed some fifty people, mostly guests. The leader of the coup was said to have been General Medbouh, the highest-ranking officer of the Royal Armed forces who had just come back from the United States where he had learned about an alleged corruption affair involving the king. The August 1972 coup started from the Moroccan Air Force base in Kenitra, where the United States at that time had a military base as well. The Moroccan fighter aircraft vainly

attempted to shoot down the king's Boeing as he flew back from Paris. Oufkir was reported as having shot himself during a discussion with the king hours after the coup's failure. See Esch-sch'abi, op. cit.

24. Both the air force and the cadets of the military school in Ahermoumou were reported to be carefully selected Berbers of particular loyalty to the king.

25. See note 19.

26. This was Morocco's contribution to pan-Arab solidarity during and after the war of October 1973.

27. The text of the treaty is published in *Maghreb*, no. 32, March–April 1969, pp. 42–3.

28. See Manfred O. Hinz (ed.), *Le droit à l'autodétermination du Sahara Occidental*, Bonn, Verlang Progress Dritte Welt, 1978, p. 68.

29. See the brief but excellent analysis in Hodges, op cit., pp. 149–56, and for the Polisario Front, pp. 157–66. See also Barbier, 1982, op. cit., pp. 98–103. The latter is especially informative about the smaller groups representing different facets of Saharawi nationalism, the most important of which turned out to be the Polisario Front.

30. All other organizations of the Saharawi people were either set up by Spain or Morocco and/or lacked popular support. They were the Mouvement de Résistance des Hommes Bleus (MOREHOB), the name of which stems from the fact that the Saharawis mostly wear indigo-coloured cloth which tans their skin. This movement was founded in Morocco in 1971 and was completely dependent on the palace. It never had any influence among the population. Another Moroccan-sponsored movement was the Front de Libération et de l'Unité (FLU); it had regular Moroccan troops in its ranks and operated for some time in 1975 from bases in southern Morocco from where there was an easy access across the border into northern Western Sahara. Finally, there was the Partido de la Union Nacional Saharawi (PUNS), which was sponsored by Spain and claimed autonomy for the Western Sahara in close association with Madrid.

31. See the programme of the Polisario Front as agreed upon at its second congress in August 1974 at Ain Ben Tili and the letter sent to King Hassan II asking him to give up his plans to annexe the Western Sahara. Hinz, op. cit., pp. 111–19.

32. This conveyor belt is the longest in the world (99 kilometres). It was built with the help of the West German firm Krupp, Essen.

33. See especially Barbier, op. cit., pp. 103–14.

34. See the very detailed analysis of Barbier, op. cit., pp. 117–31.

35. See for instance the formation of the MOREHOB and the FLU.

36. For instance the diplomatic recognition of Mauritania in 1970 and the diplomatic contacts with the Mauritanian government starting in 1969 through Algerian mediation, as well as the attempts to come to an agreement with Algeria.

37. As a consequence of the abortive military coup carried out by the Moroccan air force on 16 August 1972 (see above), American–Moroccan relations had become very poor. The Soviet Union had started to deliver equipment to the Royal Armed Forces. Thereupon the American government changed its personnel completely at the Morocco–United States Liaison Office (MUSLO) in spring 1973 and from October 1973 military relations between both countries were resumed slowly. At the end of 1973 MUSLO delivered to the

king an armoured command vehicle in which he could hide in case of another military coup and get in touch with still loyal elements of the army. At the end of 1973 King Hassan also ordered from the United States some eighty M-60 tanks (which at that time corresponded to one-tenth of the yearly American production) sixty rocket-equipped helicopters, field hospitals and communication systems. Normally, such deliveries last over four to six years. Hassan, however insisted on complete delivery by autumn 1974. A very detailed and extremely trustworthy analysis of the arms trade in the region is to be found in Jean-François Clément, 'Le conflit Saharien', a manuscript paper presented at the *Colloque sur les Transferts d'Armements et Conflits Locaux*, Institut Français de Polémologie, Paris, 21–22 March 1985.

38. In the Madrid Agreement which was signed on 14 November 1975 and published on 21 November, Spain, Morocco and Mauritania agreed that Spain would leave the territory at the latest by 28 February 1976, and that until then two vice-governors, one proposed by Morocco and the other proposed by Mauritania, would assist the Spanish Governor-General in his functions. This is the basis on which the legally absurd justification of the take over of administrative control by Morocco and Mauritania stands. Although the document invokes the principles of the UN Charter, in fact, it is in complete contradiction with it (the text of the agreement is to be found in Elsa Assidon, *Sahara Occidental—un enjeu pour le nord-ouest africain*, Paris, François Maspero, 1978, p. 154. There were annexes to the Agreement, especially concerning the economic exploitation of the Western Sahara, but up to now they have not been fully published.

39. See Barbier, op. cit., for a careful and brilliant analysis of the diplomatic process which led to the Madrid Agreement, especially pp. 155–74.

40. The mission clearly stated that the decolonization of the Spanish Sahara had to respect the aspirations of the Saharawi people, including the Saharawis living abroad in political exile or as refugees (see UN document A/10023/Rev.1, vol. II, chapter XIII, pp. 12–133).

41. The UN General Assembly had called upon the International Court of Justice in December 1974 to give an advisory opinion on the question concerning possible juridical links in the pre-colonial period between the Western Sahara on the one hand and Morocco and Mauritania on the other. On 16 October 1975 the Court ruled that according to the UN principles relating to decolonization the Saharawi population should exercise its right to self-determination. See the chapters in this volume by Thomas Franck and George Joffé.

42. See again Barbier, op. cit., pp. 155–65.

43. Hodges, op. cit., p. 217 only notes that Alfred Atherton, assistant to the American secretary of state Henry Kissinger met King Hassan on 22 October 1975, while the deputy director of the CIA General Vernon Walters went to Madrid. Barbier, op. cit., p. 169 note 33, gives the same information.

44. Later on, in 1977, Senegal even permitted France to use the air base near Dakar for direct intervention by French aircraft in the conflict, when France used napalm and phosphoric bombs against the Saharawi People's Liberation Army (see Barbier, op. cit., pp. 249–50).

45. The Moroccan–Tunisian dispute over the recognition of Mauritania is analysed in detail in Ruf, op. cit., 1969, pp. 133–4. In this case as well Tunisia

followed the interests of France which created the state of Mauritania and appointed Mokhtar Ould Daddah, in order to secure French iron ore exploitation at Zouerate.

46. It seems, however, that Libya stopped its military support for the SADR as early as 1981 or 1982. The reasons for that decision are believed to be the deterioration of relations between Algeria and Libya as well as Libyan pressure upon the SADR not to participate in an OAU summit conference scheduled in Tripoli. Therefore, the 'union' between Morocco and Libya which was signed in Oujda in August 1984 did not bring about an essential change for the Polisario Front. On the contrary, it provoked support for the SADR among anti-Libyan African states such as Nigeria. For the change in Libya policy towards Morocco see John Damis, *Conflict in Northwest Africa: The Western Sahara Dispute*, Stanford University, Stanford, Calif., Hoover Institution Press, 1983, pp. 110–13. See also V. Thomson and R. Adloff, *The Western Saharans: Background to Conflict*, London, Croom Helm, 1980, pp. 258–60. The Treaty of Oujda was revoked by King Hassan in August 1986.

47. Hodges, op. cit., p. 217 refers to the arms negotiations which took place in Paris in 1974 and 1975. Without any question these talks were closely linked with Morocco's preparation for the conflict. However, he does not give enough background on the motives behind French policy.

48. Barbier, op. cit., p. 25.

49. For the year 1969—when fishing techniques were much less sophisticated than today—Barbier, op cit., p. 24 gives a table according to which some 1,281,500 tons of fish were caught off the coast of the Western Sahara by the fishing fleets of Japan, the Canary Islands, Spain, the Soviet Union, South Africa, South Korea, Italy, Portugal, Poland, Bermuda and others.

50. See John Mercier, *Spanish Sahara*, London, George Allen & Unwin, 1976, pp. 184–95, for mineral resources and mining.

51. Barbier, op. cit., p. 252. See as well *Middle East Economic Digest* (MEED) 27 July 1985 and 3 August 1985, and Victoria Brittain, 'Polisario's battle for the wall', *The Guardian*, 21 February 1986, p. 10.

52. See Hodges, op. cit., pp. 125–6.

53. Cf. Barbier, op. cit., pp. 163 and 246–7.

54. As representative for such positions see Damis, op. cit., p. 119: 'The United States enjoys close political relations with the moderate, pro-Western government of Morocco. Because of Morocco's strategic position commanding the southern access to the Mediterranean, Washington has a vested interest in a friendly government in Rabat. Washington and Rabat share much the same assessment of the destabilizing potential in Africa of the Soviet Union, Cuba and Libya. . . .'

55. In spite of the war in the Western Sahara King Hassan dispatched troops to Zaïre in 1977 and 1978 in order to crush rebellions in the mineral-rich province of Shaba.

56. King Hassan, speech of 6 July 1963.

57. See Barbier, op. cit., pp. 104–6.

58. Very realistic accounts are to be found in Hodges, op. cit., pp. 210–25 and in Barbier, op. cit., pp. 158–67. In his otherwise apologetic book Attilio Gaudio, *Le Dossier du Sahara Occidental*, Paris, Nouvelles Editions Latines, 1978,

pp. 272–8, gives a good picture of the march, and how the well organized 'spontaneity' was used as propaganda in Morocco (see also note 61).

59. The advisory opinion of the International Court of Justice has given rise to an enormous amount of literature which is almost all presented and briefly but extremely well discussed in the exhaustive bibliography of Barbier, op. cit., pp. 390–2. A very thorough analysis which puts the conflict into its international setting and links it with American interests is Thomas M. Franck, 'The Stealing of the Sahara', *American Journal of International Law*, 70, no. 4, October 1978, pp. 694–721.

60. 'The opinion of the Court can only mean one thing. The so-called Western Sahara was part of Moroccan territory over which the sovereignty was exercised by the Kings of Morocco, and the population of this territory considered themselves, and were considered to be Moroccan ... Today, Moroccan demands have been recognized by the legal advisory organ of the United Nations.' (Quoted in Hodges, op. cit., p. 210.)

61. There was, without any doubt, an extraordinary national enthusiasm about the Green March. It has, however, to be kept in mind that the whole enterprise was prepared in an almost military fashion. Transport, food, water, tents etc. for the marchers had to be prepared as well as thousands of green flags and copies of the Koran, which gave the whole affair the dimension of a peaceful *jihad*. Each commune in Morocco had to provide a fixed number of marchers. It is not difficult to imagine the kind of people the commune administrations conscripted; they were mainly dispensable lumenproletarian elements. For them it was a big event; never were they so well fed. According to Gaudio, op. cit., p. 274 each marcher received daily bread, sugar, dates, figs, concentrated milk, oil, soap and a packet of cigarettes. Ten per cent of the marchers were women, mostly prostitutes. All this gave the operation 'an ambience of popular festivity' (see as well Hodges, op. cit., p. 213). Finally on 6 November 1975, the marchers crossed the border, stepped a few miles into the Western Sahara but were stopped by the Royal Armed Forces before they reached the Spanish defence lines.

62. The Madrid Agreement is published in Damis, op. cit., pp. 129–30, and in Assidon, op. cit., p. 154. See also note 38.

63. According to the convincing juridical analysis of Barbier, op. cit., especially pp. 169–70.

64. Barbier, op. cit., p. 177 speaks of 'real massacres'.

65. Only a very brief overview can be given here. For more details there is a huge literature—besides the two 'classics' Barbier and Hodges—especially newspaper coverage in *Le Monde* and the publications of the Polisario Front like *Sahara Libre* and *Sahara-Info*. Because of censorship of military secrets, there is practically no realistic report on the war in the Moroccan press.

66. See note 44.

67. In the period 1976–80, France intervened as many as fourteen times in African conflicts (see Werner Ruf, 'Krisenherd Mittelmeer', *Die Zukunft der Sicherheit in Europa*, in Jahrbuch für Frieden—und Konfliktforschung, vol. XI, Schriftenreihe der Arbeitgemeinschaft für Friedens—und Konfliktforschung e. V (Afk), Lothar Brock and Berthold Meyer (eds), Baden-Baden, Nomos-Verlagsgesellschaft, 1984, p. 139. It seems there is little difference between conservative and socialist governments. The latest example (1986) is France's

involvement in the Chad war where again the French air force took off from the airport of Bangui in the Central African Republic—in a state formally outside the conflict—to bomb the bases of the anti-governmental forces of GUNT.

68. In fact, the road from the military coup of 19 July 1978 to the peace agreement was a very complicated one. In order to maintain Mauritania's claim over 'its' part of the Western Sahara, King Hassan supported Mauritania with some $15 million, while Saudi Arabia gave a grant of $100 million (see Barbier, op. cit., p. 265). After one year of cease-fire and with no move from the Mauritanian government the SADR lifted its cease-fire in July 1979 and attacked the town of Tichla taking many prisoners, including the Mauritanian prefect. It was this military action which finally brought Mauritania to the negotiating table.

69. This was relatively easy in so far as Moroccan troops were already inside the 'Mauritanian' part of the Western Sahara in order to secure the most important towns and especially the iron mines of Zouerate. By bringing airborne troops into Dakhla, Morocco immediately increased its military potential.

70. Members of the Polisario Front explain that it takes some time to repair the electronic equipment because this must generally be done by the French and American military experts who alone are qualified to handle the sophisticated equipment. During a visit to the Polisario refugee camps in the Tindouf area in September 1985, I was able to interview several groups of Moroccan prisoners taken in different clashes during July, August and September 1985.

71. See *Sahara-Info*, FRG, 7, no. 1, January 1986, p. 11. See as well *The Guardian*, 20 February 1986.

72. This is the result of several interviews with Moroccan prisoners. They reported that part of their food was sold by their officers on the black market in El-Ayoun or Tan-Tan, that life behind the walls—aside from the unbearable climatic conditions—was extremely demoralizing because for months nothing happened, so that they had sometimes actually wished that the SPLA would attack. Most of them were very worried as well about the economic situation of their families at home.

73. In fact, there are two versions on the motives for the elimination of General Ahmed Dlimi. One is that Dlimi opposed a possible move of the King towards the Polisario Front. The other says that Dlimi himself had made contacts with the Polisario Front. This is the version put forward by the Polisario Front. Since Dlimi must have known best about the situation in the army this reason seems by far the more probable. In addition the King has made no move towards Polisario since then. As debatable as these hypotheses may still be, the King must have felt threatened by the political ambitions of the commander of his troops.

74. See table in Barbier, op. cit., p. 295.

75. Barbier, op. cit., pp. 321–43, who deals with the question until the end of 1981.

76. In fact, Morocco behaved in a very flexible way, speaking again and again about self-determination and voting. Whenever it came down to concrete measures, however, it appeared that Morocco would not admit the slightest concession. It may have been these contradictions which upset a number of African states.

77. According to the statutes of the OAU a member has one year for reflection

before withdrawal becomes definitive. As Rabat has not changed its position since, it is no longer considered a member of the OAU.

78. The text of the UN resolution is to be found in *Sahara-Info*, FRG, 7, no. 1, January 1986, p. 12.
79. The resolution was passed with ninety-one votes in favour, seven against. The African governments which voted with Morocco were the extremely reactionary states of Zaïre, Gabon, Equatorial Guinea and the Central African Republic. Libya did not participate in the vote . . . (ibid., p. 13).
80. Just as Morocco intervened twice in Zaïre in order to save Mobutu's regime, it permanently maintains 400 men in Equatorial Guinea for the protection of its regime. See *Streitkraefte 1981/2,* Munich, Bernard und Graefe, 1982, p. 150 (German edition of 'The Military Balance 1981/82', International Institute for Strategic Studies, London, 1982).
81. The above mentioned UN resolution was voted for by the Western European states of Austria, Finland, Greece, Sweden and Spain and also by the socialist states of Eastern Europe. At the West European level, pressure on the Western European governments as well as on Morocco is growing as the international conference, 'Peace for the Saharawi People—a European Concern', held in Paris on 23–4 November 1985 has shown. A great number of European political parties participated in the conference. See Werner Ruf, conference report in *Verfassung und Recht in Übersee*, vol. 19, no. 2, Baden-Baden, Nomos-Verlagsgesellschaft, 1986, pp. 215–19.
82. Ibid., pp. 4–5.
83. Esch-sch'abi, op. cit.
84. For instance the Casablanca riots of 1965 which saw several hundred people killed.
85. A thorough analysis of the Moroccan economy is to be found in the research by leading Morocco economists like Fathallah Oualalou, Abdelaziz Belal and others. The subject, which would require detailed analysis, cannot be dealt with here. However it is of central importance for a better understanding of Moroccan political behaviour, as well as the annexation of the Western Sahara.
86. Committee on Foreign Affairs, House of Representatives, Subcommittee on International and Scientific Affairs and on Africa, 98th Congress, 1st session 15 March 1983, US Government Printing Office, Washington DC., 1983, p. 9.
87. Reading through the *Middle East Economic Digest (MEED)* one finds a lot of projects which are either delayed or given up, like the expansion of the airport of Agadir ($100 million) (*MEED*, 4 January 1985) or the postponement of the Ait Youb dam construction until the 1990s (*MEED*, 9 October 1985) for which another $53 million was foreseen. Another example is the delay in the completion of the solid fertilizer unit at Jorf Lasfar (*MEED*, 14 December 1985), etc. Of course the shelving and delays to projects cannot be linked directly either to the import of weapons or to preferential investments in the occupied Saharan territories. But at least indirectly they are linked to the consequences of the war on the economy and the steadily growing Moroccan debt.
88. See as well for the following data, 'Phosphates: Emerging from Recession?' in *MEED*, 1 March 1985, pp. 12–13.

89. Fertilizer imports dropped partly because of the reduction in state subsidies to farmers especially in the United States but also in the EEC, and because of growing ecological concern.
90. See table in *MEED*, 1 March 1985, p. 13.
91. 'Morocco's never ending debt' in *MEED*, 31 August 1985, pp. 12–14, and *MEED*, 24 August 1985.
92. *MEED*, 31 August 1985, p. 12.
93. See *MEED*, 29 July 1985, 17 August 1985, 31 August 1985 and 9 November 1985.
94. 'Marokko, wirtschaftliche Entwicklung', Cologne, Bundesstelle fuer Aussenhandelsinformation, 1984, p. 6.
95. *MEED*, 28 April 1985.
96. *MEED*, 20 July 1985.
97. *MEED*, 4 January 1985.
98. For the extremely advantageous conditions given to the prospecting firms see *MEED*, 1 February 1986, p. 25. Participation of the Moroccan government in exploitation will be limited to 35 per cent. Amortization of all costs including drilling is set at 200 per cent, no payment of royalties is due on the first four million tons of oil and there are many more substantial advantages. See also the contract signed by the Australian BHP for another concession near Dakhla (*MEED*, 27 July 1985).
99. The contract has been concluded by the Norwegian firm GECO. See *MEED*, 3 August 1985.
100. *MEED* over the year 1985.
101. When it was unable to pay back about $6 million to Western governments at the end of the year 1985 Morocco blamed the delay on friendly Arab states' failure to meet their aid commitments (*MEED*, 21 December 1985).
102. *MEED*, 3 August 1985.
103. *MEED*, 22 March 1985.
104. *Sahara-Info*, FRG, 7, no. 1, 1986, p. 9. This figure is estimated to be 'nearly correct' by experts of the International Institute for Strategic Studies in London. Richard B. Parker; *North Africa: Regional Tensions and Strategic Concern*. Council on Foreign Relations, New York, Praeger, 1984, p. 29, states that the cost of the war was up to $1 million per day in 1978. He goes on: 'That figure should at least be doubled and probably trebled to make it current.' This, in fact, would bring the costs in 1985–6 close to the $4 million per day mentioned above.
105. *MEED*, 30 November 1985.
106. As far as the international arms trade is concerned France appears to be more unscrupulous than any other nation in the arms export business. Even the Socialist government in France has always insisted that arms exportation was vital for France as about one-third (some 90,000) of all workers in the armaments industry are working solely on export orders.
107. It may happen that because of unpaid bills in the armament business civil airplanes are confiscated in order to speed up delayed payment. This occurred in the case of a Boeing 737 belonging to Royal Air Maroc at Paris airport in March 1982 (see Clément, op. cit., p. 106).
108. Clément, op. cit., p. 101.
109. Clément, op. cit., p. 102.

110. According to the Pentagon's congressional presentation on security assistance for the financial year 1986, Algeria was to receive $100,000 under the International Military Education and Training Programme and arms worth $60,000 on the grounds that 'IMET and FMS [Foreign Military Sales] ... should result in improved relations between the US and Algerian military establishments, provide Algerian officers with exposure to Western military thought and political traditions, and enable us to strengthen relations with a key Arab, African and Mediterranean government. The US training should help to balance non-Western influence, particularly at a time when prospects are excellent for the increased diversification of purchases of defense material and services by Algeria ... In addition, it is expected that Algeria will make modest commercial purchases of military equipment under FMS procedures' (Congressional Presentation, Security Assistance Programs FY 1986, p. 122).

111. This results clearly from *The Military Balance 1981–1982*, International Institute for Strategic Studies, London, 1982; German edition, Bernhard and Graefe op. cit., pp. 130–1 and 149–50. Additionally it must be kept in mind that military service in Morocco lasts eighteen months, in Algeria only six months. The Algerian army is engaged nation-wide in different forms of public work. Therefore, it can be assumed that the military training of the average Algerian soldier is far below the level of his Moroccan counterpart.

112. See Hodges, op. cit., pp. 354–5, and Barbier, op. cit., pp. 254–6.

113. Barbier, op. cit., p. 254.

114. See Damis, op. cit., p. 120.

115. Congressional Presentation, Security Assistance Programs, FY 1986, general presentation, p. 3.

116. Ibid.

117. See for example the statement of David T. Schneider, Deputy Assistant Secretary, Bureau of Near Eastern and South Asian Affairs, Department of State, in: Hearing before the Subcommittees on International Security and Scientific Affairs and on Africa of the Committee on Foreign Affairs, House of Representatives, Ninety-eighth Congress, First Session, 15 March 1983, US Government Printing Office, Washington DC 1983, pp. 9–12. See as well the fact-distorting statement of Dr I. William Zartman (as early as 1977) in: Hearing before the Subcommittees on International Organizations and on Africa of the Committee on International Relations, House of Representatives, Ninety-fifth Congress, first session, 12 October 1977, pp. 15–18, US Government Printing Office, Washington DC, 1977.

118. See Hodges, op. cit., note 47, p. 366.

119. Ibid., p. 359.

120. *The Military Balance* 1981–2, op. cit., p. 150.

121. The Hoover Institution's chief ideologist on African Affairs, Peter Duigan, in his Editor's Foreword to Damis, op. cit., p. xii.

122. For more details, see Hodges, op. cit., p. 360.

123. Ibid.

124. *Le Monde*, 13 February 1982.

125. The 'Impact of US Foreign Policy in Seven African Countries'. Report of a study mission to Ethiopia, Zaïre, Zimbabwe, Ivory Coast, Algeria, and Morocco, 6–25 August 1983, and a staff study mission to Tunisia, 24–7

August 1983 to the Committee on Foreign Affairs, US House of Representatives, US Government Printing Office, Washington DC, 1984.

126. Hodges, op. cit., p. 365.

127. Ruf, 'Krisenherd Mittelmeer', op. cit., pp. 125–40.

128. *MEED*, 1 February 1985.

129. *MEED*, 8 February 1985.

130. *MEED*, 13 July 1985 and 23 November 1985.

131. Attempts in this direction have been made several times by the Moroccan government through statements alleging that Cuban or East German experts were fighting alongside the Polisario Front. Such attempts at internationalization of the conflict may also achieve the goal of bringing American and French personnel closer to the front, an escalated risk which may also increase the possibility of direct clashes between the armies of Morocco and Algeria. Another attempt by Morocco to provoke an escalation on the regional level occurred when Morocco tried to arm a separatist guerrilla movement in the Kabylia mountains in Algeria in 1978. A Moroccan Hercules C-130 dropped armaments for the potential guerrillas (see Hodges, op. cit., p. 329).

132. During one of the trials of persons alleged to be leaders of the hunger riots in January 1984 (according to King Hassan, 'a plot organized by Marxists, Zionists and followers of Khomeini') a group of Muslim fundamentalists on trial in Casablanca declared that the war in the Western Sahara was against the principles of *ijm'a* (consensus) in Islam. The court was not the place to debate issues on religious dogma, but, it can be argued that the Muslim fundamentalists are closer to the Moroccan masses than the official political parties, whose basis has been systematically liquidated by the Palace (see especially the persecutions against the leftist USFP and the trade unions according to the reports of Amnesty International).

133. See conference report and project of the United Nations in *Revue Algérienne des Sciences Juridiques, Economiques et Politiques*, **21**, no. 1, 1984, pp. 217–26.

5 Morocco at war

DAVID SEDDON

Introduction

For over ten years, Morocco has been at war in the Western Sahara. The declared objective of King Hassan II is to achieve an effective and definitive annexation of the territory, its resources and its people with a view to complete incorporation within the Moroccan state. To this end, the Moroccan army and air force have been deployed since 1975 against the Polisario Front and the Saharawi Arab Democratic Republic (SADR) in an attempt to crush the military resistance to Moroccan annexation; at the same time, in those areas of the Western Sahara that have come under Moroccan control, systematic efforts have been made, on both the political and the economic fronts, to reduce opposition and to encourage and promote collaboration and cooperation with the programme of 'Moroccanization' of the occupied territories.

In this chapter, I shall examine the three dimensions—military, political and economic—of the struggle for the Western Sahara with a view to evaluating the capacity of the Moroccan regime to sustain its involvement in the area and to achieve its declared objective. I shall argue that while the Moroccan regime has so far managed to maintain effective control over an important part of the territory (the so-called 'useful triangle' in the northwest), the cost has been very great. Furthermore, given the continuing commitment by the SADR and Polisario to regain control over the entire Western Sahara (re-affirmed in February 1986 at the 10th anniversary celebrations of the SADR) and the undoubted growth of political and diplomatic support from outside (sixty-seven countries recognized the SADR by the end of 1986)—which in turn is likely to increase the flow of resources in support of the SADR and its struggle—the orchestration by the Moroccan regime of the three dimensions of its 'Sahara policy' is likely to become more problematic in the future.

The military dimension

Moroccan blitzkreig and occupation: 1975–6

On 15 October 1975 a United Nations investigative mission, which had visited the territory in May, reported that the majority of the Western

Saharan population favoured political independence and the end of Spanish colonial rule. The next day, the World Court at The Hague ruled in favour of self-determination for the Western Sahara. In response to this ruling King Hassan—who had brought the case to the World Court with a view to securing a judgment in favour of Moroccan sovereignty over the Western Sahara, and was already poised to intervene in the territory in pursuance of Morocco's claims—announced plans for his 'Green March', in which some 350,000 Moroccan civilians were recruited to cross the frontier between Morocco and the Spanish Sahara at the beginning of November—as 'a demonstration of the popular will in Morocco to reclaim the Sahara'.

While public attention was focused on the Moroccan–Saharan border at Tarfaya near the Atlantic coast, as a consequence of the Green March, Moroccan forces moved into the territory from the northeast with the aim of crushing the popular liberation front which opposed Moroccan irredentist claims as well as continued Spanish colonial occupation, and sealing off the border with Algeria. Ground forces supported by aerial bombardment overwhelmed the resistance organized by Polisario and during the remaining weeks of 1975 forced both them and the civilian population of several settlements in the northeast of the territory (Mahbes, Jdiriya, Haousa, Amgala, Tifariti and Bir Lehlou) to retreat into the desert. The camps in the desert were then systematically bombed (phosphorous and napalm were also used). Meanwhile, a tripartite agreement between Morocco, Mauritania and Spain had been signed on 14 November 1975, committing Spain to withdraw by the end of February 1976 and hand over the territory to a joint Moroccan–Mauritanian administration. But the Moroccan regime was not prepared to wait that long, and moved quickly to secure military control of as much of the territory as possible: Moroccan forces occupied Smara on 27 November, against strong Polisario opposition and then drove down the coast to take the town of El-Ayoun (the capital of the Spanish Sahara) on 11 December. Further south, Polisario had entrenched itself at La Guera on the border with Mauritania, but, after Polisario launched several attacks on military posts in northeast Mauritania in mid-December, La Guera was attacked by Mauritanian forces, and 'Moroccan jets, airlifted troops and artillery took the stronghold—in the name of the tiny Mauritanian army—after a ten-day siege'[1]

Thus, between November and December 1975, the Moroccans invaded the Spanish Sahara and took control of several key towns as well as the so-called 'useful triangle' in the northwest which included El-Ayoun and the phosphate mines of Bou-Craa. The Polisario forces, small and relatively poorly equipped, were no match in this blitzkreig for the Moroccan army and airforce. In 1975, the Moroccan army numbered some 65,000 men, with possible reinforcement by 50,000 para-military troops. Its tank force consisted of 120 Soviet T-54s, twenty-five old American tanks and 120 French AMX-13 light tanks; and its air power consisted of French Fouga Magisters and American Northrop F-5s. It is estimated that the Moroccan troops deployed in the initial invasion of the Spanish Sahara numbered roughly 20,000,[2] while figures for the Polisario forces suggest under 5,000,[3] but it was the air strike capability of the Moroccan forces that proved decisive in this phase of the war. From the earliest stages of the war, Morocco received substantial material assistance from France. As soon as the invasion began, for example, the French hastily delivered fifty tanks; and within a few months, Mirage jet fighters were delivered. Subsequently, France was to be Morocco's major supplier of arms.

The signing of the tripartite agreement in November 1975 and the Moroccan armed intervention in the Western Sahara drew an angry reaction from Algeria, which stepped up its support for Polisario and threatened military intervention itself. In January 1976 during a battle at Amgala between the Moroccan army and Polisario forces, the Moroccans captured about one hundred Algerian troops supporting Polisario, but since then Algeria has not been involved in direct military intervention. It has, however, provided financial and material assistance including weapons, to Polisario.

In January 1976, the Spanish abandoned Villa Cisneros (Dakhla), the main town in the southern part of the territory; both the Mauritanians and the Polisario failed to occupy the town, and the Moroccans moved in. On 27 February 1976 near Bir Lehlou Polisario announced the formation of the Saharawi Arab Democratic Republic (SADR).

Moroccan forces in the north proved unable to cut Polisario off entirely from its rear bases in Algeria and many of the refugees went eastwards to establish camps in the area of Tindouf; others continued to remain within the territory in smaller refugee camps. A large concentration gathered at Guelta Zemmour, which was sheltering some 25,000 Saharawi refugees by March 1976. Throughout the first few months of 1976, the Moroccan airforce bombed the refugee camps; the use of napalm against civilians was confirmed by the International Committee of the Red Cross in January 1976 and by a team of Swiss doctors in May.[4] In mid-April, following the signing on 14 April of the 'Rabat agreement' which divided the Western Sahara unequally between Morocco and Mauritania, Moroccan forces made a major assault on Guelta Zemmour. Artillery and air bombardment pounded the Polisario positions; napalm and phosphorous were freely used. The battle lasted five days and ended with the fall of the Polisario stronghold.

Guerrilla war and escalation: 1976–8

By April 1976 the Moroccan forces had established garrisons in most of the small outlying settlements of the Moroccan controlled zone, as well as securing a firm hold over the larger towns. Polisario, recognizing its inability to meet its overwhelmingly stronger adversaries head-on and deprived of its earlier strongholds within the territory, began to develop a new strategy of guerrilla warfare in the desert.

During 1976 and early 1977, Polisario launched a number of long-range attacks with columns of up to one hundred vehicles which afterwards returned to Tindouf, where by October 1976 some 50,000 refugees had established camps, or to the 'liberated' areas of the eastern part of the territory. But these long-range attacks made them vulnerable and on one or two occasions—notably a raid on the Mauritanian capital Nouakchott in June 1976 when they lost 450 men killed or captured, including Polisario's first secretary-general El Ouali Mustapha Sayed—they suffered heavy losses. Increasingly they developed a different strategy, that of converging on an objective from small mobile bases in the desert, scattering after the attack and of seldom travelling in large groups, at least in daylight.

Given the greater strength of the Moroccan forces, Polisario focused its attention on Mauritania. The Mauritanian army, which was rapidly built up from about 2,000 men in 1975 to 12,500 by 1978, not only had to defend scattered settlements and outposts in the southern zone of the Western Sahara (known as Tiris el Gharbia) but also had to combat Polisario raids deep into Mauritania itself. The air force initially consisted of a few reconnaissance and transport planes although orders were placed in 1977 for a number of Argentinian Pucara JA-58 fighter-bombers. During the second part of 1976 and the first part of 1977 Polisario attacks were remarkably effective, and on two occasions raids into Mauritania reached the outskirts of Nouakchott and enabled the Polisario forces to shell the presidential palace; attacks on the mining centre of Zouerate in May 1977 and on the railway between the mines and the Atlantic port of Nouadhibou threatened to bring the iron-mining industry to a halt.

On 13 May 1977, the government of Ould Daddah signed a defence pact with Morocco under which 9,000 Moroccan troops were to be deployed in Tiris el Gharbia and Mauritania over the following year. Early in 1978 there were at least 6,000 Moroccans in Mauritania. The Moroccan presence was poorly received by the Mauritanian troops, and there were violent clashes, notably at Dakhla, Bir Moghrein and Nouadhibou, with deaths on both sides; in 1977 Mauritanian troops at Nouadhibou mutinied in protest at their lack of pay and their posting to the harsh interior while Moroccan troops were garrisoned in the port.

A Franco–Mauritanian agreement was signed in September 1976 and widened in scope in January 1977 to allow French military personnel to be sent to Mauritania. During the May attack on Zouerate, Polisario had taken six French expatriates hostage (two more had been killed) and two more Frenchmen were seized during a raid on the railway on 25 October; during the second half of 1977 the French involvement in the war in support of Morocco and Mauritania escalated. By November, a complete aerial survey had been made of the desert and a ground control network for strike aircraft based in Dakar established in northern Mauritania, the posts manned by French units. In early December 1977, during Operation 'Lamantin' Jaguars of the French air force, from their base in Dakar, bombed Polisario forces raiding the Mauritanian post of Ben Lanouar, near Nouadhibou. 'By

CARL A. RUDISILL LIBRARY
LENOIR RHYNE COLLEGE

December the French "facility" at Dakar held six Jaguar strike aircraft with their supporting reconnaissance Breguets and mid-air refuelling C-135s, together with Noratlas transports and their cover and rescue Puma helicopters; the Jaguars, unlike Morocco's F-5s have both the range and the counter-missile electronics necessary for operating against Polisario'.[5] On 14 December Polisario announced the release of the French prisoners, but French air strikes continued using napalm, phosphorous and explosive rockets; in May 1978, the French airforce attacked Polisario forces at Oum Dreiga. In February 1978, President Giscard d'Estaing had announced that French aid to Mauritania would continue indefinitely, and during the first half of 1978 French military personnel in Mauritania were increased for 'defensive' purposes, while military training schools were established under French and Moroccan officers.

Meanwhile, French assistance to Morocco was increased. 'During the first two years of the war, the French had claimed neutrality whilst continuing to supply weapons to Hassan.'[6] Arms continued to be supplied to Morocco during 1977 and 1978, notably in the form of jet strike aircraft and a Crotale anti-aircraft missile system (at the cost of some $200 million) designed to counter any possible Algerian military involvement. But, in fact, the Algerian air force, with a significant number of its 200 combat planes based at the ready in Tindouf, did not intervene in the military conflict.

The air attacks certainly inflicted setbacks on the Polisario guerrilla forces and forced them to reduce their daylight raids. But the offensive against Mauritania continued and undoubtedly contributed materially to the growing economic and political crisis in Mauritania.

Sabotage attacks on the vital Zouerate–Nouadhibou railway continued, and the Mauritanian economy slid into an almost unmanageable crisis. To the costs of the war were added devastating droughts and a dramatic deterioration in the terms of trade due to spiralling oil prices and a slump in world demand for iron. The balance of payments lurched heavily into deficit, and by April 1978 the total public external debt had climbed to $711 million, equivalent to over 170 per cent of the country's GNP . . . As the economic crisis drifted almost beyond control in 1977–78, the country's technocratic elite, in business and government alike, recognised that peace was a precondition for recovery. The army officers, meanwhile, were dismayed by their units' losses and humiliated by the ever-larger Moroccan troop presence. During the night of 9–10th July 1978, the armed forces seized power in Nouakchott. Two days later, Polisario announced a 'temporary halt' in military operations in Mauritanian territory as a 'gesture of goodwill' to the new regime.[7]

One year later, frustrated by the Mauritanian regime's failure to withdraw from Tiris el Gharbia, Polisario lifted its ceasefire and attacked the village of Tichla. This prompted an immediate response: on 5 August 1979, the Islamic republic of Mauritania signed a peace agreement with the SADR in Algiers, in which it 'solemnly declared that it does not have and will not have territorial or any other claims over Western Sahara' and 'decided to withdraw from the unjust war in Western Sahara'. In a secret addendum, the new government undertook to 'put an end to its presence in Western Sahara and to hand over directly to the Polisario Front the part of the Western Sahara that it controls within seven months from the date of signing the present agreement.'[8] But the secret addendum was never in fact implemented. Moroccan troops were gradually withdrawn from Mauritania but Moroccan forces seized control of Dakhla and on 14 August Tiris el Gharbia was proclaimed a Moroccan province under the name of Oued ed Dahab (Arabic for Río de Oro).

Polisario on the offensive: 1978–80

Morocco's military difficulties dramatically increased after the July 1978 coup in Mauritania, for the Polisario forces were now able to give their undivided attention to the war with Morocco. Given Moroccan control of the majority of settlements and towns and the strength of the Moroccan airforce, Polisario had recognized early on that 'though it could recoup these piecemeal, it could never hold them for long since it had no air cover. Instead, its major tactic has been the lightning strike by the highly mobile force, typically a couple of all-terrain vehicles carrying machine guns, recoilless cannon, rocket launchers and anti-aircraft guns'.[9] Officially, Polisario maintained that 80 per cent of its weapons and equipment were captured from the enemy, but both Algeria and Libya supplied weapons and equipment and the Polisario forces were equipped with a range of relatively sophisticated weaponry from Kalashnikov automatic rifles at one end to SAM 7 missiles at the other by early 1978. Indeed, Polisario claimed to have destroyed at least fourteen Moroccan jet aircraft and even to have hit a number of the more sophisticated French Jaguars (which have missile defence systems), an indication of the effectiveness of their anti-aircraft weaponry, and of their training (in Algeria, Libya and Cuba) in its use.

After the military coup in Mauritania Polisario began raiding into southern Morocco as well as maintaining its operations within the Western Sahara. The death of President Boumedienne in December 1978 was followed by a major campaign during 1979–80 named 'the Houari Boumedienne Offensive' in his honour. For the first time during the war, larger Moroccan-held towns and bases were assaulted and their defences breached. On 28 January 1979, for example, a large guerrilla force fought its way into the centre of Tan-Tan, a provincial capital in southern Morocco with a garrison of several thousand troops and an airbase; on 11 August the Moroccan positions at Bir Enzaren, 150 miles east of Dakhla, were partially overrun. On 24 August a base at Lebouirate in southern Morocco fell to the Polisario forces; on 6 October several thousand guerrillas broke through Smara's defence lines and evacuated 700 local residents to Algeria; and on 14 October Polisario seized Mahbes, a base in the extreme northeast of the Western Sahara which had fallen to the Moroccan forces in the blitzkreig of 1975, killing a fifth of its defenders. Other raids were mounted as far north as the Bani mountains and the southeasterly slopes of the Anti-Atlas, while attacks using pneumatic launches were also made against fishing boats off the Atlantic coast. One of the main targets of the Polisario guerrilla offensive was the phosphate mining complex at Bou-Craa, which is linked by a vulnerable 99 kilometre conveyor belt to the port at El-Ayoun. Constant harassment along the conveyor belt seriously affected production during the early years of the war (1976–80).

As the military successes of the Polisario forces became more frequent, the Moroccan army was obliged to abandon many of the smaller, more remote outposts they had occupied in the early months of the war. A gradual process of retrenchment began, and the defences of the more important towns were heavily reinforced. Thousands of fresh troops were sent south to the Sahara and it is estimated that by September 1978 the Moroccan armed forces numbered some 80,000 men, supported by over sixty combat planes, armoured cars, tanks, transport planes and heli-copters.[10] King Hassan himself admitted that there were 80,000 Moroccan troops in the Western Sahara by January 1983.[11]

'Moroccan energies, after the initial phase, were concentrated on defence fortification, the main posts being ringed with concentric trenching and barbed wire. From time to time, a large contingent crosses the open desert, either on a supply run or to help another post under siege by the Saharawis'.[12] Rather like the Soviet troops in occupation in Afghanistan, control was limited by the end of the decade to the larger centres where troops, equipment and weaponry were massed in overwhelming strength, but remained unable to extend that control systematically over the remainder of the territory.

In this situation, reports of demoralization, indiscipline and corruption among the troops of the occupying army and of general antipathy towards both the war and the Moroccan regime which initiated it were, not surprisingly, common. Late in 1977, for example, the Algerian press reported that a battalion of the Moroccan army drawn from the Atlas and the south of Morocco had mutinied and attempted to join the Polisario forces, but had been caught near Haousa and destroyed by Moroccan airplanes.

Taking advantage of its ability to mount its attacks from an effectively 'liberated' zone, the SPLA continued to attack Moroccan positions and installations in the Moroccan occupied areas of the Western Sahara. Even as the Moroccan army of occupation began to strengthen its defences further in the El-Ayoun–Smara–Bou-Craa triangle during the latter part of 1980, the SPLA was able to penetrate the existing defences in several places; in January 1981 it attacked the heavily defended Bou-Craa mines. Further north, on the same day, it attacked the Moroccan garrison at Rous Lakhyalat near Ras el Khanfra on the Moroccan border; as a result, it was claimed, over 200 Moroccan troops were killed and a large quantity of arms and vehicles were destroyed or captured. A few days before that, two

Moroccan planes were shot down at Rous Lakhyalat—one a Mirage F-1 and the other an American-built F-5.

Moroccan forces on the defensive: 1981–6

In August 1980, after several costly failures, the Moroccan armed forces succeeded in gaining control of a strategic pass through the Zini mountains, to the southwest of the Ouarkziz mountain range, near the border with the Western Sahara, and the construction of a continuous defence line southwards to Smara, sixty miles away, was initiated. By March 1981 a 'wall' of fortifications, heavily defended and equipped, had reached Smara; by mid-May 1981, it had been extended to Bou-Craa, and by May 1982 it had reached the sea to the south of Boujdour.

The 'wall' consisted of sandbanks, between six and eight feet high for the most part, protected by barbed wire and minefields, intermittent artillery placements and observation posts, and equipped with electronic ground sensors and radar equipment to detect movement up to several miles across the desert beyond. The wall was manned along its entire length, with protective dug-outs and more elaborate underground quarters for the troops concerned. This defence perimeter, which extended over 250 miles, sealed off an area of some 17,000 square miles—roughly one-sixth of the Western Sahara. Apart from this—the 'useful triangle' in the northwest of Western Sahara—Moroccan armed forces maintained a permanent presence in only one other region, a heavily fortified enclave of a few hundred square miles around the towns of Dakhla and Argoub in the south. The rest of Western Sahara was abandoned in November 1981 following a devastating Polisario attack on Guelta Zemmour the previous October, in which its 2,600-strong Moroccan garrison suffered serious losses and five Moroccan aircraft were shot down by ramp-launched SAM missiles in the space of ten days.

Even as the Moroccan forces constructed their defensive wall, the build-up of weaponry and equipment in the occupied areas continued. By 1978, the Moroccan military budget had reached $760 million, nearly 14 per cent of government expenditure. In 1979 the war was estimated to be costing between $2 and $5 million per day,[13] while by 1980, the American embassy in Rabat was reporting claims that 'Morocco's defence-related expenditure actually diverts no less than 40 per cent of the consolidated national budget'.[14] A significant proportion of this war expenditure relates to the cost of maintaining a large army in the Western Sahara, but an important proportion of the budget has gone on the purchase of arms and equipment from abroad. These include tanks, armoured personnel carriers and armoured reconnaissance vehicles, artillery, anti-tank weapons (both guns and missiles), anti-aircraft defences, combat aircraft, attack helicopters, air-to-air missiles, air-to-ground missiles and electronic and radar defence systems. A very significant number of the more advanced weapons and equipment was built in France or the United States (see Appendix 1).

Despite France's acknowledgement in 1979 of the right to

self-determination of the Western Sahara, France has remained Morocco's principal arms supplier: delivery of fifty Mirage F-1 aircraft and twenty-five Alpha-Jets began in 1980. This ambiguous policy has continued under the Mitterrand government, despite the French Socialist party's long-standing relations with Polisario[15]

French arms supplies to Morocco in recent years have been on a large scale and span the entire spectrum from light arms to heavy weaponry to a Crotale anti-aircraft missile system. These armaments include 60 Mirage F-1CH jet interceptor aircraft, 24 Fouga strike planes, 24 Alpha Jet tactical support aircraft, 40 Puma troop-carrying helicopters, and 400 VAB armoured personnel carriers. The total value of French arms sales to Morocco between 1974 and 1981 is probably in the range of $1.5–$2 billion, not including weapons supplied through military credit. French military support has included France's willingness to accept large Moroccan arrears in payment.[16]

After the fall of the Shah of Iran and Somoza of Nicaragua in 1979, President Carter dropped an earlier ban on the sale of certain kinds of aircraft to Morocco and agreed a multi-million dollar arms package for Morocco. In January 1980, the Pentagon announced plans to sell $232.5 million worth of Northrop F-5E jets, OV-10 'Bronco' counter-insurgency aircraft and Hughes helicopter gunships to Morocco; and in March 1981, a State Department official told Congress: 'Morocco is important to broad American interests and occupies a pivotal strategic area. We intend to maintain and reinforce our historically close relationship with reliability and consistency as our watchwords.'[17] Congress raised the budgeted level of military aid to Morocco from $30 million in 1980 to $45 million in 1981 and secretary of state Alexander Haig approved, early in 1981, the sale of six OV-10 'Broncos' and 108 M-60 tanks to Morocco.[18] American assistance was intensified after the Moroccan disaster at Guelta Zemmour in October 1981. American military instructors arrived at Morocco to join French instructors in training special troops in counter-guerrilla operations and to teach anti-missile tactics to Moroccan pilots. In 1982, a joint American–Moroccan military commission was established by the American secretary of state, and the Reagan administration planned to treble its foreign military sales credits to Morocco from $30 million in Fiscal Year 1982 to $100 million in FY 1983. In May 1982 Morocco signed an agreement giving the American Rapid Deployment Force transit facilities at Moroccan air bases. In July 1982 it was revealed that the United States was supplying anti-personnel cluster bombs to the Moroccan airforce,[19] The justification for the large-scale military aid provided to Morocco by the United States, in the words of the Reagan administration's official budget request to Congress in 1985, is that 'it helps to maintain the stability of a pro-Western country' which has played 'a moderating role' in the Arab world *vis-à-vis* Israel and since 1982 has 'agreed to access and transit rights in certain contingencies to assist the deployment of US forces to Southwest

Asia'.[20] Loan facilities to finance foreign military sales dropped from $39 million in 1984 to around $8 million in 1985 and only $1 million in 1986, but grants under the Military Assistance Program which began in 1983 rose from $30 million in 1984 to $40 million in 1985 and, though they fell slightly in 1986 ($33.5 million), were budgeted to rise to $60 million in 1987. Allocations under the International Military Education and Training Program increased between 1984 and 1986. In 1986 the entire security package approved by Congress was worth $74.35 million—slightly more than the $66 million allocated to Morocco for development and food aid.

Other important sources of arms sold to Morocco have included Austria (whose government in 1977 sanctioned the sale of 102 Kurassier-type tanks manufactured by the Steyr–Daimler–Puch concern to Morocco, and in 1985 approved the sale of fifty similar tanks to replace those captured by the SPLA) and South Africa (the Moroccan army in 1984 had some eighty Ratel 20 armoured personnel carriers manufactured in South Africa). As regards to the latter, a group of South African officers are reported to have visited the area under Moroccan occupation during 1985 to inspect the equipment provided by the Pretoria government, and to review military training schools and the 'wall' defences; this visit was one indication of the important relations that exist between South Africa and Morocco. Spain has also supplied arms to Morocco sporadically since 1975, albeit on a relatively small scale, and has recently renewed its arms supplies.

But, despite the arms build-up within the occupied territories of the Western Sahara, particularly since 1981, the Moroccans remain essentially on the defensive. Throughout the last five years, the SPLA has been able to keep the Moroccan armed forces on full alert by selective strikes and thrusts, both against the 'wall' and through the Moroccan defences.

Against the persistence of the SPLA and its ability to penetrate the Moroccan defences in unpredictable sorties and lightning attacks, the Moroccan armed forces have basically two responses—the airstrike and the further strengthening of the defensive structures surrounding their occupied areas. As the anti-aircraft weaponry of the SPLA has been significantly improved over the past few years by the acquisition of new artillery and ground-to-air missiles and by experience and training in the use of this equipment, so the airstrike has become a costly and only partly effective tactic. Consequently between December 1983 and May 1984, two new 'walls' were built, by an estimated 30,000 Moroccan troops. One which amounted to a southeasterly extension to the original wall, ran fifty miles due east from Bou-Craa to Amgala, and then north to rejoin the old wall north of Smara; the other was a more ambitious defence system, starting from Zaag in the southeast of Morocco and extending in a southwesterly direction, via Jdiriya and Haousa, to Smara. A fourth wall was built around the Moroccan base of Mahbes in the extreme north east, near the border with Algeria, in 1985. Later that year, the construction of a fifth 'wall' to run south and southwest from near Amgala to south of Dakhla on the coast was initiated; this new structure—a 600-kilometre-long barrier of sand, stone, artillery, manned positions and radar—was designed to encompass part of the enormous Oued ed Dahab area (former Tiris el Gharbia) in the south of Western Sahara.

However, the capacity of the Moroccan armed forces to man and defend effectively this system of defensive walls extending over a vast area in the desert must be questionable. Already at the end of 1984 the Moroccan forces—estimated to number perhaps 100,000 in the territory—were greatly extended. Polisario has demonstrated since then that it is still able to mount effective hit-and-run attacks on the Moroccan walls at virtually any point along their considerable length; the effect of this is to maintain all the Moroccan troops on constant alert and to prevent any concentration of Moroccan forces and equipment (and thereby some saving in the enormous cost of sustaining an adequate defensive capacity throughout the territory). Reports of demoralization and dissaffection among the Moroccan troops in the Western Sahara have become more common, although the reliability of these is open to some doubt[21] and the attraction of double or even triple pay for postings in the occupied territories remains considerable in the light of high unemployment rates and the rising cost of living in Morocco.

As Tony Hodges has remarked,

the Saharan conflict is a classic example of a war of attrition. The guerrillas do not have to break through the Moroccan defence lines and seize El Ayoun to achieve their objectives. They simply have to remain a permanent threat, forcing King Hassan to keep a huge number of troops and a vast arsenal of weaponry in the Sahara, at a cost, in financial terms, that Morocco can ill afford. Polisario's strategy hinges, in fact, on the belief that Morocco will be unable to sustain this war indefinitely and that, if King Hassan does not end it, he will eventually lose his throne.[22]

The suggestion is that, as the commitment to an unwinnable war progressively drains the resources of the Moroccan regime, the economic repercussions will become increasingly deeply felt and thereby indirectly contribute to undermining the present Moroccan regime. It is also conceivable, however, that the Moroccan intervention in the Sahara will become a direct political liability for the regime as casualties mount, opposition within the occupied territories and possibly terrorist attacks within Morocco develop and international opinion moves increasingly against the military occupation.

The political dimension

International politics and diplomacy: the United Nations and the OAU[23]

Certainly, in international opinion, the Moroccan regime has become progressively isolated over the last ten years over its military intervention in Western Sahara. The ruling of the International Court of Justice in October

1975, which recognized the right to self-determination of the people of Western Sahara, was followed in December 1975 by two votes at the United Nations General Assembly in favour of upholding the principle of self-determination and a role for the United Nations in its effective implementation. The tripartite agreement of November 1975 and the subsequent formal partition of Western Sahara between Morocco and Mauritania in April 1976 directly opposed the rulings and resolutions of the World Court and the United Nations General Assembly, and when the Swedish UN ambassador Olof Rydbeck visited Western Sahara to examine how the United Nations might proceed, he was so struck by the scale of Moroccan military presence, the repressive political atmosphere, the developing guerrilla war and the exodus of refugees that he advised the secretary-general Kurt Waldheim that a genuine consultation of local views was impossible. Consequently, the United Nations decided that the essential conditions for the exercise of self-determination were not fulfilled.

During the first two years of the war in Western Sahara, the Organization of African Unity (OAU) equivocated on the issue: at summit meetings in 1976 and 1977 it decided to refer the matter to an extraordinary summit which, however, was never held. During this period, the Moroccan government managed to dissuade both the United Nations General Assembly and the Non-Aligned Movement at its summit in August 1976 from taking positions on the Western Sahara, largely by pointing to the decision of the OAU to discuss the matter and by extensive lobbying. In July 1978, however, an *ad hoc* committee of five African heads of state was set up by the OAU to consider all the facts of the matter; in July 1979 the next OAU summit endorsed that committee's proposals, which included an immediate ceasefire and the exercise by the people of Western Sahara of their right to self-determination through a general, free referendum enabling them to choose one of the two following options: (a) total independence, (b) maintenance of the status quo. In December 1978, the UN General Assembly adopted two resolutions—one, backed by Morocco (adopted by sixty-six votes to thirty, with forty abstentions) appealing to states not to impede the efforts of the OAU, and another (adopted by ninety votes to ten with thirty abstentions) reaffirming the inalienable right of the people of Western Sahara to self-determination and independence.

The Algiers Agreement of 1979 (in which Mauritania signed a peace treaty with Polisario and effectively withdrew from the conflict) not only served to isolate Morocco, as the only state directly impeding the self-determination and independence of the people of the Western Sahara, but also prompted the OAU and the United Nations to take somewhat more decisive steps to support the rights of the Western Saharans. The sixth Non-Aligned summit, held in Havana in September 1979, deplored Morocco's annexation of Tiris el-Gharbia. From 1979 onwards Morocco was obliged to vote against or abstain on the resolutions on Western Sahara adopted by the UN General Assembly (in 1986 it boycotted the vote). In November

1979, and again in November 1980, the General Assembly affirmed the inalienable right of the Western Saharans to self-determination and independence, deplored the continued occupation of Western Sahara by Morocco and the extension of that occupation to the south of the territory and urged Morocco to join the peace process and to terminate its occupation. Both resolutions recognized Polisario as 'the representative of the people of the Western Sahara' and recommended its participation in 'any search for a just, lasting and definitive political solution of the question of Western Sahara'.

Morocco refused to attend a meeting of the OAU *ad hoc* committee in December 1979. Its boycott was regretted by the heads of state comprising the committee, who called upon Morocco to withdraw all its troops from Western Sahara. The meeting repeated the earlier OAU proposals regarding a cease-fire and referendum, and suggested sending an OAU peacekeeping force to the area. At the OAU summit in July 1980, a narrow majority of OAU members (twenty six out of fifty) recognized the SADR and favoured its admission to the OAU as a member state. Morocco threatened a walkout from the OAU and offered to end its boycott of the *ad hoc* committee but continued to oppose the referendum proposal. However, such inflexibility clearly threatened to isolate Morocco further in international political and diplomatic circles, and King Hassan promised at the next OAU summit in June 1981 that Morocco would accept a controlled referendum framed to take into consideration not only the *ad hoc* committee's objectives but also Morocco's conviction regarding the legitimacy of its rights. This enabled Morocco to remain within the OAU and prevented the SADR from inclusion as a member state, although by the end of 1980 a total of twenty-seven African states had bilaterally recognized the SADR (as had eight Asian states, ten states in Latin American and one in Oceania).

Throughout 1981 and 1982 the OAU 'implementation committee' set up for the referendum was unable to make any real progress; Morocco's active lobbying and a concern over the dangers of splitting the OAU, as well as Morocco's refusal to recognize Polisario, even as an adversary, rendered the OAU committee incapable of arranging a cease-fire. In February 1983, pressure from Algeria and other pro-SADR states regarding the SADR's membership of the OAU enabled the republic to take its seat as the fifty-first member–state, but eighteen other African states joined Morocco in a walkout and the OAU was thrown into disarray; only a voluntary and temporary 'withdrawal' by the SADR enabled a summit to take place eventually in June 1983. Then, for the first time, Morocco and Polisario were named as the parties in conflict and both were urged to undertake direct negotiations to reach an agreement on a cease-fire and the conditions for a peaceful and fair referendum under the auspices of the United Nations and the OAU (Resolution AHG/104). Both Morocco and the SADR sent representatives at the invitation of the implementation committee to a meeting in September 1983, but when asked to meet around the same table,

Morocco refused—although Polisario agreed. Since then Morocco has consistently refused to recognize or to negotiate directly with Polisario, although in fact an exploratory meeting had been secretly held in April 1983, suggesting that if formal recognition remains unlikely unofficial meetings are not necessarily precluded.

After King Hassan's pledge at the June 1981 OAU summit, the UN General Assembly resolutions, adopted in November 1981 and again in November 1982 with overwhelming majorities, focused on the need for peace talks between Morocco and Polisario. The June 1983 resolution adopted at the OAU summit, referring to the crucial need for direct negotiations between the parties to the conflict, was incorporated into a resolution adopted by consensus by the UN General Assembly in December 1983, although Morocco (which accepted the consensus) had already rendered it ineffective by refusing to talk with Polisario under the auspices of the OAU implementation committee. In 1985, Morocco made it quite clear to the UN General Assembly that it was not prepared to consider further discussion of the Western Sahara issue and would boycott all proceedings on the subject. In November 1985 Morocco—politically and diplomatically isolated within the OAU—withdrew from the organization when the SADR was finally able to take its seat without serious challenge. At the following summit, in July 1985, the SADR's president, Mohamed Abdelaziz, was elected one of the OAU's vice-presidents.

Morocco's continuing intransigence on the matter of peace negotiations has cost it dearly in international political and diplomatic circles. By mid-1984 the number of states recognizing the SADR had grown to fifty-eight, and by the end of 1986 this had reached sixty-seven; recent additions include India and Yugoslavia (see Table 5.1). In September 1986 the Non-Aligned summit in Zimbabwe endorsed the OAU peace plan adopted at the 1983 OAU summit; in September 1985 the Inter-Parliamentary Union (IPU), at its 74th conference in Ottawa, also supported the settlement terms spelled out in the OAU resolution. In December 1985 and again in October 1986, the United Nations General Assembly voted overwhelmingly in support of the OAU call for direct negotiations between Morocco and Polisario. In April–May 1986, Morocco eventually agreed to participate in indirect proximity talks under the aegis of the UN secretary-general and the chairman of the OAU. This concession, after ten years of refusal to consider negotiations with Polisario, must be seen as a consequence of growing diplomatic and political pressure on the Moroccan regime to compromise and as a diplomatic advance for Polisario. However, nothing came of the talks, owing to Morocco's continued refusal to engage in direct talks with Polisario. Important though the pressure from outside may be, political developments within the occupied territories and within Morocco itself are likely ultimately to prove of decisive significance.

Table 5.1 Countries recognizing the Saharawi Arab Democratic Republic
(to December 1986)

Africa				
1. Madagascar	28.2.76		2. Grenada	20.8.79
2. Burundi	1.3.76		3. Guyana	1.9.79
3. Algeria	6.3.76		4. Dominica	1.9.79
4. Benin	11.3.76		5. Saint Lucia	1.9.79
5. Angola	11.3.76		6. Jamaica	4.9.79
6. Mozambique	13.3.76		7. Nicaragua	6.9.79
7. Guinea-Bissau	15.3.76		8. Mexico	8.9.79
8. Togo	17.3.76		9. Cuba	21.1.80
9. Rwanda	1.4.76		10. Costa Rica	30.10.80
10. Seychelles	5.10.77		11. Venezuela	3.3.82
11. Congo	3.6.78		12. Surinam	21.8.82
12. São Tomé and Príncipe	22.6.78		13. Bolivia	14.12.82
13. Tanzania	9.11.78		14. Ecuador	14.11.83
14. Ethiopia	24.2.79		15. Peru	8.9.84
15. Cape Verde	4.7.79		16. Columbia	27.2.85
16. Ghana	24.8.79		17. Guatemala	10.4.86
17. Uganda	6.9.79		18. Dominican Republic	24.6.86
18. Zambia	12.10.79		19. Trinidad and Tobago	1.11.86
19. Lesotho	9.10.79		20. Belize	18.11.86
20. Sierra Leone	28.3.80			
21. Libya	15.4.80			
22. Swaziland	28.4.80		Oceania	
23. Zimbabwe	3.7.80		1. Vanuatu	27.11.80
24. Chad	4.7.80		2. Papua-New Guinea	12.8.81
25. Mali	4.7.80		3. Solomon Islands	12.8.81
26. Botswana	14.5.80		4. Kiribati	12.8.81
27. Mauritius	16.7.82		5. Nauru	12.8.81
28. Mauritania	27.2.84		6. Tuvalu	12.8.81
29. Upper Volta (Burkina Faso)	4.3.84		Asia	
30. Nigeria	12.11.84		1. North Korea	16.3.76
31. Liberia	3.8.85		2. South Yemen	2.2.78
			3. Vietnam	2.3.79
Europe			4. Kampuchea	10.4.79
1. Yugoslavia	28.11.84		5. Laos	9.5.79
			6. Afghanistan	23.5.79
Latin America and Caribbean			7. Iran	27.2.80
			8. Syria	15.4.80
1. Panama	23.6.78		9. India	1.10.85

The politics of occupation

In 1963 with the creation of partly elected municipal councils and a provincial council, and in 1967 with the formation of a wider-based assembly (or Djemaa) for the whole indigenous population, the Spanish authorities had begun to develop the formal apparatus for a gradual progression to Saharan self-determination under the protection of the colonial power in the territory, although that was not Spain's intention when it first set up these bodies. None of the councils at local or provincial level had any real power and the Djemaa was (in the view of the United Nations' investigative mission which visited Western Sahara in May 1975) considerably dependent for guidance on the Spanish authorities and representative largely of the older and more conservative elements of Saharan society.[24] In effect, the territory was governed as a Spanish military colony. In some towns and settlements troops outnumbered Spanish civilians.

While a minority of the local population appeared willing to collaborate with the Spanish authorities, opposition to Spanish colonial rule grew significantly during the 1960s. In June 1970, a demonstration organized in El-Ayoun by the Spanish authorities in support of the province's continued association with Spain triggered off a counter-demonstration against colonial rule and led to violence in the streets. The counter-demonstration was organized by the Liberation Organization of Saguia el Hamra and Oued ed-Dahab, a recently formed urban-based nationalist movement led by Sidi Ibrahim Bassiri. The Spanish Foreign Legion fired on the anti-Spanish demonstrators and many, including Bassiri, were arrested. Bassiri never reappeared and was probably murdered; the Liberation Organisation disintegrated as a result of the Spanish repression.

But over the next three years, a nucleus of Saharawi students and intellectuals living abroad began to lay the foundations of a new movement. On 10 May 1973 the Polisario Front was born—as the 'unique expression of the masses, opting for revolutionary violence and the armed struggle as the means by which the Saharawi Arab African People can recover its total liberty and foil the manœuvres of Spanish colonialism'.[25] Ten days later, Polisario launched its first guerrilla attack against the occupying forces; over the next two years, it staged a succession of small hit-and-run strikes, with virtually no support from outside, apart from one small consignment of arms from Libya. The extent of popular support for Polisario was revealed when the United Nations' mission toured the territory in May 1975; the mission reported that 'at every place visited, the Mission was met by mass political demonstrations and had numerous private meetings with representatives of every section of the Saharan community. From all these it became evident to the Mission that there was an overwhelming consensus among Saharans within the territory in favour of independence and opposing integration with any neighbouring country.'[26] It also stated that 'The Mission believes, in the light of what it witnessed in the Territory, especially the mass demonstrations of support for one movement, the Frente POLISARIO . . . that its visit served as a catalyst to bring into the open political forces and pressures which had previously been largely sub-merged'.[27]

Nevertheless the Spanish authorities were unprepared to accept such a view. In September 1974 they had created a Saharawi Progressive Revolutionary Party whose role was to seek independence in collaboration with Spain; in the absence of any support for this 'creation', the project—and the party—were stillborn. Undeterred, a further attempt was made, in October 1974, to launch a new party, the Party of Saharawi National Unity (PUNS) but the party failed to attract any real local support and when the appointed secretary-general absconded with party funds to Rabat in May 1975, to swear allegiance to King Hassan, the party fell apart. Before the end of the year, the PUNS had virtually ceased to exist as a political entity. Finally convinced of the impossibility of countering the popular support for national independence and the Polisario Front, Spain appeared prepared to withdraw, and on 29 May 1975, the Djemaa was officially informed that the Saharawi people should prepare themselves for a 'precipitate' transfer of power.[28] There were several meetings between the president of the Djemaa Khatri Ould Jamani and the secretary-general of the Polisario El Ouali between the spring and late summer, and early in September the Polisario secretary-general met with the Spanish foreign minister 'in a small village in a foreign country'[29] to discuss relations between Spain and Western Sahara after independence.

Despite all this, when Spain signed the tripartite agreement with Morocco and Mauritania on 14 November 1975, it was concluded that Spain should proceed immediately with the institution of a temporary administration in the territory in which Morocco and Mauritania would participate in collaboration with the Djemaa, and that 'the views of the Saharan population, expressed through the Djemaa, would be respected'.[30] But, in an extraordinary session of the Djemaa, held under Polisario auspices at Guelta Zemmour on 28 November 1975, sixty-seven of the Djemaa's 102 members proclaimed the assembly's dissolution and their unconditional support for the Polisario Front, as the sole and legitimate representative of the Saharan people, and established a Provisional Saharawi National Council.

On 12 December, however, the day after Moroccan troops had taken El-Ayoun, eighty-five members of the Djemaa met under Moroccan auspices, according to official announcements in Rabat, having been joined by ten of those who had participated in the Guelta Zemmour meeting; and on 16 February 1976, fifty-seven members of the Djemaa met and voted unanimously to give full approval to the reintegration of Western Sahara with Morocco and Mauritania.

Since the beginning of the occupation, the Moroccan authorities have been concerned to encourage and promote the collaboration of the

Saharawis who remained within the area under Moroccan control with the process of 'incorporation' of the occupied territories. The political aspect of this process involves the establishment of a formal provincial structure of government and administration. Three provinces were set up, with capitals in El-Ayoun (renamed Laayoune), Smara and Cape Bojador, renamed Boujdour; governors were appointed to head the new provinces. In April 1976, the Moroccan government organized a Council of Sahara Youth in Tangier (well away from the conflict in the south) in what has been described as 'an unprecedented and imaginative example of the Rabat authorities' campaign to enlist the cooperation of the region's youth'.[31]

Most of the hundred or so delegates were former members of the PUNS or other groups prepared to envisage the development of the Western Sahara as an integral part of Morocco. Resolutions adopted at the meeting in Tangier included those which expressed support for the training of local administrative cadres for the territory. By 1979, two of the three governors heading the new provinces were Saharawis and, by the end of the decade, according to the Moroccan authorites, some ninety per cent of all *pashas*, *caids* and *khalifas* (local administration posts) in the Saharan provinces were Saharawis, while all of the 213 lower level officials (*mogaddems* and *shaykhs*) were local inhabitants.[32] In April 1977 the first Saharawi was appointed minister of Saharan affairs in the Moroccan government and in June he was elected with seven other Saharawis to the new Chamber of Representatives in Rabat. When, in August 1979, the south of the territory was taken over from Mauritania and renamed Oued ed Dahab, a similar process was initiated. Three hundred and sixty tribal 'notables' were flown to Rabat to swear allegiance to the throne and a visit was undertaken by the minister for Saharan affairs in October 1979 who toured the area for the organization of municipal elections in Dakhla.

A second aspect of the process of incorporation of the occupied territories involved the economic and social 'development' of the region. In a speech on 17 November 1975, King Hassan declared: 'we did not conquer the Sahara because it has phosphate deposits . . . but to build schools, hospitals . . . and to guarantee peace, well-being and prosperity',[33] adding that the anticipated revenue from the Bou-Craa mines would provide only two-thirds of what Morocco planned to spend annually in its Saharan 'provinces'. In March 1976, the Moroccan minister of finance diverted some 600 million dirhams for the 'development' of Western Sahara; stated priorities were agriculture, health, roads, schools and other services.[34] The government's overall policy was defined at a meeting in Smara in December 1977, attended by the governors and elected representatives not only of the new 'provinces' but of Agadir, Tan-Tan, Tiznit, Ouarzazate and other parts of the deep south of Morocco. Among the measures proposed at this meeting as prerequisites for the economic and social development of the region was the development of communications (roads, airfields, ports and broadcasting stations) and such industries as mining, fishing and tourism.

This laid the basis for a so-called 'emergency plan' for 1977–80, one of whose objectives was to settle the few remaining nomads in the towns.

The programme for the effective incorporation of the occupied territories into the Moroccan state has both political and economic objectives, but the two are closely intertwined. Economic and social development within the region serves to encourage collaboration and cooperation with the political process established by the Moroccan authorities. It is undoubtedly the case that, largely as a result of the massive investment in the occupied territories by the Moroccan government, and despite the constant threat of disruption and destruction by Polisario raids and attacks within the occupied territories, there has been substantial and visible 'development', notably in the improvement of communications and in the extraordinary growth of certain urban centres. Both of these, however, are closely related to the needs of the Moroccan army and cannot be said to represent the basis for a broad-based economic development of the region. Furthermore, despite the declared hope of King Hassan that the local inhabitants should not be 'overwhelmed by an influx of administrators and technicians from the north',[35] the 'development' of the occupied territories has been accompanied by a massive influx of Moroccans. The rapid and dramatic growth of such towns as El-Ayoun and Boujdour, as a consequence of huge transfers of state funds and associated private investment, has led to the creation of an artificial 'boom' within the urban areas of the region; as a result, Western Sahara has acted as a magnet for the unemployed and underemployed, whose numbers have been growing over the last ten years at an alarming rate within Morocco itself. The demographic change that has occurred and continues to take place, has potentially far-reaching social and political implications: the local population is threatened with effective submersion under a wave of Moroccan immigrants, and their officially recognized 'voice' in the future development of Western Sahara under Moroccan occupation risks being drowned.

It is difficult to know, given the relative lack of information and analysis of this crucial subject, what potential exists, after ten years of Moroccan occupation, for effective opposition from within the occupied territories. Certainly, the Moroccan authorities have always been very aware of the danger of a Polisario 'fifth column' within the territory under their control, and have done much to ensure that this danger does not develop to any appreciable extent. But, despite the undoubted collaboration of some Saharawis with the Moroccan occupation and the strategy of incorporation, it is almost certain that opposition still exists among the local population to Moroccan occupation.

The Moroccan authorities, while encouraging and supporting those explicitly committed to integration within the Moroccan state, have also dealt harshly with those opposed to their policies. Those known to be, or suspected to be, supporters of Polisario, or even sympathetic to Polisario, have been kept under strict surveillance, and in many cases subject to arrest, interrogation, imprisonment and torture.[36] Under such conditions, political opposition and resistance to Moroccan incorporation appears to have little choice but to follow the path of subversion and violence. The response of the Moroccan authorities to such a development is likely to be harsh in the extreme, but they might find a campaign of urban terrorism and sabotage difficult to cope with, particularly if the targets include Moroccan soldiers on leave or temporarily posted behind the front line in the urban centres of Saguiet el-Hamra. Then the Moroccan troops would experience the fact, all too bitterly, that the 'wall' has two sides, and their commitment to the occupation of Western Sahara might be expected to decline (despite double or even triple pay).

Government policy and Moroccan politics

Moroccan policy in the Western Sahara must be understood, ultimately, in terms of Moroccan domestic politics; not only does the regime work to create public opinion and to implement its own policies, it is also obliged to respond to the changing balance of forces in Moroccan politics. One important factor since the early days of the Moroccan independence movement has been the existence of a strong ultra-nationalism. Between its formation in 1944 and Moroccan independence in 1956, the Istiqlal (Independence) Party was concerned not only with the eventual reunification of the Spanish and French protectorates, but also with recouping portions of Western Sahara at that time under French and Spanish colonial rule. When in December 1953 an all-Moroccan 'alternative' government was formed, it included the Istiqlal and the Parti Démocratique de l'Indépendance (PDI) as well as independent nationalists. The two major parties, although competitive in seeking power, were nevertheless agreed on the goal of a Greater Morocco. During 1955, an Army of Liberation was formed under Istiqlal auspices in northern Morocco; by early 1956 it was well entrenched in southern Morocco. Over the following two years it spearheaded attacks against French and Spanish forces in the Sahara, as far afield as Tindouf and northern Mauritania. Although after Moroccan independence in March 1956 the Army of Liberation was formally integrated into the Moroccan army, there remained among its troops a hard core of ultra-nationalists who continued to support actively the Istiqlal's irredentist programme. In 1956, the leader of the Istiqlal Allal el Fassi claimed that only parts of the historic Greater Morocco had achieved their independence:

so long as Tangier is not liberated from its international status, so long as the Spanish deserts of the south, the Sahara from Tindouf and Atar and the Algerian–Moroccan borderlands are not liberated from their trusteeship, our independence will remain incomplete and our first duty will be to carry on action to liberate the country and to unify it.[37]

Following this speech in March 1956, the Istiqlal newspaper, *Al Alam*, published in July a map of 'Greater Morocco' which included all of Western Sahara and Mauritania as well as substantial areas of south-west Algeria and a part of north-west Mali. In March 1957, the Istiqlal leader toured southern Morocco, where he announced that 'the battle for the Sahara has just begun'.[38]

The strength of support for the Istiqlal in Morocco was very considerable immediately after independence, and it is not surprising that the irredentist cause was formally embraced by the Moroccan government in 1957 and publicly endorsed by King Mohamed V during a speech in the southern oasis town of M'hamid on 25 February 1958, where he declared Morocco's claims to the Western Sahara between the Oued Draa and the Saguia el-Hamra, stating that 'we have decided to so orient our activities as to integrate that province into the national territory'.[39] When Mauritania achieved independence in 1960 and joined the United Nations, the Moroccan government refused to recognize the new state; and in 1963 Morocco went to war with Algeria in pursuit of its claims to Tindouf and other parts of the Algerian Sahara.

But after King Hassan came to power in 1961 he was frequently criticized by the ultra-nationalist opposition parties (notably the Istiqlal) for his close relations with General Franco—he visited Spain for three summit meetings in 1963, 1965 and 1969—and his lack of open and enthusiastic commitment to the Moroccan claims to the Western Sahara. The evidence suggests that, during the 1960s at least, King Hassan was concerned to improve relations with his neighbours and to consolidate his own position within the country less by accepting the irredentism of the Istiqlal Party than by dividing the opposition and disarming it through a combination of royal patronage and political incorporation. On 15 January 1969, a twenty-year 'treaty of fraternity, good neighbourliness and cooperation' was signed between Algeria and Morocco, in which both states were committed to submit all issues between them to bilateral commissions; on 27 May 1970, at a summit meeting in Tlemcen, a joint commission was set up to resolve their border dispute, and two years later Morocco recognized its *de facto* border with Algeria (though this was subsequently not ratified by Morocco). The *rapprochement* with Algeria was accompanied by a belated recognition of Mauritania: a treaty of friendship was signed between Mauritania and Morocco in June 1970. In July 1970, following a meeting with Franco in Spain, King Hassan declared, in a press conference, that

instead of going purely and simply to claim the territory of the Sahara, I went to request that a popular consultation take place there, assured as I was that the first result would be the departure of the non-Africans and that then one would leave it up to the people of the Sahara to choose whether to live under the Moroccan aegis or their own aegis or any other aegis.[40]

After a tripartite meeting between the heads of state of Morocco, Algeria and Mauritania, held in Agadir in July 1973, a joint communiqué was issued, endorsing the United Nations' call for self-determination in Western Sahara. This communiqué affirmed their 'unwavering attachment to the principle of self-determination and their concern to ensure that this principle was implemented in a framework which guaranteed that the will of the inhabitants of the Sahara was given free and genuine expression in conformity with the United Nations decisions on this question'.[41]

Throughout the decade from 1965 onwards, King Hassan faced increasing political pressure from within Morocco. After the so-called 'constitutional experiment' of 1961–3, the deteriorating economic situation generated increasing opposition to the regime, which culminated in strikes, demonstrations and ultimately riots in the late spring of 1965. In June that year, after several ineffectual attempts to persuade the main political parties to join him in government, King Hassan declared a state of emergency and took full power into his own hands. In October 1965, seven months after he had been sentenced to death *in abstentia* for fomenting 'illegal opposition', Ben Barka, the radical leader of the Union National des Forces Populaires (UNFP) was assassinated. For the next five years politics in Morocco entered a state of suspended animation, and by the end of 1969, when local and municipal elections were eventually held, 'non-political' candidates gained over 70 per cent of the votes.[42] But the pressure-cooker of monarchical control over political life blew in the early years of the next decade, when two attempted *coups d'état*—in July 1971 and August 1972—very nearly ended the regime of Hassan II. By early 1973, the king was seeking to broaden and popularize his political constituency within the country, but a new plot to overthrow the regime involving militants of the UNFP was discovered in March 1973. This resulted in a definitive split within the UNFP (hitherto the most radical of the 'opposition' parties) and the formation of the more 'moderate' Union Socialiste des Forces Populaires (USFP), and alerted the king again to the need to create broad all-party support for his regime, and to seek a 'unified' national strategy capable of dissolving or at least stifling serious opposition. The 'recoupment' of the Sahara provided a ready-made focus for Moroccan ultra-nationalism and a new rallying-cry for the king.

When in July 1974 the Madrid government announced its policy for withdrawal from the Western Sahara, involving a period of internal self-government prior to full independence, King Hassan immediately warned that 'we will not accept seeing a puppet state erected in any form in the southern part of the country', and appealed to his subjects to make 1974 'a year of mobilization at home and abroad to recover our territories'.[43] When Spain announced in August 1974 that a referendum would be finally held under United Nations' auspices during the first half of 1975, King Hassan declared that if the United Nations held a referendum on independence, 'it is evident that not only will Morocco reject it but it will be the first time that it disavows a decision emanating from the United Nations Organization'. Furthermore, he warned, 'Morocco prefers to take a diplomatic, political and peaceful path, instead of resorting to no matter what other means; however, if Morocco ascertains that this path will not lead to the recovery of its territories, it will certainly not hesitate to find these other means'. Following this speech, King Hassan began to deploy Moroccan troops in the south of Morocco.

The sense of 'national unity' fomented and fostered by the King over the next year, and exemplified in the Green March which accompanied the initial blitzkreig stage of the war in the Sahara, combined with the support obtained from virtually all of the recognized political groupings within Morocco for the king's Saharan policy, enabled the regime to permit a degree of political freedom within the kingdom. By late 1976, 'the King at last felt secure enough to hold the long-awaited elections'.[44] Municipal elections were held in November 1976; these were followed by provincial elections in January 1977 and elections for professional and vocational chambers the following March. In all of these, pro-government candidates won nearly 75 per cent of the seats. The Istiqlal and the USFP objected to electoral irregularities and administrative interference, but agreed never-theless to join the government. In the national elections in June pro-government 'independents' won a total of 141 out of 264 seats in the new Chamber of Representatives; Istiqlal and the Mouvement Populaire won forty-nine and forty-four seats respectively, the USFP sixteen seats and other opposition parties fourteen altogether. The new government included members of Istiqlal and the Mouvement Populaire and the king was able effectively to incorporate within the government the leadership of the major part of the official 'opposition'.

The Istiqlal party, under the leadership of M'hamed Boucetta after the death of Allal el-Fassi in 1974, immediately threw its weight behind the king's policy in the Western Sahara, as did the other major parties, including the USFP and even the Moroccan equivalent of the Communist party—the Parti du Progrès et du Socialisme (PPS) under Ali Yata.

Not only did Ali Yata of the PPS and Maître Abderrahim Bouabid of the USFP participate in the King's diplomatic offensive to win international support in 1974–75, but they outdid Hassan in their proposal for developing the Western Sahara and in their denunciation of Algeria. Paul Pascon, a Moroccan sociologist associated with the PPS, even drew up a detailed programme for settling the Sahraoui nomads in the coastal region of Saquiet el Hamra.[45]

Since 1975, and the early stages of the Moroccan intervention in the Sahara, the leaderships of virtually all Moroccan political parties and political groupings have strongly endorsed the irredentist policy now adopted by the regime. In 1978, the Istiqlal and USFP party congresses reaffirmed their determination to stand by Moroccan claims to sovereignty in the Western Sahara; the USFP ridiculed the notion of a Saharan 'people' or 'state' and vowed not to cede the smallest corner of the territory. Members of the OAU *ad hoc* committee who talked with leaders of the USFP and PPS were struck by the identity of their views on the Sahara, despite marked ideological differences between them and the king on other issues. Even the radical UNFP made an exception of the Sahara when condemning the government's policies, and the newly formed National Grouping of Independents (RNI) outdid the Istiqlal at its constituent congress in October 1978 by its members' insistence on 'recouping' Tindouf and the Touat oases, and by their denunciations of Algeria.[46]

There must be some doubt as to how far the party leadership speaks for the party rank and file, let alone for the majority of the prudently 'non-political' Moroccan voters. But an indication of popular support for the war may be provided by the ability of the regime to raise very large sums of money from the public explicitly for the war effort. During 1984 and 1985, state bonds were issued, which raised 450 million dirhams (about $47 million) and well over 1 billion dirhams respectively by all accounts. Other commentators have been struck by the extent to which 'the prophets of Hassan's imminent eclipse have been confounded by the advocacy on the part of all strata of Moroccan society of an ever more aggressive Saharan policy'.[47] Such views, however, are based on general impression rather than on a detailed investigation of popular opinion, and it may well be that support for the war comes from rather specific social groups and strata, and is far less deeply rooted than often suggested. Certainly, an increasing proportion of the population is aware of the real cost, in both human and in material terms, of the war, as casualties have been not inconsiderable and the expenditure enormous. The consequences of the latter have been felt throughout the Moroccan economy, which during the late 1970s and early 1980s moved deeper into crisis.

Although there has been no sign of any fracturing of the national consensus on the Sahara, the hardships which have been forced upon the country have occasioned mounting opposition. A number of strikes took place in the winter of 1978–79 and the spring of 1979; textile, banking, dock and railway employees, as well as some 60,000 teachers, all came out for higher wages, and managed to organise demonstrations—which were dispersed with considerable brutality. In response to these demands, industrial and agricultural minimum wages were raised by 30 per cent and 40 per cent respectively on May 1st 1979, but these gains were very quickly cancelled out by high rises in the cost of basic foodstuffs later in the year and in 1980.[48]

As the economic situation deteriorated in the early years of the 1980s, political opposition to the regime has increasingly found new channels to express itself. Discontent exploded into mass demonstrations and open riots in June 1981 when the government raised the price of basic (hitherto considerably subsidized) commodities and the poor people of Casablanca took to the streets. Again, in January 1984, increases in the cost of living—notably bread and sugar—sparked off riots in several Moroccan cities.[49] To date these upsurges of popular protest remain relatively unorganized, although various underground political tendencies, including the Muslim fundamentalist groups, were undoubtedly involved in the recent riots, and some even referred explicitly to the 'unjust war against fellow Muslims in the Sahara'; as the economic crisis deepens, however, a greater degree of orchestration can be expected in the future. It is not irrelevant, in this context, that the relatively poorly paid lower ranks of the state salariat have been involved in every major confrontation with the regime in the last five years and have shown themselves to be among the more vocal opponents of the regime within Morocco; the recent clashes in Egypt between the police and the army may provide some indication of the kind of tensions that exist, even within the state security forces.

At a different level, the rumours of a military plot and of disagreement at the highest level concerning negotiations with Polisario, which circulated when the commander of the Moroccan forces in the Sahara General Dlimi died in mysterious circumstances in Marrakesh on 25 January 1983, may indicate that now, as in the early 1970s, some high-ranking army officers are not as firmly committed to the regime and its policies as they might at first sight appear. Certainly, the role of the armed forces in Moroccan politics has always been ambiguous, and the king must feel concern as well as satisfaction at the growing importance of the war in the south, and the very considerable power of the higher-ranking officers.

It seems that, so far, even if the popular enthusiasm for the war in the Sahara has undoubtedly waned over the past ten years, there is no sign of an orchestrated and coherent political opposition to the war. Given the failure of the existing opposition parties to serve as effective channels for the expression of popular opinion, however, this is not surprising and cannot be taken as conclusive evidence of mass support. What have been increasing are the indications of widespread social unrest in Morocco, rooted in the growing inequality and poverty within Moroccan society. The deepening economic and social crisis of Morocco is itself creating conditions for political crisis. The role of the war and of the Moroccan occupation of Western Sahara in exacerbating this crisis is not insignificant.

The economic dimension

The cost of the war and occupation

Estimates of the effective cost of the war and occupation to Morocco vary considerably and tend, on the whole, to be on the high side. Recently it has been argued that recurrent expenditure on 'national defence' runs at about four billion dirhams ($420 million) a year or ($1.15 million a day), while the cost of equipping the army alone has averaged nearly 1,500 million dirhams ($158 million) over the last two years. In addition, there are three special accounts at the national Treasury, of which 97 per cent is allocated to the acquisition and maintenance of military equipment, amounting to a further 800 million dirhams ($84 million) annually.[50]

However accurate these estimates may be—the current estimates suggest a daily cost of about $1 million—it is also the case that in addition to the direct costs of the war are the expenditures associated with the occupation and 'stabilization' of the Western Sahara within the 'wall'. In January 1978, for example, a $292 million Sahara Development Programme was announced providing for the settlement of the nomadic indigenous population and the creation of a viable economy. Spending on construction and the development of welfare facilities (housing, hospitals, schools, etc.) within the occupied territories for their growing population has been enormous also, and constitutes a real drain on Moroccan resources.

Over the last few years, the sum spent on the 'improvement' of El-Ayoun, the 'capital' of the Moroccan-occupied territories, has reached the total of 6 billion dirhams ($630 million), and centres like Boujdour and Dakhla are expanding rapidly, largely as a result of the resources being poured in by the Moroccan state.

Not all of the investment in the occupied territories, however, can be said to be directly for the war or for the 'stabilization' of the region; there has been investment in facilities and industries capable of providing significant returns. For example, a new port has been under construction at El-Ayoun. The investment involved amounted to roughly 400 million dirhams ($42 million) and the port is expected to be able to handle ten million tons of phosphates by 1991, compared with 3.7 million at present. Mining resumed at Bou-Craa in July 1982, although heavy investment was required to rehabilitate damaged installations and exports have remained well below the levels achieved before the start of the war: in 1983, exports totalled roughly 678,000 tons, about one-quarter of the 2.6 million tons exported in 1975.[51] In addition, it is estimated that some 2,130 metres of dikes and 755 metres of quay at the new port will handle 50,000 tonnes of fish and 30,000 tonnes of general cargo a year.[52] The contractors are a joint Moroccan–French venture, Matrap. Other foreign investors are being attracted to the occupied territories, despite the warnings given by Polisario that they collaborate with the Moroccan occupation at their own risk and will be liable to sabotage and attack by the SPLA. Foreign investors are, it seems, confident in the capacity of the Moroccan armed forces to secure the 'useful triangle'.

There can be no doubt that the potential return on investments in Western Sahara is considerable, particularly in the fields of mining and fishing. Infrastructural development and the provision of basic communications facilities are important prerequisites for the development of the territory, as well as for the maintenance of security both from sabotage and subversion within and from attack from outside the 'walls'. But in the short and even medium term, there must be serious doubts as to whether the returns are likely to be commensurate with the levels of investment required. For foreign investors the dangers of sabotage and attack by Polisario or their supporters must be a real consideration, despite the present apparent security of installations and operations within the defensive 'walls'. For the Moroccan government, the very high level of investment, much of which is unproductive in an economic sense, has already had important implications for the level of investment in economic and social development within Morocco itself. Since the mid-1970s, the drain of resources to the occupied territories has meant a significant decline in the funds available for development projects in industry and agriculture and has led, in several instances, to the curtailing of major projects planned for implementation or even actually under way. More generally, the cost of the war in the Sahara and the maintenance of the occupation of the region, are together aggravating the deepening economic crisis faced by the Moroccan regime and experienced by the Moroccan people.

The growing economic crisis in Morocco

The most obvious indication of Morocco's economic crisis is the enormous foreign debt: in 1984 this was

over $11 billion and debt servicing alone rose from over 700 million dirhams ($73 million) in 1976 to 2,500 million dirhams ($263 million) in 1980 and reached an estimated 5,000 million dirhams ($526 million) in 1983. The critical balance of payments problem situation results from internal problems, world price changes, increasing Common Market competition and protectionism and the cost of the war in the Sahara.[53]

In 1975 the foreign debt was a mere $1.7 billion. By 1983, over one-third of earnings from exports of goods and services was being recycled out of the country to service the foreign debt. The balance-of-trade deficit has also worsened during the last decade: the overall value of exports has grown slowly—from 6,200 million dirhams in 1975 to 7,300 million dirhams in 1979—but in the second half of the 1970s the cost of imports rose steeply, from 10,440 million dirhams in 1975 to 14,300 million in 1979. In the 1950s, Morocco was a net exporter of cereals, but by the late 1970s between 40 and 50 per cent of the country's cereal requirements were being imported. Earnings from remittances and tourism have failed increasingly to cover the deficit, and Morocco has become ever more dependent on aid and loans.

Efforts in late 1983 to reschedule about $350 million of its debts owed to commercial banks (which fell due between September 1983 and the end of 1984) ran into considerable difficulties. In September 1983 the International Monetary Fund formally approved a programme of 'economic stabilization' that it had earlier recommended and made a condition for further loans: this included a creeping devaluation of the dirham, the rescheduling of part of the foreign debt, severe cuts in public expenditure (including investment) and the removal of subsidies on basic goods. August 1983 saw the first round of price increases. The Moroccan government must have approached the measure to reduce subsidies on basic commodities with some trepidation, given the experiences of 1978–9 and 1981 when strikes and mass demonstrations involved very large sections of the urban Moroccan population in protest at government policies—and in the latter instance gave rise to violent clashes with the security forces and bloody rioting. There was no dramatic immediate response; but if the price increases did not immediately bring the Moroccan people onto the streets in open protest, they certainly contributed to the growing sense of desperation and frustration of the large majority whose living conditions had remained stagnant or deteriorated over the previous five years.

At the beginning of December 1983, negotiations with major American and European banks to reschedule part of the country's foreign debt were nearly complete. But the prospects for the following year or so looked grim even at that time. Just servicing the foreign debt would absorb at least 40 per cent of Morocco's hard currency income, while the visible trade deficit—which the government had reduced by around 27 per cent during 1983, largely by restricting imports and stifling domestic demands—would remain high. Officials projected that the investment budget for 1984 would decline by roughly a third, compared with the 1981–5 Economic Development Plan projections; the figure for 1985 was thought likely to drop to 40 per cent below initial projections. Given this bleak outlook, and pressure from the IMF to maintain tight control on expenditure, the Moroccan government was inclined to reduce still further the 'burden' of subsidies—rather than, for example, reduce expenditure in the Western Sahara—and the draft budget for 1984 contained proposals to raise prices again.

Even in 1971 the rate of unemployment was estimated at around 35 per cent of the labour force in the urban areas, with half of those recorded as unemployed being aged under twenty-four; the situation has worsened, if anything, over the last fifteen years. With high levels of unemployment and underemployment, very large numbers of households subsist on low incomes; among the mass of workers and small producers, even multiple activities often fail to maintain subsistence levels of income. In 1981 the World Bank estimated that well over 40 per cent of the Moroccan population was living below the absolute poverty level. For those able during the past twenty years to improve their incomes—certain sectors of organized labour, the better-situated small businessmen and the middle classes as a whole—the rising cost of living has been associated with improved standards of living, but for those unable to keep pace with rising prices—notably the 'unorganized' workers and some sections of the traditional petty bourgeoisie—the rise has meant declining living standards and pauperization. The introduction to the 1973–7 national plan recognized that in the previous five years 'the overall improvement in living standards far from diminishing differentials in standards of living has to a certain extent accentuated the differentials'.[54] Between 1973 and 1977 food prices rose by an average of 11.1 per cent a year, substantially faster than wages, which in any case rose significantly only for organized workers in the private sector, leaving many public-sector employees (particularly the low paid) and most of those in the vastly expanded 'informal sector' worse off than before. Between 1973 and 1983 Morocco's cost-of-food index more than tripled; and in the five months between July and October 1983, largely as a result of the August price increases, the cost-of-food index rose 10.6 per cent and the general cost-of-living index 8 per cent. A second round of price increases in December 1983 and the prospect of more to come in 1984 and 1985 were sufficient to bring to a head the despair and anger that had been steadily growing over the previous few years; once again, as in 1981, the urban poor and unemployed took to the streets in protest at government policies and in broader opposition to the Moroccan regime.

Since 1973, the Moroccan government has pursued 'open door' or 'liberal' economic policies orientated towards 'export-led growth'. These policies—adopted at the time of deepening international recession and growing protectionism—have not only contributed to the national economic crisis but also exacerbated the glaring social and economic inequalities within Morocco and hereby sharpened the potential for social and political conflict. The crisis of the Moroccan economy will not be easily resolved in the near future and the Moroccan government certainly recognizes the potential for social and political conflict. It was made very clear during 1984 that none of the officially recognized political parties is likely to take advantage of the growing popular discontent to threaten the Moroccan regime, but it is certainly the case that 'the degradation of economic and social conditions, amidst glaring social inequalities, has encouraged the spread of Islamic fundamentalism and other radical creeds, and generalised discontent, especially in the urban areas'.[55] King Hassan himself identified Muslim fundamentalists as significantly involved in the mass protests of January 1984, even if he dismissed them simply as agitators (together with the 'communists and Marxist–Leninists' and the agents of the Israeli secret service), and a systematic policy of arrest and interrogation of known activists was adopted at this time. The Communist party was harassed and its newspaper *Al Bayane* seized for several days running; left-wing revolutionary groups like Ilal Amam were also targets, as were the many small Muslim fundamentalist groups; even the USFP was suspect—and some hundred cadres of the party rounded up 'for preventive reasons' in cities like Rabat and Casablanca—despite the fact that its leader Abderrahim Bouabid was a member of the king's cabinet. The prospect of a continuing growth of radical opposition to the regime and its economic and social policies is a likely one for the immediate future. Under such circumstances, it might appear that a continuing commitment to the war in the Sahara, as part of an ultra-nationalist strategy designed to maintain national unity in political life, offers the best option for the Moroccan government and for the king, but the appeal of ultra-nationalism may tarnish as the relationship between the economic crisis at home and the cost of the war and occupation in Western Sahara becomes more evident. The king is, above all, a shrewd politician and may well come increasingly to recognize the dangers of an ultra-nationalist strategy that depends on a continuation of the war in the Sahara but fails to resolve the growing sense of injustice and inequality within Morocco itself. Efforts to orchestrate a loyalist national following to ensure continuing support for the king may begin to focus more on domestic issues than on the recoupment of the Sahara, but such a change in emphasis will certainly not take place over night.

Foreign aid and assistance

For the time being, moreover, it appears that certain foreign interests are prepared to contribute to shoring up, and ensuring the continued survival of, the Moroccan regime by providing aid and assistance, in the form of loans and grants. Morocco's evident failure during the first half of the 1980s to resolve its continuing economic crisis—the trade deficit up by 30 per cent, international debt of around $13 billion and a bill for imported cereals of about four billion dirhams (over $400 million) in 1984—did not, apparently, put off the international bankers. Led by the World Bank (which early in 1985 provided a short-term loan of $200 million) and the International Monetary Fund (which agreed a new stand-by loan of $250 million), they agreed to reschedule the $1.3 billion due in 1985. It seems that they were impressed by the very severe austerity measures imposed during 1983 and 1984.

Such financial support for an ailing economy encourages the Moroccan regime to pursue its policy of financial austerity and political repression at home and to further encourage the 'free market' and the production of exports with a view to promoting economic growth. It also reduces the pressure on the government to cut its expenditure in Western Sahara. For one of the major objectives of this externally financed programme of economic liberalisation and political repression is to reduce the real burden of the war in the Sahara. With new loans from the international banks to add to the sizeable aid and assistance provided from other sources, King Hassan has been able to envisage a programme of military development over the next five years involving expenditure of $1 billion.

We have already seen how important to the Moroccan regime is the military aid and assistance of the United States, much of which is directly spent in Western Sahara. But the entire package of military aid (around $74 million in 1986) aimed at supporting the Moroccan occupation of the 'useful triangle' of Western Sahara, is only slightly larger than the $66 million allocated for development and food aid. During the 1980s, to date, the United States government has provided, in loans and in grants, an average annual amount of around $140–50 million to the Moroccan government. But if the American contribution is very substantial, it is dwarfed by that from France. Together with the IMF and the World Bank, these two Western powers have displaced the once important but now greatly reduced flow of aid from Morocco's conservative desert Arab ally, Saudi Arabia, which until the slide in oil prices had been contributing up to $500 million a year.

If foreign aid and assistance proves insufficient to enable the Moroccan regime to wage war and maintain its occupation of Western Sahara, King Hassan clearly hopes that it will be possible to raise additional resources from the Moroccan public. In March 1985 roughly 450 million dirhams were raised by the issue of a government bond and in September another effort, aimed at raising more than twice that amount from the savings of Moroccans at home and abroad, was surprisingly successful. The new bond was explicitly issued to help provide for civil as well as military requirements in Western Sahara, but was closely connected to King Hassan's plan to modernize the army over the next five years, at a cost of $1 billion.

For the moment the Moroccan regime has been able to raise the funds needed to pursue its Saharan policy, but at enormous cost both economically and socially. All the indications are that the war will continue without a decisive military victory and that the occupation will continue to be an extremely expensive affair. As the drain on the resources of the Moroccan economy, and the Moroccan people, continues with very little sign of ending, even the international bankers and the main sources of material aid and assistance—the United States, France, Saudi Arabia, the IMF and the World Bank—may begin to have second thoughts and to consider whether they are themselves, by offering loans and credit on such a scale, contributing to the deepening crisis and thereby increasing the vulnerability of the Moroccan regime. A first indication of such a re-thinking may be the imposition of more conditions on loans, with special emphasis on cuts in expenditure in Western Sahara.

Conclusions

The military situation and prospects

The war has reached a stalemate. Polisario is committed to 'all of the fatherland or martyrdom' and is prepared to continue its strategy of guerrilla warfare, arguing that time is on its side. The building of the 'wall' by the Moroccan armed forces has reduced the level of conflict, but commits the Moroccans to an expensive strategy of prolonged defence. Reports of growing demoralization among the Moroccan troops are common, although their reliability is difficult to assess. There may be growing pressure from high-ranking officers to negotiate with Polisario.

The political situation and prospects

On the international front, Morocco is increasingly isolated and discredited, and the possibility of growing support for and recognition of the SADR is strong. The major support from other states for Morocco comes from the United States, France, Spain, and Saudi Arabia, although of these only the United States is prepared to support Morocco openly in international forums. Recent political developments make it unlikely that the French or Spanish governments will move decisively towards recognition of the SADR, while American foreign policy ensures continuing support for the Moroccan regime for the foreseeable future; it is even possible that Morocco is included in plans for the strengthening of NATO in the western Mediterranean. Within the occupied territories and within Morocco itself, the Hassan regime is likely to face growing problems. Particularly in the Moroccan cities, economic and social disadvantage and inequality are creating increasing pressure for radical change; new political tendencies are beginning to emerge. Under such conditions, the possibility of a military coup to preempt the growth of radicalism and political disruption within the country cannot be ruled out. The example of Mauritania in 1978 may yet prove instructive. It may be that a consideration of such political dangers will encourage the king to take seriously the negotiations initiated recently under the auspices of the United Nations and the OAU.

The economic situation and prospects

In the short term, foreign aid and loans may stave off economic crisis but the prospects are still not good, although the decline in oil prices must help. Rising costs of living and reductions in public expenditure, particularly on subsidies, will create increasing inequality; growing numbers will be forced into poverty and unemployment. The economic cost of the war and occupation will become relatively (and absolutely) larger, and new returns on investment in Western Sahara will hardly begin to cover that cost in the near future. These economic problems will certainly have political repercussions within Morocco and may even of themselves force crucial policy changes by the government.

Appendix 1: Moroccan armed forces, 1984

Personnel
Military forces

Army	130,000
Air force	13,000
Navy and naval infantry	6,000
Total	149,000

Para-military forces

Gendarmerie and internal security forces	30,000

Army

Major units

Unit type	Brigades/ regiments	Independent battalions	Independent companies
Armoured		5	
Mechanized	1	3	
Infantry	11		
Camel corps		9	
Desert cavalry		2	
Paratroops	1		
Commando		3	
Armoured car			4
Total	13	22	4

Small arms

Personal weapons

9mm MAT 49/56 SMG

9mm Beretta MAB 38/49 SMG

7.62mm AK-47 (Kalashnikov) AR

7.62mm G-3 AR

7.5mm MAS 49/56 SAR

Machine guns

12.7mm (0.5″) Browning M-2 HMG

7.62mm M-60D GPMG

7.62mm RPD (Degtyarev) LMG

7.5mm AA-52 MMG

7.5mm Chatellerault M-24/29 LMG

Light and medium mortars

82mm M-43

81mm ECIA

81mm M-29

60mm M-2

Light ATRLs

RPG-7

Strim 89

Tanks

Medium quality

M-48 A5 (upgraded) (USA)   140

Kurassier (Austria)   115

Low quality
T-54	40
AMX-13	80
Total	375

On order: 108 M-60 A3 (USA)

APCs/ARVs
High quality
M-113 A1/A2 (USA–Italy)	360
AMX-10 RC (France)	100
VAB (Saviem Creusot-Loire) (France)	400
Ratel (South Africa)	80
RAM (unconfirmed) (Israel)	250
	(sub-total 1,190)

Others
AML-90	100
EBR-75	35
M-3 half-track	100
OT-62	70
M-8 ARV	55
UR-416	15
	(sub-total 375)
Total	1,565

On order: 140 M-113 (USA–Italy)

Artillery
Guns and heavy mortars
high quality
155mm M-109 A1 SP howitzer	36
155mm (AMX) F-3 SP howitzer	48
155mm M-114 howitzer	36
152mm howitzer	12
130mm M-46 gun	12
105mm AMX 105-A SP howitzer	24
	(sub-total 168)

Others
105mm M-101 howitzer	160
100mm Su-100 SP gun	40
120mm mortar	320
	(sub-total 520)
Total	688

MRLs
122mm BM-21	36

Anti-tank weapons
  Missiles
    BGM-71A TOW
    FGM-77A Dragon
    MILAN
  Guns
    106mm M-40 A2 recoilless rifle
    90mm

Anti-aircraft defences		
Short-range missiles		launchers
Crotale (France)		
MIM-72A Chaparral (USA)		30
SA-7 (Grail)		
Short-range guns		
57mm M-1950 (S-60)		
37mm M38/39		
20mm M-163 Vulcan SP	(unconfirmed)	40
Total		150

Air Force

Aircraft—totals	
Combat aircraft	85
Transport aircraft	38
Helicopters	128

Combat aircraft		
Strike and multi-role aircraft		
High quality		
Mirage F-1 (France)		50
Others		
F-5E/F-5F (USA)		20
F-5A/B and RF-5E (USA)		15
	(sub-total	35)
Total		85

On order: 10 Mirage F-1 (France)

Transport aircraft	
KC-130 refuelling	3
C-130H Hercules	20
DC-3 Dakota (C-47)	8
Beechcraft King Air	3

Dornier DO-28 D-2	3
Gulfstream	1
Total	38

Training and liaison aircraft

Beechcraft T-34 C-1	12
S1A1 Marchetti SF-260M	28
Alpha Jet	24
AS202/18A Bravo FFA	10
Broussard	12
CM-170 Fouga Magister	24
Total	110

Helicopters
Attack

SA-342 Gazelle (France)		12
Agusta A-109 (Italy)		6
	(sub-total	18)

Heavy transport

CH-47C Chinook		11

Medium transport

SA-330 Puma		40
AB-212		12
AB-205		34
Kaman HH-43B Huskie		4
	(sub-total	90)

Light transport

Alouette III		4
AB-206 Jet Ranger		5
	(sub-total	9)

Total	128

On order: SA-342, AB-206

Advanced armament
Air-to-air missiles

AIM-9J Sidewinder (USA)	320
R-550 Magique (France)	

Air-to-ground missiles
AGM-65 Maverick (unconfirmed)
(USA)
Anti-aircraft defences
Radars
Westinghouse AN/TPS-43
AN/MPQ-49

Long-range guns
100mm M-49
Military airfields   13
Agadir, Benguerir, Boulhout, Casablanca (Nouasseur), Fez,
Kenitra, Khouribga, Larache, Marrakech, Meknes, Oujda,
Rabat, Sidi Slimane
Aircraft maintenance and repair
capability:
for all existing models, in airfield, including overhauls

Navy
Combat vessels
MFPBs
Cormoran/Lazaga   4
Missile frigates
Descubierta   1
Mine warfare vessels
Sirius class   1
Gunboats/MTBs
PR-72 class   2
Patrol craft
P-32   6
VC large patrol craft   1
Le Fougeux (modified), 53 meter   1
CMN Cherbourg, 40.6 meter   1
Acror 31   3

Total   12
On Order: 4 Comoran/Lazaga class

Landing craft
Batral (Dubigeon, Normandie, 750 ton) landing ship
logistics   3
Edic (Chantiers Navals Franco–Belges, 290 ton) LCT   1

Total   4

Naval bases
Agadir, Casablanca, Kenitra, Safir, Tangier

Ship maintenance and repair capability
at Casablanca—156 meter dry dock, repairs up to 10,000
DWT; at Agadir—minor repairs

Source: *The Middle East Military Balance, 1984*, Jaffee Center For Strategic Studies, Tel Aviv
University, Jerusalem, The Jerusalem Post Press, 1984, pp. 156–61.

Notes

1. J. Mercer, *The Saharawis of Western Sahara*, Minority Rights Group Report no. 40, London, Minority Rights Group, 1979, p. 10.
2. Ibid., p. 9.
3. Ibid., p. 11.
4. Ibid., p. 10.
5. Ibid., p. 13.
6. Ibid.
7. T. Hodges, 'The Western Sahara file', *Third World Quarterly*, **6**, no. 1, 1984, p. 102.
8. *Sahara Libre*, no. 88, 22 August 1979.
9. Mercer, op. cit., p. 11; c.f. J. Howe, 'Western Sahara: a war zone', *Review of African Political Economy*, no. 11, January–April 1978, p. 86.
10. Mercer, op. cit., p. 12.
11. Hodges, op. cit., p. 104.
12. Mercer, op. cit., p. 12.
13. V. Thompson and R. Adloff, *The Western Saharans: Background to Conflict*, London, Croom Helm, 1980, p. 292.
14. Hodges, op. cit., p. 105.
15. D. Seddon, 'Mitterrand's Middle East', *Middle East*, no. 139, May 1986.
16. J. Damis, 'The role of third parties in the Western Sahara conflict', *Maghreb Review*, **17**, nos. 1–2, January–April 1982, p. 7.
17. Hodges, op. cit., p. 113.
18. D. Seddon, 'Review of *The Western Saharans* by Thompson and Adloff' *International Journal of African Historical Studies*, **16**, no. 1, 1983.
19. *New York Times*, 22 July 1982.
20. Cited in the *Western Sahara Newsletter*, no. 4, September 1985.
21. J. Marks, 'Behind the wall', *Middle East*, no. 135, January 1986, p. 8.
22. T. Hodges, *The Western Saharans*, Minority Rights Group Report no. 40, London, The Minority Rights Group, 1984a, p. 13.
23. I shall not consider in this chapter the very important role of the United States, France and other world powers in the conflict. For further details see Damis, op. cit.; D. Seddon, 'Morocco at war', *DEV Discussion Paper*, no. 190, School of Development Studies, Norwich, April 1986, pp. 30–6; or Werner Ruf in this volume.
24. C.f. Hodges, 1984, op. cit., p. 82.
25. Ibid., p. 85.
26. Ibid., p. 86.
27. Ibid.
28. Thompson and Adloff, op. cit., p. 131.
29. Ibid., p. 132.
30. Hodges, op. cit., p. 96.
31. Thompson and Adloff, op. cit., p. 294.
32. *Middle East Journal*, June 1979.
33. Cited in Thompson and Adloff, op. cit., p. 294.
34. M. Ben Madeni, 'The Western Sahara: an historical survey', *Maghreb Review*, no. 1, June–July 1976, p. 15.
35. Cited in Thompson and Adloff, op. cit., p. 295.

36. 'Morocco', Amnesty International Briefing Paper no. 13, London, Amnesty International Publications, 1977; 'Morocco and Western Sahara', Amnesty International 1978 Report, London, Amnesty International Publications, 1978; 'Morocco and Western Sahara', Amnesty International 1979 Report, London, Amnesty International Publications, 1979; 'Morocco and Western Sahara', London, Amnesty International Publications, 1980; 'Morocco and Western Sahara', London, Amnesty International Publications, 1981; Report of an Amnesty International Mission to the Kingdom of Morocco, London, 1982; 'Morocco and Western Sahara', Amnesty International 1984 Report, London, Amnesty International Publications, 1984.
37. Cited in Hodges, 1984, op. cit., p. 88.
38. Thompson and Adloff, op. cit., p. 223.
39. Ibid.
40. Cited in Hodges, 1984, op. cit., p. 90.
41. Ibid., p. 91.
42. D. Seddon, *Moroccan Peasants: A Century of Change in the Eastern Rif, 1870–1970*, Folkestone, Wm. Dawson, 1981, pp. 276–7, 187.
43. Hodges, 1984, op. cit., p. 93.
44. *The Middle East and North Africa, 1979–80*, London, Europa Publications, 1979, p. 583.
45. Thompson and Adloff, op. cit., p. 307.
46. Ibid., p. 289.
47. Ibid.
48. P. Sluglett and M. Farouk-Sluglett, 'Modern Morocco: political immobilism, economic dependence' in *North Africa: Contemporary Politics and Economic Development*, R. I. Lawless and A. M. Findlay (eds), London, Croom Helm and New York, St. Martin's Press, 1984, p. 82.
49. D. Seddon, 'Winter of discontent: economic crisis in Tunisia and Morocco', *MERIP Reports*, no. 127, **14**, no. 8, 1984.
50. *Western Sahara Newsletter*, no. 4, September 1985.
51. Hodges, 1984a, op. cit., p. 13.
52. Marks, op. cit., p. 8.
53. Seddon, 1984, op. cit., p. 15.
54. Ibid., p. 12.
55. Hodges, 1984a, op. cit., p. 13.

Part III: Refugees and human rights

6 Al-Mukhtufin (the disappeared): a report on disappearances in Western Sahara

TERESA K. SMITH

An indescribable climate of terror reigns. The abduction and arrest campaigns often occur at home or in the streets. Searches by the police are systematic. Everyone is suspect. Even the cowards are not saved. Since 1975 there have been many disappearances.

Aminettou Mint Ali Ould Mohamed,
January 1984

International concern about Western Sahara began in 1964 when the United Nations General Assembly passed its first resolution affirming the Western Saharan people's right to self-determination. On 12 May 1975 a United Nations Mission of Inquiry arrived in Western Sahara and later reported these findings:

At every place visited, the Mission was met by mass political demonstrations and had numerous private meetings with representatives of every section of the Saharan community ... From all these it became evident to the Mission that there was an overwhelming consensus among Saharans within the Territory in favour of independence and opposing integration with any neighbouring country ... [The Mission believes] in light of what it witnessed in the Territory, especially the mass demonstrations of support for one movement, the Frente Polisario, ... that its visit served as a catalyst to bring into the open political forces and pressures which had previously been largely submerged. It was all the more significant to the Mission that this came as a surprise to the Spanish authorities, who until then had only been partly aware of the profound political awakening of the population.

Despite the evidence that the majority of Saharawi people were in favour of independence, Spain derogated from the norms of decolonization and abrogated its promises to the Saharawi people. By virtue of the Madrid Accord or Tripartite Agreement of 14 November 1975, Spain handed over its colony to Morocco which took the northern two-thirds, and to Mauritania which annexed the southern third. On 27 February 1976 the Saharawi Arab Democratic Republic (SADR) was proclaimed. The Polisario Front is now the political-military wing of the SADR.

By spring 1976, the Moroccan and Mauritanian military forces had occupied the whole of Western Sahara. The Polisario Front then turned the armed liberation struggle it had begun against Spain on 20 May 1973 against Morocco and Mauritania. By concentrating its attacks against the weaker link first, it forced Mauritania to sue for peace in 1979. Mauritania has since renounced its claims on Western Sahara and in February 1984 it recognized the SADR. Morocco still occupies roughly two-thirds of the territory. Its some 100,000 troops are concentrated behind an earth-works defence wall (*berm*) equipped with sophisticated radar and surveillance devices. The wall encloses the capital, El-Ayoun, the Bou-Craa phosphate mines, Dakhla, Smara and a few smaller towns. Saharawis are not free to travel outside the towns occupied by Morocco.

A large part of the Saharawi population fled to camps organized by the Front, far away from the cities, when the invasion began. After napalm and phosphorous bombings, they sought refuge across the border in south-west Algeria. An estimated 165,000 Saharawi refugees are in the Tindouf area.

The war in Western Sahara has resulted in a steady deterioration of human rights in the territories occupied by Morocco. One of the most horrifying violations of human rights in the Western Sahara is disappearance. Since 1975 there has been a consistent pattern of individuals disappearing from Moroccan-occupied Western Sahara and southern Morocco through the complicity, consent and conspiracy of the Moroccan government forces. This practice has contravened both Moroccan law and the international human rights instruments to which it is bound.

The phenomenon of disappearance has victimized hundreds of Saharawi civilians. These missing persons are the victims of state terrorism. Morocco has employed the practice of disappearance to eliminate political activists, dissidents or other perceived enemies of the government.

Amnesty International has confirmed the disappearance of approximately 100 Saharawis taken by the Moroccan security forces as long ago as 1975 from southern Morocco in the context of the Western Sahara war.[1] Amnesty suspects that the actual number of disappeared persons may amount to several hundred. Amnesty International continues to investigate the fate of the disappeared Saharawis whose detention and whereabouts the Moroccan government has never officially acknowledged.[2] Through cross-checking various lists, the Swiss Support Committee for the Saharawi People confirms the disappearance of 180 Saharawis during the period of 1975–81.[3]

In February 1980 twenty-six Saharawi political prisoners (who were counted among the disappeared until their whereabouts were traced), drew up a long testimony which confirms the hundreds of disappearances reported by the Saharawi Red Crescent. They concluded:

More than 1,600 Saharawis of all ages—from infants to the elderly—disappeared during the wave of arrests in 1975–76 and since then we have no knowledge of their fate. The abductions have not stopped and among us, there is not a family which has not been affected, has not experienced an arrest, a victim of repression, or a murder by the Moroccan regime.[4]

Disappearances are carried out by the security forces and the paramilitary forces with the complicity and consent of the Moroccan government, in a way that seeks to avoid government accountability. These disappearances are not ransom-seeking kidnappings; rather they are politically motivated abductions. Amnesty International notes that massive disappearances are often effected in areas where the Moroccan government mistrusts the local population.

This happened during 1973 in the Middle Atlas region; and since 1976 when the Moroccan army became engaged in the Western Sahara, detention camps have been established, not only for prisoners of war, but also for members of the civilian population suspected of sympathising with the Polisario guerillas. The number held in this way in Morocco itself is estimated to be between 100 and 150. The Moroccan authorities maintain great secrecy about the names and number of those detained; and in the Western Sahara there may be several hundred members of the local population held in army camps. Fear of such treatment has caused many thousands to flee from southern Morocco and Western Sahara into Algeria.[5]

According to the Swiss Support Committee, the arrests which lead to disappearance are made by the police, the National Security, the gendarmerie, the Auxiliary Forces, and the Royal Armed Forces.[6] The abductors often wear civilian clothes. Sometimes they identify themselves as officers of the National Security. They can strike at any hour and no regular military or police force interferes with their mission. In one case, evidence surfaced which directly implicated members of the military forces in a wave of disappearances.[7] When the Polisario Front seized the Lebouirate garrison in southern Morocco in August 1979, three telegrams sent by the Commander of the Third Group of the Moroccan Armoured Squadron (GEB), based in Lebouirate, fell into its hands. The telegrams told of recent arrests and led to the discovery of two Saharawis who had disappeared during 1975–76. Still the Moroccan authorities have made no efforts to bring any of the abductors before the law.

Generally, independence-minded Saharawis are those who are at the greatest risk of vanishing in Moroccan held areas of Western Sahara, but target groups cannot be clearly identified. The disappeared come from the entire Saharawi population. Most are simply critics of the Moroccan occupation of Western Sahara; others are politically radical, openly in favour of Polisario. A few of the disappeared are suspected of acts of violence against the Moroccans: of blowing up Moroccan military vehicles, for example. Some are relatives of the abducted, while others apparently disappear at the whim of the abductor, or simply because they are Saharawis. Amnesty International suspects several hundreds are held in secret detention because of their ethnic links with the Western Sahara, whereas some Saharawis disappear by 'mistake'.

Tony Hodges, reporting for the French newspaper *Le Matin*, learned of some forty disappeared Saharawis during a visit to El-Ayoun in 1978.

Noteworthy in his account are the possible political objectives behind the disappearances as well as the Moroccan government's denial of knowledge.

The central prison of El Ayoun capital of Western Sahara, is a dismal, windowless building which resembles a warehouse. Located near the head-quarters of the Moroccan Auxiliary Forces, the locals call it the dungeon (*calabozo*). Two Saharawis indicated to me that on May 20 and during the days which followed, fifty-six civilians were arrested and that most of them are still detained in the *calabozo*. May 20 was the fifth anniversary of the first guerrilla attack mounted by the Polisario Front against the Spanish occupation forces. The two Saharawis furnished me with the names of forty-five of the detainees—all save five, are women.

'The Moroccans reckoned that anyone wearing new clothes that day was celebrating May 20,' explained a young Saharawi. That's what explained the wave of arrests.

According to a completely reliable informant, thirty-five persons are stilll being held in the *calabozo*. He claims to have proof that at least one of them, a woman, has been tortured. He had seen electric shock torture marks on her back and she had to be admitted to hospital.

At the central hospital of El-Ayoun, a director confirmed that seven of the detained were hospitalised. But he refused to provide any details, and he pointed out to me that if I wanted to pursue my inquiries, I would need police authorisation.

However, at the headquarters of the Royal Moroccan Gendarmerie, Commander Mattaich, Moroccan officer in charge of maintaining order, claimed that he knew 'nothing' about the arrests on May 20. He declared himself 'amazed' upon reading the list of detainees that I gave him and promised that he was going to make a 'complete investigation'.

The same reluctance at the office of the royal public prosecutor in El Ayoun, Mohamed Lanssar, who was prepared to show me a large file listing all the arrests made in El Ayoun but refused to verify the list I gave him. 'I was in El Ayoun on May 20,' he said, 'and I can say that May 20 means nothing here. May 20 doesn't exist in El Ayoun.' Mohamed Lanssar stated that in the Western Sahara 'People are not arrested for crimes of opinion.' Yet, he added that 'there is not a single person arrested for political reasons who has not been tried.' And he claimed that the detainees in the hospital, all of whom are women, were prostitutes about to give birth.[9]

The Saharawi Red Crescent reported a wave of arrests and disappear-ances which followed peaceful demonstrations on 14 November 1980, in protest against the anniversary of the Madrid Accords.[10] Targeted areas were El-Ayoun, Smara, Dakhla, Boujdour and Tan-Tan. Five Saharawis detained then were: Lehsen Ould Absalla, Ould Labid Doutabaa, Taher Ould Tayeb, Ould Abeylil, and Mohamed Fadel Ould Yehdih Ould Ebheya. Thirteen Saharawis, whose names are not known, disappeared from Dakhla after participating in a similar demonstration there.

A French journalist who travelled incognito in El-Ayoun in 1981 reported that 'people suspected of wanting independence disappear in the middle of the night from their homes. They are accused of taking down the Moroccan flag from above their door. It is the police or the informers themselves who tear down the flags which fly above the homes in order to have a pretext, or immediate grounds for arrest.'[11] This is a clear example of the illegality of the practice of disappearance and of the fear it instils in people.

The Swiss Support Committee has noted that arrests, disappearances and systematic torture of Saharawi civilians has intensified since the summer of 1981 following the announcement that a referendum on self-determination of the Saharawi people would be held in the territory.[12] This development is in keeping with Morocco's plan to eliminate all opposition to its designs on Western Sahara. Sid-Ahmed El Fillali, who had been detained in mid-August 1981, during which time there were demonstrations against the Moroccan presence in the Western Sahara,[13] died later from the torture inflicted on him in a secret detention centre. Even a Saharawi worker in France, Brahim Ould Khneibila, a worker at the Renault-Flins factory, was kidnapped on 17 August 1982, and later incarcerated in Agadir. There has since been no news of him.[14] In December 1982, L'Houcine Mezzine, a young Saharawi student of the upper-sixth level in Agadir, was arrested in Goulimine and he too has never reappeared.[15] Faced with such examples, the Saharawi children are taught that if they show the slightest form of resistance, if they protest against the Moroccans, they risk being arrested, taken away never to appear again.

In Western Sahara, the perpetrators of disappearance direct terror not only against their perceived enemies, but against the families of their enemies as well. Husbands and wives have disappeared together with their children. Some evidence suggests that the daughters and sisters of the disappeared are often raped and then carried off too. According to *Afrique Asie*, the Royal Armed Forces have abducted women, children and the elderly.[16] The French journalist cited earlier reports that 'whole families are arrested in retaliation after a Polisario raid. The only explanation put forward by my sources was that the families had ties, direct or indirect, with the known members of the Polisario Front.'[17] Every family has a relative in Polisario and thus every family faces disappearance.

The Swiss Support Committee too reports Saharawi family disappearances. 'Whole families are taken by force out of the cities without their belongings. They are installed in camps where they cannot survive thanks to the meagre food rations that are distributed.'[18] This practice of family disappearances finds a precedent in Morocco itself. Following the government's announcement in March 1973 of the discovery of the third plot to overthrow King Hassan II, after the failed coup attempts of July 1971 and August 1972, 2,000 people were arrested, including whole families.[19]

Testimony from former disappeared persons, who subsequently escaped or were released, suggests that the Saharawis abducted are routinely subjected to imprisonment, torture and death.

It must be kept in mind that information on disappearances is extremely difficult to obtain. It is a crime for a Saharawi to inquire as to the whereabouts of a disappeared person. The Swiss section of Amnesty International notes that one cannot speak openly about the disappeared.[20] The Moroccan government has persistently, save in one instance, denied any knowledge of disappeared persons in Western Sahara or southern Morocco. Through unfailing efforts, the whereabouts of twenty-six disappeared Saharawis were discovered in April 1980. Of the three years they had spent in incommunicado detention, some six months were in secret police centres and in the remaining time, many were transferred from one prison to another, or from prison to hospitals, before they were subsequently brought to trial and released. These twenty-six Saharawis were the only disappeared persons that the Moroccan government has ever admitted to holding in official custody.[21]

The Moroccan government has refused to respond to inquiries on disappearances made by foreign individuals or human rights groups. In a February 1981 mission to Morocco, Amnesty International reports that it:

raised this matter with officials and gave them a list of approximately 30 such cases which Amnesty International groups have been investigating. After stating that it was difficult for any government and, in this case, for the Moroccan Government to know with certainty the whereabouts of any named individual—especially in southern Morocco which was described by the officials as a war zone where much of the population is nomadic—officials at the Ministry of Justice promised to make inquiries about the individuals on the list and to send Amnesty International any information they succeeded in obtaining. The list was also given to officials of the Ministry of the Interior who made a similar promise.

. . . On 27 February 1981, Amnesty International's Secretary General sent a letter to officials at the Ministry of Justice reiterating Amnesty International's request for further information on this matter. To date there has been no reply from the Moroccan government.

. . . Since February 1981 Amnesty International has been able to confirm the 'disappearances' from southern Moroccan towns of 63 other people.

. . . Amnesty International is seriously concerned at the pattern of such 'disappearances' and fears that, if other reports reaching the organization are true [which Amnesty International has not yet been able to confirm], the number of such cases may amount to several hundred. Amnesty International urgently requests the Moroccan authorities to inquire into the whereabouts of all the individuals named by Amnesty International who have reportedly 'disappeared', and consistent with their promise to Amnesty International's delegates, to communicate the results of their inquiry to Amnesty International.[22]

The Moroccan government has never officially acknowledged the whereabouts and detention of the approximately one hundred Saharawis whose detentions have been confirmed by Amnesty International, despite repeated inquiries from the organization.[23]

Tony Hodges also experienced the Moroccan government's refusal to investigate disappearances, in 1978.

In Rabat, too, one comes up against the same wall of silence on the part of the Moroccan authorities. Last July, I had sent to the secretary of the interior, Driss

Basri, a list of 114 Sahrawis who were arrested in Tan Tan, Goulimine, Agadir and other Southern Moroccan towns. The list was drawn up in 1976 by a French educator, Gilles Gauthier, who was expelled from Morocco for 'subversive' activities. But, Basri, despite his promises, could not find anything to say to me during a new meeting, in November, four months later.[24]

Many of the disappeared have been killed. During a visit to El-Ayoun in 1983, this writer was told that Saharawis had been thrown out of helicopters and airplanes and drowned in the Saguia el-Hamra river and in the sea. The Saharawis Red Crescent reported the discovery in January 1981 of three mutilated corpses on the beaches of the Dakhla peninsula. The three Saharawis had disappeared from Smara and Tan-Tan.[25] Several of the testimonies included in this report tell of the deaths from torture of disappeared Saharawis.

The majority of the disappeared are secretly detained. They are the disappeared in official custody whose detention is not acknowledged by the authorities. The some hundred Saharawis confirmed as missing persons by Amnesty International are presumed to be detained in secret centres. In 1981 Amnesty International had received serious allegations indicating that several hundred additional Saharawis from the southern Moroccan towns of Goulimine and Tan-Tan and from Western Sahara itself were in custody and were being held in secret detention centres in southern Morocco as well as in police detention centres.[26]

Amnesty International believes that a large number of Saharawi civilians are detained in the Western Sahara by the Moroccan forces.[27] Expressing its concern in 1978–9 Amnesty noted: 'It is thought that several hundred may be detained in the Western Sahara itself; but it is difficult to obtain information. Some are reportedly held in the 'Calabozo' prison in El-Ayoun, and some are reported to have undergone 're-education' programmes.[28] In December 1978 the Swiss section of Amnesty International released a document on Saharawi civilian prisoners. It reported that 'during 1976 and 1977, 150 Saharawi civilians, at the least and potentially many more, had been placed in detention without trial in Morocco. No charge has been made against them and they are presumed to be in Morocco.[29]

In addition to the army camps and the prisons in Western Sahara which serve as detention centres for the disappeared Saharawis, secret penal colonies are said to exist in the south of Morocco: a fort at Ait Benhaddou (near Ouarzazate), a camp at Agdz, at Tagounite (near Zagora), and at Tazmamart (near Rich).[30] Some sixty women and scores of others who have fallen ill are said to languish at Fort Ait Benhaddou.[31]

It is possible that some Saharawis have been sent to Morocco's main secret detention centres in Casablanca. One is in the Moulay Cherif area and the other at the old, abandoned airport. Two other centres, one between Rabat and Kenitra, and the other near Oujda, may also hold Saharawis.

The practice of disappearances is in flagrant violation of Morocco's own laws, as well as the International Covenant on Civil and Political Rights to which it is a party. This chapter now turns to examine certain illegal practices which directly implicate the Moroccan government with the responsibility for disappearances.

Illegal practices

Certain aspects of the practice of *garde à vue* (incommunicado detention) create the conditions for disappearances in Morocco and Western Sahara. Individuals who have been arrested because their political opinions have made them suspect, have been detained for years without trial and without communication with their families. They are counted among the disappeared. Amnesty International has conducted the most thorough investigation of incommunicado detention as practised by the Moroccan government:

After arrest the suspect is held for police inquiry under *garde à vue*. During this period, the suspect is in the sole custody of the police. Although the police are under the authority of the public prosecutor they are not under his direct supervision, and are not monitored in their behaviour by any independent authority. Under the code of criminal procedure [Code de procédure pénale—CPP] of 1959, *garde à vue* could last for forty-eight hours in routine cases, with a possible extension of twenty-four hours upon the written authorization of the public prosecutor. These periods were doubled in cases involving the internal or external security of the state (CPP, Article 68). For cases involving the internal or external security of the state, these periods were again doubled in 1962 (decree No. 1-59-451, Article 2); they now stand at eight days *garde à vue* and four days extension. In addition, the courts have often rejected appeals against repeated extensions of the *garde à vue* period. In practice, therefore, the period of police inquiry and *garde à vue* may be indefinitely prolonged . . . At each extension of *garde à vue* the suspect should be brought before the public prosecutor ('except in exceptional cases'—CPP, Article 82). This is apparently not done.[32]

Under *garde à vue*, the detainee cannot contact a lawyer and has no opportunity for a proper legal defence. The detainee also has no access to an independent doctor and cannot communicate with his family or friends. Families of the detainees are not officially informed of their whereabouts or even of their arrest. A family dare not ask 'where are they?' Herein lies the conditions for disappearance.

In the conclusion of its report on a 1981 mission to Morocco, Amnesty International described a number of blatantly illegal practices which 'have led to serious human rights violations involving the "disappearance" of large numbers of people and the deaths in custody of others . . .'[33] Concerning the practice of *garde à vue* and ill treatment,

Amnesty International believes that Moroccan officials are falling in their legal and moral obligations to arrested individuals by routinely arresting without showing warrants (in violation of Moroccan law); by not informing families and lawyers of the arrest or of the arrested person's place of detention; by extending repeatedly the *garde à vue* period so that it often lasts months and sometimes more than a year (interpreting the relevant provisions of Moroccan law too broadly); by furnishing such extensions without seeing the detainee and doing this without providing a reasoned written explanation (as required by Moroccan law); by providing no way for the arrested person to appeal directly against wrongful arrest. The *procureur du Roi*, who is legally responsible for the observance of law and the protection of the rights of the detainee from the moment of the arrest until the case is handed to the *juge d'instruction* is particularly lax in exercising that responsibility; in many political cases the *procureur du Roi* has not exercised that responsibility in an appropriate manner and, in some instances, appears to have contravened the law.

Without the careful supervision of the *procureur du Roi* the long periods of *garde à vue* where the detainee is held incommunicado in the sole custody of the police and interrogating personnel, with inadequate medical care available, create the preconditions for torture and ill-treatment. On the basis of all the information in its possession, its assessment of the conditions of *garde à vue*, and the consistency between the numerous allegations it has received of ill-treatment and torture in Moroccan police detention centres, Amnesty International concludes that such treatment has frequently taken place and may be occurring routinely.[34]

Disappearances constitute violations of the Covenant on Civil and Political Rights which Morocco ratified on 3 August 1979. Article 6 of the Covenant states: 'Every human being has the inherent right to life. This right shall be protected by law. No one shall be arbitrarily deprived of his life.' For the authorities, the disappeared Saharawis have no life; they do not exist.

Article 7 holds that 'No one shall be subjected to torture or to cruel, inhuman or degrading treatment or punishment.' This chapter has provided evidence which indicates a clear and consistent pattern of torture during clandestine detention. Furthermore, the dehumanizing experience of disappearance is in and of itself a form of cruel, inhuman and degrading treatment.

Article 9 provides: 'Everyone has the right to liberty and security of person. No one shall be subjected to arbitrary arrest or detention. No one shall be deprived of his liberty except on such grounds and in accordance with such procedure as are established by law.' Article 14 sets down the rights to equality before the courts and tribunals and a fair trial. Testimonies from Saharawis who 'reappeared' in 1984 make it clear that many of the Western Sahara's disappeared are arrested without the benefit of any procedural safeguards. These individuals charge that the Moroccan occupation forces were responsible for the arrests and incommunicado detention to which they and scores of others were made victims. Generally, the security forces and gendarmerie were involved in either the initial arrest and detention or when the Saharawis were transferred to their custody. This amounts to an illegal situation which is further complicated by the fact that the detainees are officially denied access to a lawyer, or any other form of legal redress for that matter, and thus to any possibility of an effective legal remedy. On this note, Article 16 provides, 'Everyone shall have the right to recognition everywhere as a person before the law.' The Moroccan government denies the disappeared Saharawis this right; they have no identity before the law.

With its disappearance campaigns, the Moroccan government has consistently violated Article 17 on the right to privacy, Article 18 on the freedom of conscience and Article 19 on the right to expression. This chapter has cited numerous cases which indicate that the Moroccan government uses disappearance as a means to effectively silence the Saharawi people.

Article 10(1) provides: 'All persons deprived of their liberty shall be treated with humanity and respect for the inherent dignity of the human person.' The disappeared are treated neither with humanity nor with respect.

The phenomenon of disappearances has touched hundreds of Saharawis. These missing persons are the victims of a disregard for law, little short of state terrorism. The Moroccan government's failure to account for numerous arrests and subsequent disappearances in Western Sahara constitutes a continuing violation of human rights. A great injustice will be done to the disappeared Saharawis if the international community does not persist by asking: 'Where are they?'

Notes

1. Amnesty International, *Report of an Amnesty International Mission to the Kingdom of Morocco*, London, Amnesty International Publications, 1982, p. 42.
2. 'Morocco and Western Sahara', *Amnesty International 1984 Report*, London, Amnesty International Publications, p. 354.
3. 'Ou sont les civils Sahraouis enlevés par le régime marocain?', *Nouvelles Sahraouies*, Geneva, 22 February 1982, p. 2.
4. 'Répression en zones occupées de la République Arabe Sahraoui Démocratique', *Nouvelles Sahraouies*, 18 February 1981. Teresa K. Smith (trans.).
5. Amnesty International, *Amnesty International Briefing Paper no. 13: Morocco*, London, Amnesty International Publications, 1977, p. 10.
6. 'La répression continue en zones occupées de la République Arabe Sahraoui Démocratique et au Maroc', *Nouvelles Sahraouies*, 27, May 1983, p. 13.
7. 'Répression en zones', op. cit.
8. 'Morocco and Western Sahara', *Amnesty International 1978 Report*, London, Amnesty International Publications, p. 268.
9. Tony Hodges, 'Sahara: le mur du silence', *Le Matin*, Paris, 16 December 1978.
10. Croissant Rouge Sahraoui, *Communiqué*, 30 November 1980.
11. Jean-François Bover, 'Sahara: l'ordre marocain règne à El Aıoun', *La Matin*, Paris, 5 January 1981, Teresa K. Smith (trans.).
12. 'Ou sont . . .', op. cit., p. 1.
13. 'La répression continue . . .', op. cit., p. 13.
14. Ibid.
15. Ibid.

16. 'Disparus par ordre du Roi', *Afrique Asie*, 25 October 1982, as reprinted in *Nouvelles Sahraouies*, 26 February 1983.
17. Boyer, op. cit.
18. 'Dans les zones occupées de la République Arabe Sahraoui Démocratique', *Nouvelles Sahraouies*, **26**, February 1983, p. 6. Teresa K. Smith (trans.).
19. Amnesty International, 1977, p. 4.
20. Swiss Section of Amnesty International, *Maroc: prisonniers civils sahraouis*, December 1978.
21. 'Ou sont . . .', op. cit., p. 2.
22. Amnesty International Mission, op. cit., pp. 27–33.
23. Amnesty 1984, op. cit., p. 354.
24. Hodges, op. cit., 16 December 1978.
25. 'Une féroce répression sévit au Sahara occidental occupé,' *El Moudjahid* (Algiers), 25 January 1981.
26. 'Morocco and Western Sahara', *Amnesty International 1981 Report*, London, Amnesty International Publications, pp. 372–6.
27. 'Morocco and Western Sahara', *Amnesty International 1980 Report*, London, Amnesty International Publications, p. 349.
28. 'Morocco and Western Sahara', *Amnesty International 1979 Report*, London, Amnesty International Publications, pp. 167–8.
29. Swiss Support Committee, op. cit.
30. 'La répression continue . . .', op. cit., p. 12.
31. 'Disparus . . .', op. cit.
32. Amnesty International Mission, pp. 8–9.
33. Ibid., p. 40.
34. Ibid., pp. 40–1.

7 The Saharawi refugees: origins and organization, 1975–85

ANNE LIPPERT

In the desert region around Tindouf, Algeria, somewhere between 150,000 and 200,000 relatively unknown refugees from the Western Sahara, the former Spanish Sahara, are grouped in camps, preparing for eventual return to their homeland. Having fled the territory of the former Spanish Sahara, or, and in some cases, Mauritania or Morocco, since 1975, these Saharawis are coping with the extreme desert rigours of the region where they are settled and attempting to develop skills that will aid them develop their nation once Western Sahara's independence has been achieved.

Origins of the struggle

The refugees' struggle for nationhood has been a long one and threatens to go on even longer. Originally the colonial power against which the Saharawis fought was Spain. As early as 1476 Spaniards from the Canary Islands attempted to establish a presence on the Western Saharan coast.[1] Most colonization activity by Spain, however, did not occur until the latter part of the nineteenth century, and the interior of the region which became Spanish Sahara was not really penetrated until 1934. In the late 1950s Spain and France worked together to halt Saharawi resistance to Spanish domination of the territory.[2] In 1963 the United Nations Special Committee on Decolonization first turned attention to the Spanish Sahara, but only twelve years later did the Spanish colonists leave, handing over the administration of the territory to Morocco and Mauritania.[3]

The withdrawal of the Spanish administrators and army between November 1975 and February 1976, under the Madrid Accords with Morocco and Mauritania, occurred following advisory opinion by the International Court of Justice in October 1975 that neither Morocco nor Mauritania had compelling ties that would merit the legal integration of that territory into Morocco or Mauritania unless it were at the behest of the Saharawi people themselves.[4] At the time of Spanish withdrawal, both Moroccan and Mauritanian army troops were involved in military operations to control and subdue the territory. It was at this point that many of the refugees now in the Tindouf camps in Algeria sought refuge in the desert after fleeing Saharawi cities like El-Ayoun and Smara to avoid capture, mutilation or death. As Moroccan and Mauritanian troops moved across the Sahara destroying herds, poisoning wells and killing those who were in their path, these refugees, as well as nomads, fled before them. Bombed, strafed and napalmed by Moroccan planes in their temporary refuges in the desert of the Western Sahara, these Saharawi refugees fled finally to the Tindouf region of western Algeria where the women, children and old men found sanctuary, while the able-bodied men returned to the Western Sahara to fight the new colonizers, Morocco and Mauritania.[5]

On 5 August 1979, an agreement between the Polisario Front and Mauritania ended Mauritanian involvement in the Western Saharan war. Morocco then claimed the zone formally abandoned by Mauritania and escalated its effort to gain control of the entire territory. Seven years later that struggle continues with the Saharawis determined to regain their land, a state they proclaimed as the Saharawi Arab Democratic Republic on 27 February 1976, and that is recognized as such by sixty-seven nations, including thirty-one of the fifty other members of the Organization for African Unity.[6]

Early days of the camps

The name Saharawi is a general term referring to persons living in the Sahara. Specifically, the refugees who came from the Western Sahara, that region bordered by Morocco to the north, Algeria and Mauritania to the east, Mauritania to the south, and the Atlantic Ocean to the west, are from a number of tribes, sub-tribes and fractions of mixed Arab, Berber and black African descent. The greatest number of the refugees are Reguibat, Tekna, Oulad Delim, Arosien and Oulad Tidrarin.[7] As part of a national policy and stemming from Article Six of their Constitution (all citizens are equal before the law and have the same rights and duties), the Saharawis have minimized the importance of tribal and family origin so as effectively to erase the caste differences that existed prior to the struggle for independence. Slavery, although not widespread at the time of the establishment of the Saharawi state, was also abolished through the same article of the Constitution.

Some of the Saharawi refugees in the Tindouf camps had led nomadic lives prior to their coming to the camps, but a greater number of the former inhabitants of Spanish Sahara had lived in the cities, such as El-Ayoun, Dakhla, La Guera, and Smara or were attached to the phosphate-mining operations at Bou-Craa. Many other Saharawis, who had taken refuge in Morocco from the late 1950s and then fled repressive measures taken against them by the Moroccan government at the outset of the present war, had also grown used to a more sedentary life, and, in fact, were not used to the rough existence of the refugee camps where water is scarce, wind and sand destroy the tents and temperatures can rise to 140°F in midday or plummet to below 0°F at night, according to the season of the year.[8]

When the largest group or refugees arrived in the Tindouf camps in 1976 they came by truck or Land Rover or on foot from as far as 1,400 kilometres away. Many had fled with no more than the clothes on their backs. A large number were Saharawi women who had been active in the Polisario Front during the Spanish occupation, and who fled with their children because they feared being tortured or imprisoned since the Spanish authorities had turned over their police records to the Moroccan authorities. Their fears were not groundless. Both the Polisario Front and Amnesty International have since published lists of Saharawis who were arrested and interned in 1975–6 and have never reappeared.[9]

Life in the refugee camps around Tindouf was extremely difficult in the early days. Interviews with a number of women refugees in summer 1977 pointed to the very stark situation of the refugees in 1976. One of those interviewed, Mucina Bint Chejatu of La Guera, was one of a very small number of Saharawi women to attend a girls' boarding high school in El-Ayoun. In November 1975 when the Spanish began to abandon Western Sahara to the Moroccans and Mauritanians, her school was closed and she returned to La Guera. Mucina, who had joined a cell of the Polisario Front as a high school student in El-Ayoun and whose father was a resistance fighter captured by the Mauritanians during a Polisario strike against Nouakchott, fled the coastal city of La Guera for the interior of the territory in late 1975. She and other La Guera refugees stopped at the desert settlement of Oum Dreiga within Western Sahara, where a refugee camp had been established. The refugees out-numbered the shelters available so many slept under bushes or trees. Food supplies were minimal. In mid-February 1976, four Moroccan Mirages attacked these refugees for two days with bombs and napalm. Many of the approximately 2,500 refugees in the area were killed. Mucina survived and arrived in the Tindouf camps on 23 February. Here again there was insufficient food and shelter for the numbers of refugees arriving from all parts of the desert, seeking to escape the Moroccan and Mauritanian armed forces.[10]

Another interviewee, Bouteta, married and the mother of two children, described how she had belonged to a cell of the Polisario Front in El-Ayoun in 1973, the year of its founding. Her role in the Front had been to help organize other Saharawi women, to distribute political literature and to assist in the demonstrations for independence. According to Bouteta, on 13 November 1975, the day before the signing of the tripartite Madrid Accords, columns of Spanish tanks rolled into El-Ayoun and were stationed in every Saharawi neighbourhood. Bouteta and her two children left El-Ayoun on foot and walked forty kilometres into the desert where they lived for a month and a half with little food and clothing. A nomad group took them in hand, and they finally reached the Tindouf area. In the spring of 1976, having survived the exodus and the privations of the desert, Bouteta's children died in a measles epidemic in which about one thousand Saharawi children perished.[11]

As refugees streamed into the camps around the Tindouf area from intermediate refugee sites in the Western Sahara, the Algerian Red Crescent, which is affiliated with the League of Red Cross Societies, was on the scene. It had already appealed to the League of Red Cross Societies in late 1975 to provide urgent aid for refugees in the Western Sahara.[12] The emergency grew as tens of thousands of Saharawis fled into Algeria, assisted in their flight by the new Saharawi Red Crescent, constituted in November 1975.[13]

The area around Tindouf is an extremely arid part of the desert where there is little vegetation and water is scarce. The refugees lacked food, clothing, water and shelter and suffered from exposure, wounds, dehydration and shock. Journalists' reports and photographs of the camps at this time reveal the terrible misery which existed. There were no shelters available for these thousands of people, no doctors, no hospitals, insufficient food and water, no facilities for sanitation. Sven Lampell, a League of Red Cross Societies' representative who liaised with the Saharawi Red Crescent in 1975–7, noted in an interview in 1977 that even in the earliest days of the exodus, these were the most unusual refugees he had known in his years of work with such groups. He recalled early food distribution operations where there was not enough to go around and noted that he saw no fighting, no pushing, no theft, no corruption. Those who were lucky enough to get something shared it with others.[14] Despite the generosity of the refugees towards one another, conditions in the camps were abysmal. Tami Hultman, the first American journalist to visit the camps, noted at the time of her visit (the summer after the measles epidemic of spring 1976), that 'one in every four infants dies before the age of three months. The effects of malnutrition are visible everywhere in skinny limbs and bloated stomachs, in the rows of cots where older children die from measles, chicken pox or whooping cough. Many of the refugees are scarred and disfigured by burns and wounds received during the bombings.'[15]

Reports of the League of Red Cross Societies in 1975 and 1976 to national Red Cross societies also noted the appalling conditions faced by the refugees:

Refugee camps are set up in the heart of the desert where waterholes are rare. The climate is hostile; very strong winds stir up sandstorms and, at night, the temperature sometimes drops below freezing. Most of the refugees are women and children. People are living in improvised 'tents' or completely in the open. The refugees are in poor health. They are exhausted and suffering from cold after their long march across the desert. Considerable numbers of children are affected by severe malnutrition. There are many newborn babies in the camps. Their mothers, exhausted, have too little milk to feed them. A medical student who has 4,000 people under his care showed us all his equipment, one pair of tweezers and a hypodermic syringe. He has no medicine. A woman showed us her food store, one two-kilogram bag of flour for a family of five. The food ration for a family of six who had eaten nothing for two days was a handful of already used tea leaves and small pieces of dry bread. The parents gave it all to their four children.[16]

In 1976 there was one doctor for all the thousands of refugees. In July 1976 Médecins sans Frontières sent a medical team to assist in the camps and a Cuban medical team arrived sometime later to work there as well.[17] Calls for international assistance resulted in some help. The League of Red Cross Societies, which had launched an appeal in December 1975, raised 10.9 million Swiss francs.[18] The Office of the UN High Commissioner for Refugees (UNHCR) had contributed $700,000 by October 1976. In January 1977, the FAO provided $942,000, which supplied food for the refugees for three months. Prince S. Aga Khan, the UN high commissioner for refugees, visited the camps on 12 January 1977, and called for $13 million in assistance. The sum could supply the needs of 50,000 people for one year.[19] But even as food and assistance came to Tindouf, more refugees flocked to the camps. In mid-1976 it looked as if those thousands of refugees who had escaped death and undergone every privation in the desert of the Western Sahara, would succumb to the privations and disease prevalent in the initial stages of any refugee camp.

The immediate task of the Polisario Front, and, in particular, of the Saharawi Red Crescent, was to organize the refugee population for survival. Twenty-six camps were established in a two-hundred kilometre area along the Algerian border by 1986. These camps were organized into three *wilayat* (provinces) named after the three major cities in the Western Sahara: Smara, Dakhla and El-Ayoun. A fourth province, Aoussert, was created in 1985. The distance between these *wilayat* was sometimes almost one-hundred kilometres. The purpose for the great distances was two-fold. The first was to protect the refugee population from enemy attacks, for King Hassan of Morocco has often threatened to invoke 'hot pursuit' after Polisario attacks in the Western Sahara and as we have seen, many of the refugees had already suffered air attacks in the interim camps within Western Sahara in 1976. The second purpose, of course, was to protect the population from epidemics.[20]

Each *wilaya* was divided into six or more *dairat* (camp communities also bearing the names of Western Sahara towns or cities) and these, again, were sub-divided into several 'neighbourhoods' of tents set in rows. In 1986 each *daira* contained from five to seven thousand inhabitants. Water cisterns and garbage barrels were provided and 'toilet' sections were eventually marked off, as were areas for livestock when the refugees again began to raise some animals to replace those left behind in the 1975–6 exodus, or killed or seized by the invading armies.

In the early years of the camps each *daira* was composed of several hundred tents, when tents became available, each tent sheltering from eight to ten persons. About ten per cent of the tents were traditional nomad tents constructed of woven camel hair strips. The rest were tents provided by humanitarian organizations, but whose shape or material did not effectively resist the cold, sand and wind of the desert. Many tents were made of bits of material sewn together on the spot.[21] Today tents continue to serve as accommodation for the refugees and, as the number of refugees grows, so does the number of tents although in August 1984 severe storms destroyed large numbers of them.[22]

Each *daira* was administered by a 'Popular Council', made up of elected heads of the camp committees (health and sanitation, supplies, handicrafts, education, pediatrics, security, social affairs, commerce and herds) and an administrator and a political leader. Later the number of committees was reduced to five, including a new one, justice. In this later system of organization, which continues to the present day, the other committees are for education, crafts, health and sanitation, and distribution of supplies.[23]

A major concern of Saharawi leaders was not only the physical well-being of the Saharawi refugees but their mental, emotional and spiritual well-being as well. To reduce the depression of the refugees who had already undergone severe trauma and were continuing to suffer deprivation and fear, an effort was made to build a new society, forward-looking to the time when the Saharawis would again recover their territory and return home. For this reason each adult Saharawi refugee became a member of one of the camp committees and of a political cell. No one was forced into this membership, but most persons in the camps joined. A cell was a unit of eleven persons. The committees for each camp were made up of much larger numbers. In each small cell members discussed together life in the camp, the struggle for independence, the needs that existed in the camp, the history of the Saharawis. Cell leaders and committee heads brought the concerns of their members to the camp's Popular Council. At times these concerns were carried by the elected camp representatives to National Popular Congresses, of which there have been five to date.[24]

Of major importance to the committees, however, were the daily needs of the people. The committee charged with distribution of supplies was responsible for the equal and fair distribution of food, water and other supplies to all inhabitants. The health and sanitation committee (and the former pediatric committee) were responsible for instructing all inhabitants of the camps in the sanitation rules designed to protect the health of the camps and for visiting camp inhabitants to see that medical needs were taken care of. Mothers were instructed in the nutritional and health care of their children, methods which had to be different in camp surroundings from practices in nomad camps or in the cities of the Western Sahara.[25] Because of the high incidence of children's early deaths, the pediatric committee assisted the Saharawi Red Crescent in comprehensive immunization programmes for children and also brought ailing mothers and children to camp dispensaries or the *wilaya* hospitals set up for pre- and post-natal care. Members of these committees and other volunteers made bricks for the dispensaries and hospitals and also provided bricks for community ovens, schools, homes for families of martyrs killed in the war and schools.[26]

In 1977 and early 1978, however, despite these efforts by the refugees, visitors to the camps noted that there was still not enough clothing, shoes and blankets for the refugees. A report by the Algerian NGO Rencontre et Développement described the difficulties:

Water is also a problem. If some camps have wells where water is abundant, the others must collect it in cisterns, which in any event poses problems of containers for storage. Besides, there is a shortage of disinfectants, soap and detergents. Another problem is fuel for cooking. . . . The arid environment makes it impossible to cultivate food, and since the invaders' armies destroyed the livestock, the refugees lack food sufficiently high in proteins, vitamins and mineral salts. The consequences of this malnutrition are serious, above all for the nursing babies and young children, but also for the nursing mothers and pregnant women.

The same report noted that the main diseases in 1978 were broncho-lung diseases for the men, anaemia for the women, and diarrhoea for the children, other epidemics having been halted by the inoculation programmes.[27]

Current refugee developments

Sanitation and health care remain a major concern of the Saharawis today. In 1985 the health and sanitation committee, which also includes in its functions the responsibilities of the former pediatrics/child care committee, continues its work of preventive medicine. In 1981 efforts were made to remove the tents further from one another for reasons of sanitation. Following that improvement, a small kitchen area of mud brick with a hot plate and butane bottle was constructed at a short distance from each tent. (The lack of firewood in the area had required trips of some two hundred kilometres for wood in the early days of the camps. The Algerian government began to supply the butane bottles in 1978.)[28] Keeping cooking and waste activities at a distance from the tents has helped to control the number of flies in the living quarters. It has been important as well to keep the butane bottles out of the tents for reasons of safety.

Today each *daira* has a dispensary and each *wilaya* has a major hospital, these buildings being constructed of mud bricks. (Incidentally, although this form of construction is assuredly better than the tents, it is vulnerable to sudden, strong rains that occur occasionally in this part of the desert.) There is also a national hospital, Bachir Salah, with a capacity of 450 beds to provide for some of the more serious illnesses. This national hospital is divided into three sections: general medicine, maternity and children's units. It is equipped with operating rooms and a number of laboratories. In keeping with their policy of striving for the maximum possible degree of self-sufficiency, the hospitals and dispensaries are staffed entirely by Saharawis. The principal hospital has nine Saharawi doctors along with numerous other Saharawi health care personnel.[29] Saharawis educated in medical schools abroad have returned after completing their studies to assist in the camps.

Daily visits by health care committees to tents in each neighbourhood in each *daira* continue so that there is constant monitoring of the health of each Saharawi inhabitant. This daily vigilance has accounted for the lack of recent major medical crises. According to the present minister of health, Nema Ould Joumani, the foremost concern of his ministry is preventive medicine. 'We always prefer to prevent rather than cure. Our second concern is to care for patients when this is necessary. Our third goal is education, not only education of health care personnel, but of the whole Saharawi population as well.' Control of flies and careful hygiene by the refugee population are seen by the minister as major continuing priorities.[30]

Current health care goals and practice do not differ much from the concerted efforts of the Saharawis from 1978 on to improve health care and sanitation in the camps, but the results of their efforts are demonstrated in reduced infant mortality. Continued concern for pregnant women and the newborn remains. As soon as a woman becomes pregnant she now receives pre-natal care, including dietary supplements. Ordinarily women give birth in the *wilaya* hospitals, although certain cases in which it appears that there may be complications are sent to the national hospital. A few days after the birth of the child, once the family celebrations are ended, mother and child are placed in a special mother-care centre where both receive attention. Once they return to the camps, members of the health care committees visit them regularly to assist the mother, where this is necessary, in caring for the new child.[31]

In 1977 and 1978 a number of Saharawis, men and women, were sent to Algeria or to other countries (mostly Spanish-speaking since the second language of the Saharawis after their mother tongue, Hassania, is Spanish), to receive health care training, notably in nursing. Many of these Saharawis, like the Saharawi doctors, have now returned to the camps and provide care in the dispensaries and the hospitals. They also provide training in the schools for those Saharawis who will work in the health care and sanitation committees.[32]

Despite the very real successes of the Saharawi refugees in health care and their independence in totally directing the health care aspect of life in the camps, they remain dependent on outside sources to provide the food, medicine, equipment and training abroad necessary to maintain good health care in the camps. Even now, handicapped Saharawis are sent abroad for retraining. Burn victims, like those of 1976, are also sent abroad for treatment, as are emergency medical cases that cannot be handled in the national hospital. Since the Saharawis cannot yet return to their own independent nation and since they do not benefit from the natural resources of that nation, medical supplies, vitamin supplements, milk for children, innoculation materials, laboratory equipment and advanced training of health care personnel must all be supplied by outside humanitarian groups. The Saharawis, however, remain fiercely independent in an intrinsically dependent situation.

Since 1978 there have been efforts to develop some goat herds (especially for milk to supplement the diet of the ill) and to engage in some farming in those areas where there is sufficient water. As early as the summer of 1978, during stays in the camps, visitors recall eating a 'Mediterranean salad' (tomatoes, onions and cucumbers), watermelon and yoghurt (from goat milk), all produced by the Saharawis.[33] The Saharawis have also experimented with raising chickens and growing squash and other vegetables. Although it has been possible to produce enough food to contribute significantly to the diets of patients in the hospitals, mother-care centres and nurseries, there is not sufficient water and resources in the refugee camp areas to supply the very large population of the camps with more than a small fraction of their food needs. Thus most of the food and much of the water must be trucked into the camps. Funding for this still must come from outside sources.

The herds of camels lost by the refugees have, for the most part, not been replaced. Some goats are again being raised in the camps, as are some sheep. Fodder available for livestock is, however, at a minimum, though some is being grown in the experimental gardens. 'Agricultural cooperatives' exist in some camps and agricultural training is provided through these organizations. The 'cooperatives' raise some animals, but most goats are being raised by individual families.[34] Despite the very active involvement of the Saharawis in the development of food resources where this is possible and in the distribution of food and water supplies, in this sphere as in the case of health care, they remain dependent upon external resources for much of their maintenance. With the tripling or quadrupling of the camp population since 1976, this means a sum of from $35 to $50m. per year for minimal food maintenance of the refugees.

At the time of the exodus in 1975–6, few Saharawi men and fewer Saharawis women had received much formal education. At the time of the outbreak of the war, about 95 per cent of the Saharawi population could neither read nor write.[35] After health care to protect the population, their education became the second major priority of the Saharawi leaders. In 1976 tent schools were established in the camps to teach Arabic, the history of the Saharawis, simple mathematics, and reading and writing. Separate schools were established for the adults (mostly women) and the children. The first teachers were young men who had received some high school training in the schools of the former Spanish Sahara or in Morocco. Gradually young women and other young men were sent to Algeria or elsewhere abroad to secondary education and teacher training.[36]

Today most of the tent schools have been replaced by mud brick structures. The younger children remain at home in their camps for the first years of primary school. The later primary classes, as well as some secondary schooling, are provided in boarding schools. Kindergartens and primary schools are mixed. Particularly gifted students, both girls and boys, are still sent abroad for advanced instruction. Numerous young women are now teaching in the various programmes of instruction in the schools and are also responsible for most of the other tasks of running the boarding schools.[37]

Many young women continue their education after marriage, which may occur when they are sixteen or seventeen years old. There is a special school for women, the School of February 27, named after the birthdate of the Saharawi state. Instruction at this school is generally a one-year programme, which includes one month of military training (requested by the women through the popular congresses), seven months of general instruction and two months of specialized training. At the school women continue studies in reading and writing Arabic, as well as mathematics, and learn to type and drive, and acquire skills in crafts and health care. Physical education is also a part of the programme. Those students who demonstrate special aptitudes receive additional training beyond the first year. Most of the instructors at the School of February 27 are women, as are its directors. Nurseries and child care are provided for those women students who have children so that they may attend class and study. Over three thousand women per year have received instruction at this school.[38]

A new national school for vocational training has been constructed. In January 1984, although its buildings were nearly completed, much of the equipment and most supplies were lacking. The purpose of this school is future-orientated, for the trades to be taught include not only those necessary in the camps, but also those that will be critical in a newly independent state—among them auto mechanics, plumbers, electricians, masons, secretaries and administrative assistants, radio and refrigerator repairmen, seamstresses, designers, printers and so on. The purposes of the specialized and advanced training schools are to provide trained personnel for all camp functions, to prepare the cadres necessary for the effective functioning of a Saharawi state once independence is gained, and to ensure that all Saharawis receive adequate instruction for the democratic governing processes which form the basis of their organization and their constitution. Education is so important to this people that it is proclaimed a right in Article Seven of the 'fundamental principles' section of the constitution: 'Education, health and social protection are rights guaranteed to all citizens.'[39] Adherence to the democratic process is equally important. Article Eighteen of the Constitution states: 'The government shall ensure the execution of the programmes elaborated by the popular congresses and the popular committees under the supervision of the head of state.'[40] From primary school to specialized training school, education in the democratic process is taught through the activities of group meetings. Children are taught to express their opinions, and to listen to one another.[41]

Although the Saharawis have managed to staff their own schools in the refugee camps, they are still dependent on outside resources to provide books, other teaching and learning materials, indeed supplies of all sorts for these schools. The Saharawis expect to continue to send students abroad for more advanced technical training.[42] As one educational need is satisfied, the Saharawis find new needs and new responses for those needs. During this period of war and exile in the refugee camps, they are not remaining idle. When independence comes, they plan to be prepared with Saharawis trained to manage every aspect of their state. They do not want to become dependent on expatriate expertise as have a number of other developing nations. They have no desire to lose such a hard-won independence to any form of neo-colonialism. Their thinking is that, if the resources of the nation belong to the people, as their Constitution states,[43] it is up to the people to manage those resources once independence arrives.

Koranic schools continue to exist throughout the camps and most of the teachers in these schools are now women. One of the issues of the third and fourth popular congresses was the encouragement of religious practice in the camps.[44] The Saharawis are serious followers of Islam. The guerrillas on manœuvres stop to pray the prescribed five times a day, as do the refugees in the camps, wherever they happen to be at the hours of prayer. The Saharawis have wanted increased institutionalization of these practices. Now, as in the early days of the camps, koranic schools teach the koran and the other schools teach the secular subjects. Koranic verses, however, may make up the reading exercises in a school. In the koranic schools, children continue to use wooden boards as slates and to memorize verses. A further example of institutionalization has been the construction of mud brick mosques. Imams serve in these mosques. The first mosques in 1976 were simply areas of the camp set aside for prayer and marked off by stones.

The work of the craft committee and of the supply committee is frequently intertwined. Craft committees are not only involved in attempting to retain the traditional crafts of the Saharawis, but also are engaged in supplying the needs of the refugees for clothing, shoes, shelter and household supplies. Although much of the raw material for these crafts, that is the yarn, leather, cloth, wool and so on, is supplied by international humanitarian groups, committee members are actively involved in the production of school uniforms for all the children, sandals, tents, utensils and bowls, blankets and rugs.[46] In the craft committees, as elsewhere in these camps, self-help is the catchword. Gifts of sewing machines have eased the burden of supplying clothing to the refugees. None the less there are some items that are difficult to make on the spot. Anoraks, shoes, boots, and tents, due to lack of sufficient camel hair, are among items that are still provided by Saharawi support groups abroad.[47]

What the craft committee creates to supply the needs of the refugee inhabitants of the camps, the supply committee distributes. This committee also continues to oversee the distribution of food supplies, mostly rice, beans, couscous, tea, sugar, vegetables and some canned fruits, and to monitor the water supply. The major difficulty of the supply committee, of course, is scarcity, scarcity of water and scarcity of food. Water scarcity means that despite the washing and cleaning directions given by the health care committees, it is sometimes difficult to follow them. In those areas dependent on cisterns, there are frequently delays in delivering water and the water itself must be rationed.[48] The supply committees, like the health care committees, check regularly to see that no one is in need. None the less, food, water and other supplies remain minimal.

The justice or social affairs committees of the camps have played an important role in maintaining the spirit of the refugees. The periodic *daira* and *wilaya* meetings and celebrations centred around historic dates of the struggle for independence do this. The social affairs committees provide other activities: music and dance, both traditional and contemporary, dramatic performances, story-telling, poetry recitals.[49] The focus of much of this creative activity, although rooted in traditional forms, is the struggle for independence, highlighting such events as the death of El Ouali, the first secretary general of the Polisario Front, the death of other Saharawi martyrs, important battles against the Moroccans, and, earlier, the Mauritanians, imagined scenes with King Hassan II of Morocco, or, earlier, with Ould Daddah, the former President of Mauritania, historic dates of the Saharawis and the Saharawi Arab Democratic Republic (SADR).[50] In acting out or celebrating these events, the refugees come to grips with their present history and sustain the courage to continue the struggle.

Not all of the celebrations and social gatherings in the camps, however, have a political dimension. The Saharawis are not a people organized primarily by cell and committee meetings and political rallies. The Saharawis also celebrate the festivities of marriage and birth, even as refugees. They visit friends and relatives in the different camps and *wilayat*. They get together in the evening to talk and joke. Nation building is not so serious that the Saharawis can no longer laugh. The family remains the basic unit of their society.[51]

The development of the justice committees, as well as the present educational system with its varied training programmes, the improvements in child care, preventive health care and sanitation and the agricultural cooperatives have all arisen from the periodic popular congresses. The last was held in December 1985. The purpose of the popular congress is to define the short-term and long-term goals of the Saharawi community.[52] One need that received attention from popular meetings and found its way into the popular congress was that of assistance to women in adjudication of marriage and divorce questions. Since about 90 per cent of the adults in the camps are women, their concerns in particular have come to the fore in the popular congresses. Important issues at the third popular congress in 1976 were education for those women already married with children, and military training for all women due to their vulnerability in the camps. The results of the discussions were the creation of the School of February 27 for adult women and a military training program for all women.[53] In discussing the marriage and divorce questions, the women felt that the *qadi*, the judge, who is traditionally male, could be helped to understand women's difficulties in these cases by being advised and assisted by women in the discussions with the disputants in the arbitration of differences. This is a marked departure from traditional custom. Marriage and divorce still remain essential domestic areas of concern, for despite the fact that most of the able-bodied men serve in the SPLA, the Polisario army, these men return from time to time to the camps to spend time with their wives and children. Although some sort of family life continues, personal mis-understandings can arise between spouses in these conditions of war and prolonged separation. New marriages are now generally arranged with the mutual consent of both partners.[54] The minimum age for marriage has been fixed at sixteen for a woman and at eighteen for a man. Revisions of marriage custom that have been devised through the popular congresses include not only the changes in age for marriage and greater emphasis on the assent of both partners, but also their setting of the conditions of the marriage. Only a token dowry still exists.[55] In general polygamy was not an integral part of Saharawi social life prior to the struggle for independence and it does not appear to exist today. Divorce must be by mutual consent. This stipulation differs from traditional Islamic law that permits the husband to divorce his wife and is much stricter than laws governing divorce in many modern family codes of Islamic states.[56] To maintain family stability and to discourage divorce, however, members of the justice committee work as counsellors to the disputing parties to help them resolve their differences. The *qadi* is a member of the justice committee and is the person to sign all documents. The other members of the committee, all women, assist him by presenting the woman's point of view and work with the women involved in domestic disputes. The justice committee involves itself only in activities concerning domestic relations. Criminal matters are handled under the other judicial provisions of the constitution.[57]

A major change in Saharawi family life today, apart from the fact that the men are involved in a lengthy war and the women are living in refugee camps, is that many of the women have important responsibilities in the camps, in the women's union, in the workers' union and in the students' association. Saharawi women have been actively involved in representing the Polisario Front at international women's groups and associations and have served in the external affairs work of both the Saharawi women's union and the Polisario Front. It is not uncommon today that a Saharawi man and woman will celebrate their marriage, enjoy the several days of festivities with family and friends, and then each return separately to duties for the Polisario cause.[58] This type of existence, well known currently in the developed world, is one reason why it has been necessary to refine and change the Saharawi system of civil justice.

Conclusions on the Saharawi experience

What is most evident in the organization and administration of the Saharawi refugee camps is the determination of this people to provide for themselves wherever possible, to develop a group and 'nationhood' consciousness, to direct their own lives, to place their individual stamp on their activities. On entering the area of the refugee camps around Tindouf, one crosses from 'Algerian' to 'Saharawi' territory. This 'frontier' is clearly marked by checkpoints and signs.[59] In reality, of course, all the land on which the Saharawi camps are situated is Algerian territory, but the Saharawis from individual inhabitants to camp leaders to Saharawi Red Crescent workers, to committee and cell members, direct, maintain and organize every activity in their camps. In maintaining and asserting this independence, this group of refugees has pulled itself up from the tragedies of the exodus from the Western Sahara and the threatened genocide of 1975–6, to prepare actively and positively for the return to the Saharawi Arab Democratic Republic, once the struggle results in independence.

After a trip to the refugee camps to assist the Saharawis in the development of the new technical training centre founded in 1984, Jean-Claude Bruffaerts noted that:

1. the Polisario struggle is that of an entire people; old and young, men and women share the responsibilities and have the same determination;
2. surprisingly there is an absence of hatred toward the enemy and its allies and the will to fight is not motivated by a desire to destroy or crush a neighbour;
3. the struggle is based essentially on a plan for a society, a society that respects the positive values of tradition, democracy, sharing and sovereignty. Unceasingly the discussions one has with the Saharawis have to do with what will follow the war, the projects of reconstruction that they must prepare for.[60]

In the early days of the camps, the Saharawis' focus was on survival. As some of the fears of imminent extinction lessen,[61] more and more emphasis is placed on the future. The current focus on projects for education and technical training for all Saharawis, the experience of working together as equals, the training provided in self-management and self-expression, are all part of their nation-building. Once the war is over, the Saharawis reason, there will be much building and rebuilding of cities and towns, the construction of a complete infrastructure system for the SADR. To finance this, there will have to be careful exploitation of the nation's resources. As the Saharawis now control their lives in the refugee camps, they want to control this future exploitation themselves. This will be made that much easier by their current preparation.

Notes

1. Tony Hodges, *Historical Dictionary of Western Sahara*, Metuchen, NJ and London, The Scarecrow Press, Inc., 1982, p. 5.
2. Francis de Chassey, 'Données historiques et sociologiques sur la formation du peuple saharaoui', *Sahara Occidental: un peuple et ses droits*, Paris, Editions L'Harmattan, 1978, pp. 10–22. See also Maurice Barbier, *Le Conflit du Sahara Occidental*, Paris, Éditions L'Harmattan, 1982, pp. 52–73 and Tony Hodges, *Western Sahara, The Roots of a Desert War*, Westport, Lawrence Hill and Co., 1983, pp. 40–84.
3. Spain later claimed that it had merely transferred administrative responsibility, rather than sovereignty, to Morocco and Mauritania, and that it still advocated a referendum to enable the Saharawi people to exercise their right to self-determination.
4. *Advisory Opinion of 16 October 1975, Reports of Judgements, Advisory Opinions and Orders, International Court of Justice, Western Sahara*, The Hague, ICJ, pp. 59–60, paragraphs 161 and 162. See chapters in this volume by Thomas Franck and George Joffé.
5. Ahmed-Baba Miske, *Front Polisario, l'âme d'un peuple*, Paris, Editions Rupture, 1978, pp. 212–23. See also Anne Lippert, 'Emergence or Submergence of a Potential State: The Struggle in Western Sahara', *Africa Today*, **24**, no. 1, January–March 1977, pp. 50–6, and John Mercer, *The Saharawis of Western Sahara*, London, Minority Rights Group, Report no. 40, 1979, pp. 10–11.
6. *SPSC Letter*, (Saharan People's Support Committee, Ada, Ohio) vol. IV, nos. 3–4, April 1984, p. 7 and vol. V, no. 4, April 1985, pp. 4 and 8.
7. Tony Hodges, op. cit., pp. 341–6.
8. Interviews by the author with refugees in the camps, June–July 1977, June–July 1978, June–July 1979, and September 1981.
9. *Amnesty International Briefing: Morocco, U.S.*, Amnesty International Publications, London, October 1977, p. 10. See also *Report on Different Forms of Repression Against Saharawis in Morocco*, publication by Polisario Front 1977. The author has also received a number of written queries from Amnesty International groups in the United States requesting additional information on 'missing' Saharawis. See also 'Témoignages,' *Résistance Sahraouie*, Brussels, 5th year, no. 2, 1984, pp. 6–7, and chapter by Teresa K. Smith in this volume.
10. *A People Accuses*, Saharawi Red Crescent, Polisario Front Information Service, 1976; see also Ahmed-Baba Miske, op. cit., pp. 213–14, and Anne Lippert, op. cit., pp. 50–4.
11. Interview by author in June–July 1977. See also Maurice Barbier, op. cit., p. 211.
12. Tony Hodges, op. cit., p. 233.
13. Tony Hodges, op. cit., p. 311.
14. Interview by author with Lampell in July 1977. He was in the refugee camps at the same time as the author and was reviewing improvements made by the Saharawis in health and sanitation.
15. Tami Hultman, 'A Nation of Refugees, Western Sahara', *Response,* **9**, no. 15, March 1977, pp. 4–7 and 42.
16. *A People Accuses*, op. cit., p. 56.

17. Maurice Barbier, op. cit., p. 211.
18. Tony Hodges, op. cit., p. 253.
19. The figure of $13 million was based on the initial request by Algeria for assistance at a time when the number of refugees was given as 50,000. Subsequently the numbers of refugees increased greatly.
20. On 6 November 1977, King Hassan II had threatened hot pursuit into Algeria. The refugees had anticipated these strikes from 1976 on. See also Tony Hodges, op. cit., p. xxv. Interviews with health personnel pointed to the need to space the tents further apart. See also *Sahara Occidental, la lutte d'un peuple*, Algiers, Rencontre et Développement, May 1979, pp. 34–5.
21. Information received and observations by author in visits to the camps.
22. Reuters report in *The Blade*, Toledo, Ohio, Wednesday, 15 August, 1984, p. 9.
23. Information received by the author during visits to the camps. See also Barbara Harrell-Bond, *The Struggle for the Western Sahara, Part III; The Saharawi People*, American Universities Field Staff Reports, Hanover, New Hampshire, 1981, no. 39, pp. 3–8.
24. Discussions with Saharawi leaders in 1977, 1978, 1979, 1981 and 1983.
25. Ibid.
26. Ibid.
27. *Sahara Occidental*, Rencontre et Développement, op. cit., p. 34.
28. Discussions of author with Saharawi women committee members in the camps.
29. Member of Rencontre et Développement and delegate of Services Caritas des Diocèses d'Algérie, 'Impressions de voyage, *RASD 1984, 8 ans d'existence'*, Algiers, Rencontre et Développement, April 1984, pp. 16–21.
30. *RASD 1984*, op. cit., p. 18. See also *5ᵉ Congrès du Front Polisario, 12–16 octobre 1983*, Condé-sur-Noireau, 1983, p. 43. This latter document provides valuable information on Saharawi organization.
31. *RASD 1984*, op. cit., p. 19.
32. Discussions with Saharawis in the camps.
33. Discussions by author in the camps with Polisario leaders including Bachir Mustapha Sayed and Mohamed Lamine Ould Ahmed among others.
34. Discussions with Saharawis and observations by the writer in the camps.
35. Figure given by Saharawi leaders.
36. Discussions with Saharawi men and women in the camps.
37. Visit to teaching and administrative personnel at the school in September 1981.
38. Ibid.
39. *Western Sahara Report*, vol. 5, no. 5, June–July 1984, pp. 3–4.
40. Ibid.
41. Experience of writer in several Saharawi schools.
42. *Sahara Info*, op. cit., p. 16.
43. *Western Sahara Report*, op. cit., p. 3; Article 8 of the Constitution. Private property is also allowed.
44. Discussions of the author with imams and other Saharawis in the camps in 1981. These matters had been discussed by the base congresses in March–April 1977 and April 1978.
45. Ibid.
46. Author's observations and discussions in the camps in 1977, 1978, 1979 and 1981.
47. Reports from Saharawi support groups.

48. Observations of author during visits to the camps.
49. These poetry recitals are really more in the 'griot' tradition of improvised creation. The author was told by an elderly poet in 1981 that the warriors in Saharawi tradition were also expected to be poets and that the poet was an honored individual in traditional society. The author has attended a number of these performances in the camps.
50. Ibid.
51. Saharawi Constitution; see Article 5.
52. Discussions with men and women Saharawis in the camps in 1981.
53. Ibid.
54. Ibid.
55. Ibid.
56. In Algeria, for example, there does not need to be mutual consent for divorce.
57. Discussions with Saharawis in 1981.
58. Discussions with Saharawis in 1978, 1979, 1981.
59. Experience of author on all visits to the camps.
60. *Sahara Info*, op. cit., p. 17.
61. The new thrust in Moroccan attempts to secure the Western Sahara, that is, the erection of the five Moroccan 'walls' in the territory has reawakened these fears of possible genocidal attack. The part of the 'wall' closest to the camps is only a few kilometres from the Algerian border in the Tindouf area.

8 The Saharawi refugees:
Lessons and prospects

JAMES FIREBRACE

The Saharawi refugee camps

The Saharawi refugee camps in Southern Algeria date back to the final months of 1975. In October 1975 Morocco's Green March assembled, crossing into Western Sahara in November. This was coupled with Morocco's military invasion, while simultaneously Mauritanian troops entered from the south. This double invasion led to the flight of the Saharawi population from the towns with people leaving often only twenty-four hours before the arrival of the Moroccan troops.

Temporary camps were first set up inside Western Sahara, at places like Tifariti and Guelta Zemmour, Mudraiga and Bir Lahlou, but the Moroccan airforce bombed these sites in a series of raids—in November 1975 and January, February and April 1976—in which napalm and cluster bombs were used. The population of these temporary camps fled across the border into Algeria. Many were killed or wounded. This tragic period of Saharawi history is now relived by older refugees who can still vividly describe the stench of phosphorus burning the bodies of humans and animals alike, and by the younger generation, many of whose paintings take the theme of a Saharawi woman and child fleeing their makeshift camps in terror as bombs fall all around.

Many refugees had to make the journey into exile on foot, with only the clothes they were wearing. Others were brought to safety by Polisario vehicles. The luckiest came with camels and other possessions including the family tent. Not all the refugees came from inside Western Sahara. Many Saharawis had fled Western Sahara to neighbouring territories back in the 1950s, and some of these joined the exodus to the camps near Tindouf at the time of the Moroccan invasion. Later the refugees were joined by other Saharawis, including Saharawi workers on agricultural projects in south western Algeria and Saharawi traders from northern Mauritania.

For the first few months conditions in the makeshift camps were horrific. There was little food; many died of wounds and burns received during the bombings; there were frequent miscarriages, extensive malnutrition, and epidemics of measles and whooping cough led to high mortality rates. At one time sixty children a day were dying. Shelter, clothes and blankets were in desperately short supply and many suffered great hardships in those first winter months, sleeping out as temperatures dropped below freezing point at night.

Delivery of food and medical supplies was intermittent, and the Saharawis initially had great difficulty convincing the international community of the severity of their plight. The frustration and anger of Saharawi Red Crescent officials at this situation has not been forgotten. They tell the story of how, during these critical first months, when one European Red Cross finally responded they did so by sending Chevrolet ambulances made in the 1930s.

The grim situation of the early days has been transformed over the last decade. The camp population is comprised largely of the same people, albeit supplemented by a generation of younger children. But now the camps are lively and stable communities with a sense of purpose. However with the vagaries of aid and the shifting alliances of donors, many hardships are still endured. The drinking water supply remains rudimentary and serious shortages of many essential food items still occur.

The vulnerability of the situation of the Saharawi refugees was demonstrated dramatically in October 1986 when the region experienced the largest rains for twenty-five years. Aoussert, where half the tents had been pitched on low ground, was badly flooded and its vegetable gardens destroyed. For several days, as damaged sodden tents were repitched and attempts were made to clean blankets and floor coverings caked with mud, the population lost its usual confident and cheerful spirit.

The first refugees of late 1975 pitched their tents at the first place where water was available, in the vicinity of Tindouf in southern Algeria, not far from the frontiers with Western Sahara and Mauritania. This is now the site of the reception centre for foreign visitors named after 'Martyr Hafed'. Later the refugees were reorganized into the four existing settlement areas named after towns in Western Sahara: Smara (twenty minutes' drive from Tindouf), Aoussert (half an hour's drive and only established in November 1985 after the Smara camp had become very large), El-Ayoun (one hour's drive), and Dakhla (three hours' drive). These camps and their schools have an estimated combined population of 165,000. Sites were chosen where water was drinkable and reasonably accessible.

The landscape of this region is a barren desert of sand, rocks and dunes, where the eye is continually tricked by the gleam of mirages. The terrain is largely flat with occasional hills and small gorges. There is practically no vegetation except clumps of desert moss and the odd acacia tree, which is all that can survive in the region's very inhospitable climate. In summer, temperatures can soar into the 30s (degrees Centigrade), while in winter it is bitterly cold at night. Sand storms blow throughout the year, and the fine sand makes its way everywhere—into the tents, school classrooms and hospital wards.

The camps were dispersed also for security reasons. In the early days of their establishment, to add to all the other problems, there was the real fear that the Moroccans would strike across the border. In some camps each tent has beside it a small shelter dug into the ground. These are still maintained for the Saharawi authorities clearly believe that Morocco could, in desperation, still resort to bombing the camps. The tents themselves are supported by two vertical poles joined with a crossbar. Inside, the sleeping area can be divided off with curtains. Unlike the earlier days described by Lippert, cooking is done in small mud brick huts situated next to the tents.

Administration and social organization

The four refugee settlement areas are termed *wilayat* or the provinces by the Saharawi authorities. The population in any *wilaya* originates from anywhere in Western Sahara and effectively there has been a thorough mixing of the original tribal groupings. Each *wilaya* is subdivided into six or seven *dairat* representing the main groupings of tents into which the camp areas are divided. Each *daira* comprises four *hayy* or neighbourhoods.

Every adult over the age of eighteen, with the exception of the very old and those with specific jobs such as teachers, nurses or *wilaya* agricultural workers, plays a role in the servicing of camp life through membership of one of five committees organised in each *daira*. This total participation of refugees in the smooth running of camp life is unique. The running of the camp in other refugee situations is the task of only a few. In the difficult context of enforced exile, frustration, alienation and boredom are usually common factors. But in these camps the Saharawi administrative structure ensures the involvement of all.

The five *daira* committees meet regularly. They are:

(1) The health committee: responsible for maintaining the sanitation and cleanliness of the *daira* (this is important as children defecate in the spaces between the tents and flies have become a real problem); carrying out the chlorination of the *daira* water supply; checking on and keeping a record of the health of the *daira* population, particularly the vulnerable groups (young children, the old, pre- and post-natal women and the disabled); referring the malnourished to nutrition centres and the sick to *daira* clinics.
(2) The education committee: responsible for looking after children of nursery school age (three to six) including staffing; ensuring primary school attendance; helping organize summer adult literacy campaigns.
(3) The production committee: responsible for repairing tents, working in small workshops, and working in the *daira* vegetable gardens. Workshops are now being established in every *daira*, making clothes, sandals, carpets, leather cushions, leather tobacco pouches and rush mats. Leather is obtained from the goats of the *daira* (and cured using the pods of the acacia tree) or from outside. Training programmes have

been set up by the *daira* heads, relying on the expertise of those with previous experience of these skills.

(4) The social affairs or justice committee: responsible for the provision of services for the elderly (including their referral to old people's centres) and the disabled; organizing cultural shows; registering and organizing the social activities surrounding births and marriages (and divorce); looking after official visitors; and settling minor disputes. It would appear that levels of crime are very low and that this self-regulatory local system of justice works very well. Only occasionally are cases referred to the *daira* head and thence to the *wali* (the administrator responsible for the *wilaya*). There is a jail at each *wilaya* administration centres but these are seldom used, and the vehicles marked *shurta* (police) largely provide back-up assistance in crises ranging from a medical emergency to a flood or a major storm.

(5) The distribution committee: responsible for the distribution of food rations, for which there is a ration card system, and clothes and tents to the camp population; providing food and other supplies to the health and education institutions of the *daira*; maintaining the stores.

Individuals are assigned to the different committees according to their abilities or their expressed interest. The heads of each committee at neighbourhood level represent the neighbourhood on the *daira* council (twenty in total) over which presides the *daira* head. The running of the camps is overseen by the *wilaya* council consisting of the *daira* heads, the directors of the camp schools, health institutions, food distribution and agriculture, and presided over by the *wali*. This council meets frequently and plans a weekly programme for the *wilaya*, including an assessment of where 'popular campaigns' are needed and what the targets for production in the workshops should be. The *daira* heads can then coordinate the agreed decisions with the popular committee heads at *hayy* level. This *wilaya* council is therefore the key link with the local population. The organization of 'popular campaigns' (*hamlat sha'abia*) is a vital function and enables the immediate mobilization of a labour force of whatever size is necessary, whether for constructing a school, harvesting a vegetable plot or erecting some new tents.

The position of *daira* head is crucial to the smooth and effective running of camp life, and the choice of individuals holding the respect of the community is essential. Every year in April a 'popular basic congress' is held for each *wilaya*, followed by the 'popular congress of the wilayat', in which delegates elect the *daira* heads by show of hands. The post of *wali* is a political appointment made by the Political Bureau of the Polisario Front.

Polisario and SADR structures in the refugee camp

The Saharawi Arab Democratic Republic (SADR) government structures operate within the Saharawi camps as well as in the areas of Western Sahara outside Moroccan military occupation. SADR currently has eleven ministries, for health, education, defence, commerce, information, transport and construction, economic development, supply, justice, interior and foreign affairs. These function without restriction in the area alloted for the Saharawis by the Algerian government, which has effectively temporarily ceded jurisdiction there to the SADR until a settlement of the Western Saharan conflict has been reached. This open attitude of the Algerian authorities allows the Saharawis complete control over the administration and running of the camps and is unique in international refugee situations. The Polisario Front has a strong ideology of self-reliance and has created all the structures necessary for the running of what is effectively an independent Saharawi state operating partly from exile.

Polisario has also set up 'mass organizations' for women, workers and youth in which the camp population participates. These organize social and political activities for their members and build international links with sister organizations in sympathetic countries. They hold annual congresses which elect their executives, adopt their programmes and discuss resolutions regarding the participation of their interest group in the social, economic and political development of Saharawi society. But the most important mechanism for developing a unified understanding of the priorities and tasks of Polisario's struggle is through the structure of 'cells' (each composed of eleven people) under the tutelage of the *daira* orientation department.

The leadership positions of this Saharawi state in exile are occupied by relatively young people with very different ideas about the way forward for the Saharawi people than the Saharawi tribal leaders of the colonial period. The older generation is, however, treated with great respect and is given priority in the distribution of the scarce resources of the camps. Centres for old people have been set up in each *daira* in an important gesture to the Saharawi elders who wish to spend some time with their peers a little way from the hubbub and rigours of camp life. Old people can come here and receive better food (including occasionally meat and vegetables) than is made available to the population at large. There is also a National Centre for Old People where the elderly stay for breaks of 40 days, and have the chance of communicating with colleagues now living in other camps. The old tribal leaders are known in the camps as 'national personalities'.

Two important changes that Polisario has brought about should be mentioned here because they are essential to the cohesion and lack of conflict in the camps. The first concerns the success in eliminating tribal identification. Historically, this dates back to a meeting of Saharawi tribal leaders on 12 October, 1975 at Ain BenTili at which they decided that the national struggle against the Moroccan occupation was more important than their own conflicts. The tribal history of Western Sahara is not taught in the schools of the camps.

Polisario has also ruled against any form of racial discrimination. In Mauritania to the south, relations between the black population and the Moors are often strained and forms of semi-slavery still exist. The situation of many of the black Saharawis had been similar. The report of the UN mission which visited Spanish Sahara in May 1975 refers to a trade in slaves. Refugees in the camps recall the days when slaves (*abid*) could be beaten by their master 'as a member of the family', with no recourse to the law. No evidence of discrimination against darker Saharawis can be detected in the refugee camps. They appear to play an equal role in all activities and are well represented in positions of responsibility—there are a number of black *daira* heads and mixed marriages are not infrequent.

A significant change in attitude towards the black population began when Polisario was founded in May 1973 and accelerated rapidly with the far reaching changes of 1975–6. The loss of the camel herds meant that the blacks (who looked after the herds) lost their distinctive occupation. Their involvement in Polisario's forces added strongly to the new sense of equality and Polisario itself launched a campaign to outlaw the old racialism in favour of the unity needed for the independence struggle. The social changes that have been made in these two areas are major achievements.

The Saharawi Red Crescent

The Saharawis Red Crescent began work in 1975 directing humanitarian aid to the Saharawi people. In November 1976 it became the formal channel for all external assistance to the Saharawis people. The Saharawi Red Crescent has observer status with the League of Red Cross Societies (it cannot be a full member as the SADR is not yet a member of the United Nations) and is also recognized by the International Committee of the Red Cross as the official body which it contacts over issues concerning the rights and treatment of Moroccan prisoners of war.

The Saharawi Red Crescent operates closely with the Algerian Red Crescent which, with Algerian government backing, finances the transport of supplies from external ports to Algiers and thence to the camps and provides much of the grain which forms the basis of the camp population's diet. Other major governmental donors are Austria and Sweden. The EEC gives milk powder, butteroil, flour, sugar and dried fish, but in quantities that can hardly be seen as generous given the milk lakes and butter mountains of Europe and the continuing shortages in the camps. Since 1985 the Saharawi Red Crescent has been receiving assistance from a UN agency, the World Food Programme, to provide food aid to children and pregnant women.

The reaction of the Office of the United Nations High Commissioner for

Refugees (UNHCR), the UN agency with special responsibility for refugees, to the plight of the Saharawis in the camps of Algeria is worth examining as it illustrates how political issues have at times interfered with the provision of humanitarian aid to the refugees.

In the period 1975 to 1980 the UNHCR proved vulnerable to Moroccan pressure and gave the Saharawi refugees only limited assistance from a special emergency fund under the personal direction of the high commissioner, independent of the UNHCR's normal eligibility process. It was not until the Saharawis began to emerge from diplomatic isolation in 1980 (the year the SADR was recognized by more than half the OAU states) that the high commissioner felt able to allocate funds from the UNHCR General Fund. The UNHCR programme then grew steadily from $1 million in 1980 to $3.5 million in 1984, but the allocations for 1985 and 1986 have been held at the 1984 level without any increase, to avoid objections from Morocco.

Many European voluntary agencies also support the work of the Saharawi Red Crescent. NOVIB (The Netherlands) and Radda Barnen (Sweden) have been involved for many years and provide significant assistance. Most approaches to these non-governmental organizations have been for contributions of the always vulnerable basic essentials of the camps. In recent years, though, more and more 'development' projects are being presented for funding. War on Want (UK) has in the last few years built up a substantial programme of support, concentrating particularly on the development of the vegetable gardens.

Support Committees, made up of active, sympathetic individuals, have also raised significant contributions towards the needs of the refugees as well as carrying out information work on the plight of the Saharawis and their political rights. Such committees exist in West Germany, France, Spain, Portugal, Austria, Yugoslavia, Switzerland, Britain, The Netherlands, the United States, Belgium, Denmark, the Canary Islands, Sweden and Greece.

Providing the essentials—food and water, shelter, clothing and fuel

Apart from the still limited vegetable production in the camps, all food is provided by external donors. A large part of the basic grain ration (wheat, flour and rice) is now provided by Algeria. For other foodstuffs and in particular for the supplementary foods distributed to vulnerable groups in the nutrition centres and old peoples centres, the camp population must depend largely on the voluntary agencies. Yet there are continuing shortfalls and the Saharawi Red Crescent must make continued appeals for food aid, particularly oil, milk and sugar.

All the camps have access to water, either by using a deep borehole or by pumping from shallow wells. Water supplies are chlorinated (a task carried out by the *daira* health committee). Only Smara camp has serious salinity problems, and here water is brought into the different *dairat* by tanker and stored in reservoirs. But as water is limited, care must be taken when bathing or washing clothes.

Shelter is a major problem in the camps. All accommodation is in tents, although schools and clinics are built with clay bricks. The tents made in the traditional way from animal hair last longest, but with few animals to supply the raw materials, only a handful of these now remain. Almost all the tents are now of canvas which rots in the heat and tears in the high winds. Although tears are continually repaired, the likelihood of further tearing is increased once a tent is torn. Few tents last more than three years; those made up on site from material sent by donors do not even last this long. Effectively the whole living accommodation of the camp has to be continually replaced. The Saharawi Red Crescent estimates that tents need replacing at a rate of 4,000 per year. Donor contributions to shelter are lagging and Red Crescent officials are concerned at the accompanying decline in the standard of shelter which in this severe climate is so central to the basic living conditions of the population.

The clothing needs of the camp population are partly met by donors giving ready-made clothes. But an increasing proportion of the needs are met by the sewing workshops of the Women's School and in the *dairat*, which produce the colourful dresses the Saharawi women can now be seen wearing. Fuel for cooking and lighting is provided by gas cylinders brought in by lorry from outside. This is clearly extremely expensive but with the complete absence of firewood there is little alternative. The Saharawis are now investigating the possibility of using solar cookers. In spite of the cold winters, heating inside the tents is unheard of.

The Saharawi health services

The health status of the Saharawi refugees is now a long way from the devastating famine and epidemics of that terrible first year. Every effort is now being made to maintain the good health of the population in this difficult and unhealthy environment.

The cold winter creates most health problems, particularly bronchitis and respiratory infections, with the old suffering from rheumatism and bronchial pneumonia. In the summer, children are at risk from diarrhoea, often resulting from intestinal infestations. Flies, which can reach plague-like proportions at certain times of the year, are a major health hazard for spreading disease. With sand often blowing around in high winds, eye infections are always a problem. Following a strict policy of isolation, TB, once rife, has now been almost eradicated.

The main thrust of the Saharawi ministry of health's policy is towards prevention. The *daira* health committees play the vital role here—ensuring camp cleanliness, burning rubbish, maintaining hygiene of the latrine area (situated outside the camps behind a raised sand ridge at least one hundred metres from the nearest tents), teaching the need to boil drinking water for young children and making referrals of the sick and malnourished. The vaccination programme that has been underway for several years now achieves 100 per cent coverage and thus there have been no epidemics since 1978.

'Nutrition centres' have been set up in each *wilaya* and have been highly effective in keeping down the infant mortality rate. They are, however, very busy and full places. On my first visit to the centre at Smara, there were 434 people there (65 per cent children). Malnutrition in these well ordered camps is caused largely by the irregularities and shortfalls in the food supply. The high attendance at the nutrition centres indicates the continuing problems of ensuring that even the basic food needs are met. Malnourished children and anaemic women are referred to these centres by a member of the local health committee or by a health worker. At the centres a supplementary diet is provided (including fresh vegetables from the local gardens) until (in the case of childen) their 'weight to height ratio' is back to normal. Mothers are given basic advice on nutrition and on the prevention of diarrhoea in children. Health education posters cover the walls of various rooms.

Although the centres cater mainly for new born babies, women stay there with their babies for forty days after birth. This is the traditional Islamic period in which the mother is confined to the home. It is also the most vulnerable period for a child, so the current Saharawi practice in the camps represents an interesting adaptation of past customs. Older brothers and sisters of the newborn also stay in the centres and nursery activities— singing, drumming, games—are organized for them.

Pregnant women as a vulnerable group are given special attention. Given the Saharawi policy of encouraging a high birth rate (an important political and social card in the struggle for and future strength of an independent SADR), no contraception is provided for the camp population and pregnant women form a large and important group. They are referred by the health committees to the hospitals for regular pre-natal check-ups. It is only in the last year or so that the ministry of health has been able to offer a hospital delivery for all; the rudimentary condition of the tents is considered too hazardous to allow the risk of a home birth developing complications when the Land Rovers used for emergency trips to hospital are in critically short supply.

The curative health service is highly developed. It was clearly planned to cope with morbidity levels which were once significantly higher than those that now prevail. Many of the current institutions—clinics and hospitals— are now utilized well below capacity. The basic structure of the service is pyramidal. Each *daira* has a dispensary staffed by an 'auxiliary doctor' (trained in the central hospitals) who prescribes from a kit of twenty or so priority drugs, and is assisted by twelve locally trained nurses. These dispensaries refer to regional hospitals of which there is one in each *wilaya*.

The more developed of the hospitals have the basic essential equipment and have departments for general medicine, paediatrics, gynaecology, obstetrics, X-Ray, dentistry, as well as a laboratory and pharmacy.

There are three 'national hospitals' of around 150 beds each, the general hospital, the paediatric hospital and the maternity hospital, which act as the teaching hospitals. The SADR has only nine doctors (trained abroad in Algeria, Cuba and until 1983 Libya) who work in these hospitals in the mornings and in the regional hospitals in the afternoons. A major training programme for health workers has been underway since 1977 and has been graduating around thirty-three nurses on average every year, as well as seven 'auxiliary doctors' per year who have basic ability to diagnose and prescribe.

All the buildings of the health institutions have been constructed by 'popular campaigns' of the local people. With the exception of one nutrition centre which is still housed in tents, all are of mud brick construction with zinc roofs. But sand storms still create major problems. On a windy day, thin ripples of sand appear on the floors of the wards in a matter of hours. Funds are needed for the basic maintenance of the hospital buildings—the thick whitewash is flaking off the walls everywhere and the roofs need better sealing to keep the sand out. Supplies of basic drugs sometimes run low. There has been a renewal of interest in the traditional Saharawi use of minerals and plants from the desert as medicaments. Polisario fighters bring these back from the liberated areas and they have been used in the dispensaries when drugs run short.

The central role of education

If there is one aspect of life in the Saharawi camps that stands out above all others it is the emphasis given to education. The woman director of the Dakhla regional school expressed the spirit of it when she told me: 'our revolution is one big school'. In colonial times education was confined to a small elite and the skilled jobs needed for the extraction of Spanish Sahara's economic wealth were in the hands of foreign technicians. The Saharawi authorities are now determined to reverse past humiliations and to create their own educated cadres to staff a future SADR.

Everyone in the camps, except the very old and very young, seems to be either studying or imparting newly acquired skills and knowledge to others. Education starts at the age of three when the children go to nursery school. These exist in each *daira* but because of the lack of materials and space they operate on morning and afternoon shifts. They are joyful places where visitors are greeted with songs, the rhythms bashed out by the teacher on an old tin can.

At the age of six the young Saharawi moves on to attend a regional school which, depending on the school, provides the first four or five grades of primary education (of a total of six). These are large institutions, of which there are now two in each *wilaya*, each with several hundred children. But sadly they have to cope with the barest minimum of materials. There are only enough course books for the teachers, and there is a great shortage of paper. The curricula for the schools (primary and secondary) have been developed by a National Curriculum Committee and are designed to reflect the social, cultural and political situation of the Saharawi people.

Teaching is initially in Arabic, Spanish is introduced at grade three and after grade five used for teaching science subjects. One aspect of the Saharawi education system is the encouragement of student 'magazines'. These are large sheets of cardboard on which students' essays, poems and drawings are carefully inscribed by hand, and which can be seen hanging on the walls and corridors of all the educational establishments. There are crèches in the schools for the babies of women teachers, but toys are desperately lacking. Two nurses work full time in the school clinic supervising the use of medicines prescribed by the regional hospital. The schools are now involved in exchange schemes with children from European countries (particularly Italy and France). These are important for children living in such isolation in order to broaden their understanding, children who have for example great difficulty in visualizing a sea or a river.

Education beyond the grades offered by regional schools takes place at boarding schools outside the main camps. The emphasis on boarding, particularly in a refugee camp context, was at first surprising. The reason given for this was that a boarding school provides a more total educational environment and allows the quicker assimilation of new ideas and knowledge. This may well be true where the older generation is largely uneducated. The authorities may also want to create a certain distance between children and parents so that children, returning during the summer vacation, can more effectively teach in the adult literacy campaigns.

At the two National Schools (the '12th October' and '9th June') there is teaching of grades five and six primary, and the initial three grades of secondary level for which a curriculum has been developed. English is introduced (as the third language) at grade seven. These schools are large, with 4,000 and 2,000 students respectively, and discipline appears strict. That this has not stunted the imaginative and creative abilities of the students is obvious in the highly talented work in drawing, painting, researching Saharawi traditional stories and customs and the making of little artefacts which is displayed in various exhibitions round the camps. As a mirror image of the participatory style of the camp administration, the students in these schools play a role in the school administration. They are organized into three committees with responsibility for supervising health and hygiene, supervising maintenance, and organizing cultural activities.

Generally, the education system in the camps operates at a very high standard and has been successful in engendering a strong commitment to learning. As at the other schools, textbooks are in short supply, as are the teaching materials and visual aids (maps, posters) that other schools take for granted. The students have a brightness and maturity that would be rare elsewhere. Students reaching the end of their studies in the camps must choose from three options—enrolling at the Vocational Training School, joining the Saharawi People's Liberation Army or continuing their education in another country. A senior UN official in Algiers recently commented that Saharawi students who go on to Algerian secondary schools do extremely well.

The El-Ouali Mustapha Sayed Vocational Training School sited next to the 12th October School is a relatively recent addition (1984) to the growing list of Saharawi institutions. Its students have completed grade seven and have an assigned place (in *wilaya* administration as secretarial assistants to SADR embassies, army mechanics, and so on, to which they will go after completing their particular technical course. There are two streams at the school—administration (typing, accountancy and law) divided into classes for men and women and technology (electricity, mechanics, vehicle bodywork repairs and carpentry). Other vocational training (school teachers, kindergarten teachers, nurses, craft workers) is done at the Women's School described below.

The annual literacy campaign is one of the Saharawis' major successes. Special literacy classes are organized on a permanent basis at *daira* level for women in the later stages of pregnancy when they are relieved of their general responsibilities. But every year the ministry of education organizes a more concerted literacy campaign for the whole adult population of the camps from the end of July to the beginning of September. Secondary school students, and those taking higher education courses abroad return to the *wilayat* and are available to teach, at a time when the great heat precludes many other activities. The adult education programme is now divided into six levels. Classes of twenty take place in the tents using the primary syllabus adapted for adult use. It would seem that the adult population has accepted being taught by their sons and daughters. As one sixteen-year-old put it; 'everyone understands why they have no education; they sit quietly and want to learn.' The end of the yearly literacy campaign is marked by a Festival of Youth with celebrations, competitions, poetry recitals, cultural shows, theatre and sport.

Food production in the camps

Many of the Saharawi camel herds were lost during the period of the refugee exodus; others were given voluntarily into the SADR government's care by refugees who could not maintain their herds in exile. Now there are said to be between 200 and 400 herds 'owned' by the SADR government and looked after by government 'employees' who receive clothes and food. The herds of camels graze in the areas of Western Sahara outside the walls erected by the Moroccan occupation forces. Some of the milk is given to the hospitals and nutrition centres of the camps, and the children of the herders go to the camp schools. There are also camel herds attached to and 'managed' directly by the *wilayat* and schools, which have rights to the meat whenever animals are slaughtered.

Of more significance, in terms of providing meat (and milk) to the camp population, are the herds of goats and to a much lesser extent of sheep which now surround all the camps. There is one herd per *hayy* (the sub-division of the *daira*) and after dramatic increases in numbers over recent years the herds are now sizeable at 300–400 head each. The pens are located a short distance from the camps. Each owner feeds his goats on whatever is available—mainly the refuse from the camp, especially card-board torn into strips. Given the finite limits of camp refuse and the absence of pastures, the current levels are likely to be the largest practicable herd sizes. A few poultry are housed in clay coops and seem to be surviving well in spite of the harsh conditions. The ministry of economic development is also experimenting with cows (fed from the waste of the vegetable farms) and with a poultry project.

Vegetable production in the camps began in 1977, but the first phase of activity did not prove to be particularly successful. By 1983, however, pumps had been installed, much of the ground preparation work had been carried out and some trained Saharawi agronomists had returned from courses abroad. The programme is now extremely successful and yields comparable to those of schemes in less hostile environments are being obtained. In an area of the desert which has probably not been farmed in a thousand years (if ever) and where now practically nothing grows, the Saharawis have created oases of green. The effect on any visitor to the earliest gardens at 'Smara II' is always one of astonishment and admiration. Here, surrounded by the rock and sand of the Sahara is a small micro-environment of verdure, where fig trees and pomegranates grow among palm trees and acacia which have even attracted a population of noisy small birds.

Agriculture has now been defined (by Polisario's general congress of December 1985) as the first priority in the field of economic development, with workshop production the second. Clearly, these priorities relate to the possibilities for the population in exile. But the development of agriculture will also be a priority for an independent Western Sahara. In colonial times, there was little agriculture and the current development in the camps draws on the experience of a tiny minority of the population. But the conditions for agriculture in Western Sahara are considerably more propitious than those that exist in the Tindouf area of Algeria, and thus it makes every sense for the Saharawis to be developing cadres with relevant skills and experience.

By October 1986, there were 44.5 hectares under cultivation. The long-term plan is to make the camps self-sufficient in vegetables. A three-year plan to extend cultivation to 150 hectares has now been developed, supported with financial and technical help coordinated by the British voluntary agency, War on Want. The initial objective is to meet the needs of nutritionally vulnerable groups and all produce is currently directed to the nutrition centres, hospitals and old people's centres. The needs of the general population are not yet being met. The bulk of the area under cultivation is in gardens organized at *wilaya* level, with a permanent workforce under the direction of a trained agronomist. Other smaller gardens have more recently been developed under the responsibility of the *daira* committees, and worked by the women from the production committee of the *daira*. Popular campaigns help with the labour intensive activities—building walls, preparing the land, weeding and harvesting the crop.

Vegetable production in these Saharan conditions faces a number of problems. The extremes of temperature mean that only melon production is possible in the hottest summer months. Throughout the year, high winds create serious difficulties. Violent sand storms are common and can easily flatten the crops as well as critically increasing evaporation rates from the leaves. Each of the gardens is therefore surrounded by mud brick walls, and within the gardens wind breaks of cane or woven grass have been erected. This grass, *sbut*, is brought from areas many miles distant inside Western Sahara. This operation is expensive and investigations are now being made into alternative windbreak material. On some farms, shifting sands pile up against protective walls and efforts continually have to be made to avert this threat.

A further major difficulty is the salinity of the soil, and harmful salts must continuously be leached out with large quantities of irrigation water. In some of the sites, the existing soil must either be replaced or mixed with less saline earth brought in from nearby areas. The most successful vegetables are those most tolerant of saline conditions: carrots, beetroot, turnip, onions and white radishes.

Surprisingly for the middle of the Sahara, the availability of water has not yet proved to be a problem. In the sites currently cultivated, there are good supplies of underground water, although as the area under cultivation expands it will become necessary to tap deeper underground water sources. Again, salinity causes difficulties, some sites have been abandoned because of very high salt content (12 October School) and at others water from some wells must be mixed with that from other sources to dilute the salt level (El-Ayoun). On the larger *wilaya* farms diesel pumps are being used, while the smaller gardens at *daira* level use either the traditional *shadouf* (with a long weighted arm) or hand pumps.

Pests have yet to prove a major problem, but this situation is likely to change. Until recently, the isolation of these farms from other agricultural areas has provided effective protection, but some pests are now establishing themselves. In 1985 and 1986, the arrival of locusts caused considerable alarm. Fortunately, they arrived in the summer months when there were few crops growing and damage was limited. The refugees had no insecticides with which to tackle the problem and attempts to smoke them away proved largely ineffectual.

Fertilization of the soil has to date been entirely by use of animal manure collected from the goat pens. With further expansion, artificial fertilizer will have to be imported. It is ironic that fertility should prove a constraint with some of the world's largest deposits of phosphates tantalizingly out of reach in the refugees' own homeland.

Women in Saharawi development

Women dominate numerically in the population of the camps where they comprise an estimated 80 per cent of the adult population, as many of the men are fighting with Polisario inside Western Sahara. Women, although many receive basic military training, do not serve at the battlefront. During the colonial period Saharawi women had been denied even the slim educational opportunities available to the men and held no positions of public responsibility. Now a concerted attempt is being made to redress this, both through SADR's education policy and through the policy of involving all refugees in the five *daira* committees.

Inevitably, given that relatively few women yet have higher educational qualifications, men occupy most of the top positions. In 1974 there were only four Saharawi girls in the secondary schools of Spanish Sahara, and the traditional political structures were exclusively male. Now, however, there are two women headmistresses and three women in Polisario's Political Bureau. At the popular congress of December 1985 a woman was elected for the first time to the position of *wali* and thus effectively responsible for the welfare of a quarter of the refugee population.

Women are much better represented at the middle professional levels. They form the majority of teaching and health staff in the camps. Furthermore the authorities take seriously measures necessary to enable women's participation in social and political activities. Crèches are provided in all schools and hospitals, and the Women's School provides education and other facilities on site for the children of the women attending.

The Women's School ('27th February') opened in 1978. It is a boarding school sited a little way from Smara camp, but the residential area of tents around the main school buildings itself resembles a small refugee camp. The women live here with their smaller children and sometimes older relatives. Their husbands visit when on leave from the front. In late 1986, over 1,000 women were attending the school. Students are selected by the *daira* committees who consider the needs of the *daira* for particular skills. The school gives courses in nursing, sewing, leather work and carpet making. On completion of their courses, most women will return to their original *dairat*.

Polisario has introduced many progressive reforms to protect women's rights. One important example concerns marriage law. Traditionally marriages were arranged entirely between the couple's parents. Now the couple themselves must agree to the marriage, and the *daira* social affairs committee examines each case to ensure the couple marrying understand their obligations. The parents of the bride still formally have to agree, but it is estimated that most would now automatically respect the woman's right to decide for herself; only a minority would expect to have the right to veto her choice. The SADR has also fixed minimum ages for marriage; sixteen for women, eighteen for men. Dowries have disappeared. The *wilaya* administration provides a tent and essential household items for the newly married couple.

The changes in women's position cannot be underestimated. Women are now free to participate in their own mass organization, to discuss matters in the orientation sessions, to acquire an education, to hold administrative and political positions. These changes were often not easy to achieve. As one woman put it: 'In the beginning, women didn't know anything; they were illiterate and never took work outside the house. We had to find some with skills to teach others. Then they discovered for themselves that women can do anything. Women are now respected.' Perceptions of women's role in the division of labour have changed radically. To give one example, sewing was traditionally a man's job, but now hundreds of women have learnt the skill. Some gender division of labour is still encouraged: at the Vocational Training School, for example, men and women learn different administrative tasks. And as with other revolutions, the question must be asked—how are women's gains protected once the struggle for national liberation has been won and a different dynamic takes over?

Lessons and prospects

In recent years we have been bombarded with pictures of starvation, disease and chaos in the camps of refugees and displaced people in Sudan, Eritrea and Ethiopia. A decade ago the Saharawi camps were in a similar plight themselves, now they are stable, ordered communities with a strong sense of purpose. The changes have been far-reaching and impressive. How were the Saharawis able to achieve them?

The fate of long-term refugee camps is dependent on a number of factors relating both to their external situation, over which the refugee population has little control, and to the internal social and political dynamic of the refugee community. Of the external factors, three are most crucial. The first is the attitude of the host government towards the refugee population. This can vary between friendship to open hostility; it can support the development of a community or stifle it. The two key issues here are the host government's attitude to the delivery of essential material supplies (food, medicine, shelter) and the degree to which it allows refugee-based organizations/political groupings to control the essential services (from health care and education, to food distribution, to the maintenance of 'law and order'). In both cases, the Algerian government has played a facilitative role towards the Saharawis refugees. The Algerians have made major contributions to ensuring the delivery of outside supplies (and indeed have paid the transport bills to the remote camps). They have also given the Saharawis complete organizational and political freedom within the areas allocated to them. The Saharawi refugees therefore have a more secure base for their development than most.

A second external factor determining the development of refugee camps is the economic relationship that develops between the camp population and the surrounding population. Refugees seldom arrive as the homogeneous destitute mass that they are so often portrayed as in the Western media. They arrive with many of the disparities of wealth of their original society. Those with some capital develop trade with the local population and markets appear in the camps; those without sell their labour on nearby farms and construction sites. The refugees begin to integrate economically with their surroundings and sooner or later may be able to leave the camps for jobs and accommodation elsewhere. This will profoundly affect the development of the camps as social units. In the Saharawi case there has been no such local population with whom economic interaction might take place—the nearest population is the Algerian military, albeit with a civilian population to service it, at Tindouf, a restricted zone. Polisario leaders do not have to fear, as do many of the political leaders of populations which include a large refugee element, that the refugees will be seduced by economic opportunities away from the determination to return to their homeland. The Saharawi refugees have, for better or worse, been able to develop along independent lines, free from external economic influence but also dependent on external largesse and the vulnerability that this entails. No market economy has developed in the camps. Indeed, money appears to play an insignificant role—limited to buying cigarettes, soap, needles and thread.

The third consideration is where the refugees stand in terms of the political and military conflict which led to their flight in the first place. How identified are they with a political liberation front or armed opposition, and if so, do they enjoy sufficient diplomatic or even military support to deter aggression? This can be a critical factor: the Palestinian camps for example have always existed within a climate of pressure and tension and frequently have been the target for military attack. The Saharawi refugees have experienced this fear, as the air raid tunnels beside the tents of Smara camp testify only too clearly. But Polisario's military operation is kept separate and distinct from the civilian population of the camps. A cross-border operation against the camps by Morocco has never taken place and is, at least in the immediate future, unlikely.

The effect of the above three factors is thus to leave the Saharawis isolated but relatively secure. To appreciate the transformation of the Saharawi refugee community from the despair and destruction of 1975 to the hope and vitality of today, we must now examine its internal dynamic. Six aspects of this can be highlighted which together explain the success of the Saharawi community in exile.

(1) The Saharawi leadership consciously developed a political ideology emphasizing political unity and a new social order. This has been promoted through the structure of orientation cells which have encouraged debate at the base while the main agenda is set from above. The dangerous contradictions of the old society, between the old tribal groupings, between the hierarchies within these tribes, between owners and slaves, between rich and poor, between men and women, between a younger generation thirsting for change and an older generation more set in its ways, have been largely ruled out through the evocation of a greater good.

Certainly, to the visitor to the camps, these tensions are not readily visible. Reminders of this old order are now kept out of sight—tribal names are no longer used and the term *abd* (slave) is now only a historical reference. Instead, there is a new vocabulary in which the names of Saharawi martyrs and heroes and the dates of the milestones of the 'Saharawi Revolution' are given to the institutions of camp life. Common experiences are now stressed. The bombing of the interim camps within Western Sahara in 1975–6 and the quest for peace and return to the homeland are the two most popular themes of the paintings that now abound in the camps.

(2) The links with a common historical and cultural past are stressed. This nationalism, however, takes a new form from that of the colonial era. The old are respected, are given special attention and are given priority in the distribution of scarce resources. But it is the younger generation who spearhead this new nationalism. Pre-colonial songs, proverbs, dances and music are being researched, and those which emphasise cooperation are promoted. Traditional plants and minerals are used as medicines when drug supplies run low. Modern practice is adapted from traditional custom—women recuperate for forty days after delivery, but in the nutrition centres. Marriage customs are now very different, although elements of the old are still retained. The names of the camps and *dairas* themselves are taken from the towns and villages of Western Sahara. The best features of the old society are being developed while oppressive aspects are broken down.

(3) There is a total orientation to a future in which Saharawis are no longer refugees but citizens in their own land. The emphasis is on creating a population with the education and skills needed both to wage the political struggle for an independent SADR and to run the administrative and economic structures once independence is gained. It is this emphasis on self-reliance that provides the enormous motivation found in the schools and training centres.

(4) The refugee community itself participates at all levels, whether in camp administration, in running the camp services and institutions, in production, in ensuring local justice, or in political organizations. Everyone feels involved by both contributing and sharing the rewards;

no one is idle. The camps may be dependent on external supplies, but there is none of the apathy that accompanies such dependence in other situations. Women are given every encouragement to participate and, depending on ability, to take high office.

(5) There is a stress on the creation of a caring society in which priority is given to the needs of the most vulnerable within the camp population—young children, pregnant and post-natal women, the old and the disabled. Structures have been created to ensure that social or health problems are identified and addressed at an early stage, and special centres have been created to ensure the well being of vulnerable groups.

(6) Full use is made of existing skills among the community. In a population desperately short of basic skills, those who have relevant experience are in a key position to teach others. Former farmers play a vital role in the development of the vegetable gardens, and those with craft skills have formed the basis of the workshop production in the camps.

The Saharawi efforts to develop their society while in its enforced exile deserve international support. The health and well being of the Saharawi refugees is dependent on the continued interest of the international community. Sufficient supply in the vital areas of shelter and a nutritional range of foods is only assured after yearly negotiations with donor partners, some of whom still regard the issue of humanitarian aid to the Saharawis as politically sensitive. From one of the most tragic refugee problems of this half century a new society is being forged, but a society which cannot afford to be forgotten.

9 Women in the Western Sahara

BIANCAMARIA SCARCIA AMORETTI

In order to analyse the importance of the Saharawi woman in relation to the problem of refugees and war, it is first necessary to assess the role played by the women within their society and thus to ascertain the extent to which the survival and evolution of that society depends on them. Second, it is necessary to gauge the extent to which the situation of war and exile has pressed women into taking part in public life and further to compare current and traditional role expectations. This analysis must therefore be at once historical, anthropological and political.

In the case of the Saharawis, one could maintain that it is somewhat constraining if not strictly inaccurate to refer to them as 'refugees' as they are formally established as a state and are internationally recognized as such.[1] Furthermore, they are actively working to alter their social structures to cope with gradual modernization but without giving up their unique cultural identity. Nevertheless, the current status of the Saharawis is objectively that of 'refugees' for whom war is a grim fact of everyday life. Because of this, and despite the exceptional nature of the Saharawi political experiment and social aspirations, my particular topic falls squarely into the much wider debate regarding refugees and war.

It is not easy to draw a sufficiently clear picture of the Saharawi woman prior to the colonial period to explain the decisive influence she has had in altering Saharawi society as a whole.[2] To begin with, not only do a large number of the studies on the Saharawis date from the colonial period, but the material that is available is fragmentary. Of this region of Africa, as F. De la Chapelle states:[3]

Reporters and geographers have all dedicated a few pages; they purred with contentment over the trade routes and markets; the movements of the tribes and the preachings of the odd fanatical reformer attracted their attention; they celebrated the victories won by the dynastic armies over these nomads; they went into raptures over the wonders they saw, the plunderer's spoils and goods unloaded from the caravans. The entire north of Africa is peopled with these pious legends hailing the virtues of 'Sequia-al-Hamra', the distant Sahara river, which thus becomes the 'land of the holy'.

These sorts of comments hardly provide a reliable basis upon which to reconstruct the history of a people and a region. Even when the object of the research is defined in more detail and reference is made to the various tribal groups[4] united to form what is described today as the 'Saharawi people', the approach is too eurocentric for the results to be of use without some kind of further scrutiny.

So thus, despite the existence of numerous accounts of specific aspects of the tribes and their 'country',[5] an overall picture of the society is lacking, as is one clarifying the status of the women within that society. Where indeed there are observations that might lead us to some interesting insights into the relationships between women, importance of feelings, and so on, these tend to reflect stereotypes of feminine coquetry, jealousy or envy for a rival's dress, and the like. Even when we do encounter remarks on more substantive issues, such as those that indicate the possible existence in some groups of an ancient matriarchy, traces of which remain in a matrilineal structure,[6] or a freedom of initiative in marriage and divorce,[7] we find ourselves then having to reckon with a much more widespread literature which presents the Saharawi social structure as that of an ordinary patriarchal and hierarchical society.[8]

Yet in the same texts, one can readily find reference to the fact that the so-called Moors, although Muslims, Malikite and deeply imbued with Sufism, keep alive the ancestral Berber customs relating to marriage and conjugal life. Thus the society can be described as matriarchal and monogamous[9] and, disregarding the contradictions, we can speak of the 'family head' in terms which are in no way ambiguous.[10] This kind of inaccuracy or misinformation can also be found in other works: for example, in a list of those persons who are entitled to a particular form of respect women of course do not appear, not even when they come from prominent families.[11]

Naturally, this creates a certain mistrust of the information that the ethnologists and anthropologists have accumulated, although this mistrust is not a result, as one might think, of the fact that no mention is found of a well defined Saharawi entity but merely of this or that tribe. That the Saharawis were actually separated into tribes is well known and again such a recent phenomenon as not to create ideological or methodological problems. If it is therefore legitimate to identify the characteristics of the various groups (those characteristics in particular that enable the group to be distinguished from the others, its members to recognize one another as belonging to the same group and which, in all likelihood, are today part of the cultural heritage to which the Saharawis lay claim, in national terms, as their own) one cannot, however, always succeed in demarcating between a correct hisorical–anthropological analysis and a reconstruction of the past that might serve as a part of some political plan[12] or be conditioned by a certain political climate as in the case of the literature from the colonial period. Similarly, even if they do contain valuable information, the accounts of travellers, be they Western or Muslim, suffer the inevitable effects of the cultural prejudices of their time and of their culture. Whereas Ibn Battuta[13] remarks on the freedom of the Moorish women, others refer to their ferocity and fanaticism.[14] Of course, the plausible decoding of a stereotype is possible; if at the end of the eighteenth century the savage was still something midway between animal and man, by the nineteenth century the romantic myth of the nobility of those who have remained in contact with nature without being contaminated by industrial civilization had had its effect.[15] However, one must move ahead to the present day in order to find the Saharawis distinguished as a separate society because of the particular triangular inter-tribal structure (warriors, sages, and holy men, craftsmen and tributaries) which distinguishes them from other nomadic groups in the Sahara, and because of their social and cultural identity which is the 'fruit of a common history' of combat or alliances for the control and use of the means of production (water, pastures, trade routes, and so on).[16] With this kind of outlook one can attempt to accumulate that information, on which the sources do not disagree, regarding the subject of the 'foremothers' of the Saharawi women of today. This information, although certainly neither systematic nor exhaustive, does give an indication of the situation from which the Saharawi women set out in the process of regaining and reconstructing their historical identity. Or, if one prefers, it may represent the final link in a long chain of events which, although connected to the past, constitutes—by direct acknowledgement of those involved—the foundation on which the present is built.

Two factors appear clear: that the Saharawi woman has always run the tent, i.e. the home, and that she has always been the privileged trustee of a specific cultural tradition. Let us take a closer look at these. Running the tent in the rigorous environmental conditions of the Sahara implies assumption of the duty of guaranteeing the family's livelihood,[17] in that this is not only a matter of technical skill in erecting and dismantling the tent/ house, of utilizing the materials necessary for its upkeep and of fitting it out with the essential furniture, but also of planning how the resources, food and otherwise, should be put to use. This is also true of that part of Saharawi society which is sedentary or which has been settled for some time. Thus the female assumes a socio-economic role which is integrated into the male activity of exploitation and seeking out of resources. The most anomalous case serves as both confirmation and example of this. Especially within the framework of craft activity, in particular in that of blacksmithing, the wife is employed as part of the husband's technical labour,[18] and as such thus becomes together with him, holder of a title which awards them a well defined position within the tribal system.

To the Westerner, social relations assume the participation of women[19] whereas, in the vast majority of Muslim societies, their segregation is strictly enforced with the exception, naturally, of farming societies where the women represent an important part of the work force. Because this is not the case in the Saharawi society, the female involvement in social life acquires a special importance. It is especially notable in that this is a custom common throughout almost the entire area populated by Saharawi groups, and that the difference between the Arab and the Berber elements does not appear significant in this regard. It would suggest that here we have a distinct unitary trait belonging to that 'common history' mentioned earlier. The position of women, in that it is a factor common to all Saharawi societies, demonstrates their cultural unity and also functions as an element of social cohesion as was evidenced on the occasion of the mass exodus after the Moroccan occupation in 1975. This provides a position from which they may begin to assert themselves both externally and internally as a 'people' in modern terms.

Another major unifying characteristic is cultural. Most of the information available confirms that, before the advent of colonialism, more often than not it was the women rather than the men who passed on the culture from generation to generation.[20] Because 'culture' is not immediately productive, one might consider this a secondary function, but in the case of the Saharawis where personal prestige has a value even on the socio-economic level, the importance of culture ought not to be underestimated.[21] Culture not only gives identity to the group but also keeps alive the 'specificity' of the group in the first place and that of being Arabophone Muslim in the second. In practice, culture maintains that *asabiya* (solidarity) which according to Ibn Khaldun upholds the force and cohesion of each entity which wishes to be distinct from the others[22] and which is particularly essential among nomadic groups. On the other hand, yet further proof is provided by the fact that it is often the women, both traditionally and in the present day, who pass on the folk poetry,[23] which in a Bedouin society constitutes historical record since it is composed of comment on the major aspects of day-to-day life of the group. The importance of its composition on the political level and in the process of national identity should not be underestimated.[24] All this appears far more significant in explaining and evaluating the present-day political role of the Saharawi women than does their probable lack of institutional participation in the governing of the tribe in the past or present.[25]

Let us now look at the current situation which we have mentioned on several occasions but which merits more specific individual analysis. It is generally accepted that national movements accelerate the mechanisms of women's emancipation. The need for cadres necessitates their involvement in public activity; and further, the agreement of the masses on the ideals proposed by the movement depends largely on the women. Also not to be discounted or undervalued is the work performed by the women to ensure the efficient running of civil society during a period when the men are engaged in war activities.

So far, the Saharawi case fits into a familiar typology. The divergence, however, lies in the conscious application by Saharawi women of traditional behaviour which is then reapplied in the new socio-political context.[26] As in the past, before colonialism, which is considered an unpleasant episode the residual traces of which must be removed before the people can return to their own authentic models of life, the tent was run by women who assumed the responsibility for guaranteeing survival of both the family nucleus and the larger group. Today the refugee camps are managed in much the same way. The culture which served to strengthen their capacity to endure trying conditions again provides the women with sustenance. In addition to providing the necessary cohesion, she performs another function which does not however preclude the former; this is that of preparing for a different, better future but one which does not reject its own individuality. The Bedouin tradition, interrupted by colonialism for a good part of the Saharawi people, is thus re-established as a necessary factor of resistance and as a means by which to measure how much and in which way change is desired. This tradition is retrieved through the memory of those women who continue to carry out their task of transmitting culture. In this way, a national cohesion is created which seems to have few parallels in the current historical milieu where the acquisition of national identity is normally paid for with a wholesale rejection of the past, or begins with a process of deculturation so trenchant it is difficult to reverse.[27]

In effect then, it is the duty of the Saharawi women to turn the 'refugee' situation into an experience which will help pave the way for the introduction of an efficient, effective and modern way of life. In the same way, it is the Saharawi women's duty to use the circumstances created by the war to build a people, a nation and a state. This figures in many different aspects of their lives: the acceptance of motherhood as a political necessity as well as of social consequence (the Saharawi people are in need of demographic growth); the command of a situation in which equality of rights and duties does in fact exist, giving reality to the often abstract statement that the future belongs to the new political subjects who have to date been outcast and oppressed. This does not automatically mean that the Saharawis have embarked on the path towards liberation, as it is understood in a Western sense, from the age-old and universal oppression of women. But the delay of formal clarification of their position in the state, although it may be debatable, suggests that an attempt is being made to bypass the eurocentric analyses that have been discussed and which are no more than that even when they appear 'objectively' advantageous.

However, this brief presentation of the role of Saharawi women in their society does not appear complete or convincing without the inclusion of several examples which have been collected from the women themselves. One concerns so-called traditional medicines and the other religious practices. Although a great part of the paramedical activity in the SADR hospitals might be in the hands of the women, anyone who is a little more observant will become aware that another widespread therapeutic practice is also exercised by women. Specifically, this is the traditional medicine based either on the use of plant and mineral remedies or on a physical therapy the particulars of which are handed down from generation to generation. It can be argued that there is nothing particularly new in this.

However, this practice is not presented by its practitioners as a simple complement to official medicine but also assumes a certain political value, naïvely perhaps but of importance if one considers the risks innate in the refugee condition: inactivity, loss of manual ability, alienation with respect to the environment, and so on. The fact is, these medicines are made with herbs and minerals which are found in the Sahara, that is at home, the place to which they wish to return. Its name is never forgotten, the sense of the reality of the land from which they have been banished is kept alive, and the conviction that life in that land is possible is passed on even though for others the land might appear hostile and difficult. They understand this homeland and they know how to obtain what they need from it. But there is more to it than that. The author was informed that at times it is the sons or brothers who, on their return from the front, bring with them those herbs that their mothers or sisters have taught them to recognize and with which the ritual of preparing medicines will be repeated. There is nothing magical in this ritual but as a ritual it serves to help the threads of a social fabric to remain interwoven.

The other example concerns religious cult practices, although this expression is not actually correct. Unlike the previous case, this does not involve a practice, re-established or continued, but rather the recollection of a practice, the pilgrimage to the tombs of the holy men that are found in the Western Sahara. The women who tell of this custom assign it a significance which is more social than religious. The seasons used to regulate the visits to this or that holy man; in retrospect, the Sahara appears totally accessible and open. The destination is not important because of the religious symbolism, but because it is an occasion for meetings, for socializing, and for exchanges. There is more nostalgia for these lost journeys than for the brick houses of El-Ayoun built by the Spanish colonialists. In these pilgrimages people knew each other and recognized that they belonged to the same culture with its own specific tongue in which to express itself. Here too is one thread among many in that 'common history' which the Saharawi women continue to keep a living reality.

Notes

1. See proceedings of the international conference held in Paris on 23–4 November 1985, on the topic 'Peace for the Saharawi People: A European Concern', Rome and Brussels, 1985 and 1986. Saharaoui, Coordination des associations au Soutien du peuple.
2. I refer mainly to the sedentarization during the Spanish colonial period. However, the altered living conditions following the Moroccan occupation of a large part of the Saharawi territory also contributed to the effects of the colonial impact. (Cf. T.Hodges, *Western Sahara: The Roots of a Desert War*, Westport, Conn., Laurence Hill, 1983.
3. See F. De la Chapelle, 'Esquisse d'une histoire du Sahara Occidental' in

Hesperis, **XI**, 1939, pp. 203–96; see also, T. H. Weir, *The Sheiks of Morocco in the XVI Century*, Edinburgh, Morton, 1904.

4. Particular reference is made here to various articles appearing in the *Revue du Monde Musulman*, especially those by P. Marty, but any bibliography of that era will serve to illustrate this (cf. 'Bibliographie du Sahara Occidental' in *Hesperis*, **XI**, 1930, pp. 203–96).

5. Illustrative in this regard is the work by O. du Puigaudeau, 'Arts et Coutumes des Maures' in *Hesperis Tamuda*, 1967 (pp. 111–96); 1968 (pp. 329–427); 1970 (pp. 5–48); 1972 (pp. 183–225); 1975 (pp. 185–211).

6. Cf. H. T. Norris, *The Berbers in Arabic Literature*, London, Longman, 1982, p. 105, referring mainly to the Sanhaja.

7. Ibid., p. 125.

8. Cf. F. Beslay, *Les Reguibats*, Paris, L'Harmattan, 1984, pp. 82–7; M. Barbier, *Voyages et Explorations au Sahara Occidental au XIXème Siècle*, Paris, L'Harmattan, 1985, p. 53; and F. de Chassey, *L'Etrier, la Houe et le Livre*, Paris, Anthropos, 1922, pp. 62–4.

9. See O. du Puigeaudea, op. cit., 1972, p. 183.

10. O. du Puigeaudeau, op. cit., 1967, p. 157.

11. Cf. F. Beslay, op. cit., p. 110 and, although referring to the groups living in Mauritania, the opinion expressed on p. 137.

12. Cf. for the purposes of example the works on Ma el-Ainin, whose bibliography is in M. Barbier, *Le Conflit du Sahara Occidental*, Paris, L'Harmattan, 1982, p. 386.

13. Cited in M. Dauber, *Nomades du Sahara*, Paris, Presses de la Cité, Collection Connaissance du Monde, 1983, p. 51.

14. '. . . they buried us under insults and subjected us to the most inhumane treatment; two of my companions were reduced to a pitiful state. The women, who are far more cruel than the men, took pleasure in tormenting them. . . .' This is the way in which M. de Brisson expresses himself in his *Histoire du Naufrage et de la Captivité* (1785), presented and commented upon by A. Gaudio, Paris, Nouvelles Editions Latines, 1984, p. 35. Or again: '. . . they hastened to come and see the 'christian' . . . and the women, before insulting me, turned around and spat on the ground as a sign of contempt; the young girls too, put on dreadful airs and clenched their fists under my chin.. . .' quoted in M. Barbier, *Voyages et Explorations au Sahara Occidental au XIXème Siècle*, pp. 294–5, which quotes the passage from C. Douls' journey in 1887.

15. In addition to the texts mentioned in the previous note, cf. also, M. Barbier (ed.), *Trois Français au Sahara Occidental en 1784–1786*, Paris, L'Harmattan, 1984.

16. See F. de Chassey, 'Les multiples devenirs étatiques d'une "société sans état" saharienne' in *Enjeux sahariens*, Paris, Table ronde de CRESM, Eds du CNRS, 1984, pp. 200–1, but also O. du Puigaudeau, op. cit., 1967, p. 137.

17. Cf. M. Barbier, *Voyages et Explorations*, pp. 55, 301–2, 303, 306, and above all p. 321.

18. Cf. F. Besley, op. cit., pp. 37–8.

19. Cf. M. Barbier, *Voyages et Explorations*, pp. 135–6, where the segregation of the 'city dwellers' of Noun is mentioned as exceptional, but also O. du Puigaudeau, op. cit., 1967, pp. 156–8.

20. Cf. O. du Puigaudeau, op. cit., 1975, pp. 185–6, and op. cit., 1972, p. 214, but

also, to underline how this seems anomalous to the author, O. du Puigaudeau, op. cit., 1968, p. 395.

21. In this regard, the entire chapter dedicated to the teaching of work, quoted several times by O. du Puigaudeau, op. cit., pp. 185–211 is relevant.

22. Cf. O. du Puigaudeau, op. cit., 1967, p. 159 and Ibn Khaldun, *Muqaddima*, examined in an Iraqi edition, n.d., pp. 127 ff.

23. Verified during the course of a mission in the Saharawi refugee camps in May 1985; the old women, more than the men, including the poets, remembered the old songs, ballads, etc.

24. Cf. G. S. Colin, 'Mauritanica', in *Hesperis*, 1930, p. 134; and also B. Scarcia Amoretti, 'Reflexions sur la culture sahrawie' in *Sahara Info*, January–March 1985, pp. XXII–XXIII.

25. Cf. V. Baccalini, *Un popolo canta lulei*, Milan, Ottaviano, 1980, p. 76–7.

26. The observations which follow are based on the material produced by the Saharawis, and published in particular in *Sahara Libre*, and on information gathered during the course of a study mission in the Tindouf refugee camps (May 1985).

27. Similarly the so-called Islamic revival which has little to do historically with the civilizations which appeal to Islam as an ideal and religious referent. Cf. B. Scarcia Amoretti, 'Questione religiosa e questione nazionale nel mondo arabo' in *La Storia*, Turin (in press).

Index

WAR AND REFUGEES: *The Western Sahara Conflict*

F or over a decade a war has been raging in the former Spanish colony of Western Sahara which was ceded to Morocco and Mauritania in 1975–6. Although by 1979 Mauritania was forced to sue for peace, the Kingdom of Morocco continues to fight with the Saharan Liberation Movement, the Polisario. One result of this has been one of the largest long-term refugee communities in Africa. Despite living in an inhospitable desert environment largely dependent on others for their material needs and without a long tradition of sedentary existence, the refugees are exceptional in that they are actively using their experience in exile to create a society, quite removed from their tribal, nomadic past, which is based on self-reliance and equality.

This book resulted from an international symposium organized by the Refugee Studies Programme, Oxford University, and was attended by both Saharawis and Moroccans. It provides a history of the Saharawi peoples, their colonial experience, their emergent identity as a nation, the development of their incipient nationhood in exile, and the devastating conflict that has engulfed them and that has notable international implications.